'The Death Mother is brought out of the shadows in this engaging, scholarly, and compassionate book. By artfully juxtaposing the narratives of women who have committed infanticide with archetypal psychology, Dr Laufer offers a perspective that is unique, sensitive, and compelling. Readers will finish this insightful book with a deep understanding of the forces that can drive a mother to murder her children.'

Daniela Sieff, Ph.D., *author of* Understanding and Healing Emotional Trauma

'Brooke Laufer's look at the infanticidal mother is both heartbreaking and inspiring. Rather than judge and punish these women, as patriarchal systems often do, we should make the psychological move Brooke Laufer does: turn toward them in a bid to understand and care for them.'

Dennis Pottenger, *MFT, author of* Alchemy, Jung, and Remedios Varo: Cultural Complexes and the Redemptive Power of the Abjected Feminine

'This book is *essential* reading for all healthcare professionals. Laufer takes us into the underbelly of human life, into patterns of behavior and horror that we generally prefer to ignore yet are deeply embedded in us all. From compelling phenomenological research and clinical work with individuals and groups, Laufer brings us crucial insights regarding the significance of the social matrix of oppressive dynamics which hurt Mother.'

Evangeline Rand, Ph.D., *author of* Recovering Feminine Spirituality *and* C.G. Jung as Artisan

'In this insightful and necessary book, Brooke Laufer's clear mind, impeccable research, wisdom of experience, and compassionate heart draw us into the depths of modern expression of the Death Mother archetype, while passionately advocating for restoring the Dark Mother to her place in the wholeness of the Great Mother archetype. This wonderful book is essential reading for women, humanity, and the spirit of our time.'

Violet Sherwood, Ph.D., *author of* Haunted: The Death Mother Archetype

'Brooke Laufer ventures into the forbidding and important territory of the infanticidal mother and brings compassion and depth to this most difficult of subjects, inviting us to see these mothers in all their complexity.'

Lisa Marchiano, *LCSW, NCPsyA, author of* Motherhood: Facing and Finding Yourself, *and* The Vital Spark: Reclaim Your Outlaw Energies and Find Your Feminine Fire

'Equipped with solid scholarly research methods and a warm sensible heart, Dr. Laufer is a pioneer who ventures into the depths of horrors of infanticide to provide us with the voice of the mother who kills. This is an excellent comprehensive book for practitioners as well as researchers.'

Dr. Orit Sônia Waisman, *author of* Body, Language and Meaning in Conflict Situations

Uncovering the Act of Maternal Infanticide from a Psychological, Political, and Jungian Perspective

Using a wide range of disciplinary backgrounds, Laufer examines the topic of maternal infanticide through the lens of Jungian theory and presents an integrated and forensic view of this issue as an aggregate of personal and political moments, and as a feminine and feminist outcry urging human evolution.

The first part of the book will dissect the identity of the infanticidal mother and the Death Mother archetype, with the author providing firsthand accounts of patients that she has worked with in her professional career. The second part of the book focuses on interpreting that act of maternal infanticide, and these chapters will look to the construct of patriarchal Motherhood as a way of explaining the drive and actions of an infanticidal mother. The third and final section of the book takes the concept of evolution and transmutation a step further and addresses what is required in our modern state for the event of maternal infanticide.

This is an important new book for Jungian and analytic clinicians and scholars with an interest in maternal archetypes, as well as psychologists and psychiatrists who specialize in perinatal mental health. It would also be appropriate for forensic psychologists and legal analysts, and academics and clinicians in the fields of women's health and studies.

Brooke Laufer, Psy.D., is an independent scholar, writer, and clinician with a doctorate in Clinical Psychology from the California Institute of Integral Studies. She has analytic training and a deep interest in motherhood, perinatal mood disorders, and infanticide. Dr. Laufer treats women with postpartum illnesses and facilitates groups for women who have experienced postpartum psychosis. She lectures on the dynamics of maternal filicide. She also serves as a forensic evaluator and expert witness specializing in cases of infanticide and maternal filicide.

Uncovering the Act of Maternal Infanticide from a Psychological, Political, and Jungian Perspective

Brooke Laufer

Routledge
Taylor & Francis Group

LONDON AND NEW YORK

Designed cover image: Heart by Brooke Laufer

First published 2025
by Routledge
4 Park Square, Milton Park, Abingdon, Oxon OX14 4RN

and by Routledge
605 Third Avenue, New York, NY 10158

Routledge is an imprint of the Taylor & Francis Group, an informa business

British Library Cataloguing-in-Publication Data
A catalogue record for this book is available from the British Library

Library of Congress Cataloging-in-Publication Data
Names: Laufer, Brooke, author.
Title: Uncovering the act of maternal infanticide from a
   psychological, political and Jungian perspective / Brooke Laufer.
Description: New York : Routledge, 2024. | Includes bibliographical
   references and index.
Identifiers: LCCN 2024000081 (print) | LCCN 2024000082
   (ebook) | ISBN 9781032536224 (hardback) | ISBN 9781032536200
   (paperback) | ISBN 9781003412809 (ebook)
Subjects: LCSH: Infanticide—Psychological aspects. |
   Motherhood—Social aspects. | Patriarchy. | Jungian psychology.
Classification: LCC HV6537 .L38 2024 (print) | LCC HV6537
   (ebook) | DDC 304.6/68—dc23/eng/20240108
LC record available at https://lccn.loc.gov/2024000081
LC ebook record available at https://lccn.loc.gov/2024000082

ISBN: 978-1-032-53622-4 (hbk)
ISBN: 978-1-032-53620-0 (pbk)
ISBN: 978-1-003-41280-9 (ebk)

DOI: 10.4324/9781003412809

Typeset in Times New Roman
by Apex CoVantage, LLC

Contents

Figures

Acknowledgments

To the mothers.

All clinical material shared in this book has been used with permission or is a composite rendering. Names and identifying details have been changed.

This book is based on findings from dozens of cases of maternal infanticide for which I've provided psychological evaluation and consultation; my research interviews with 20 North American women who lived through postpartum psychosis; groups I cofacilitate for women recovering from postpartum psychosis; and women in my psychotherapy practice.

I am grateful for insights and encouragement from colleagues such as Dr. Erika Yamin, Dr. Katherine Wisner, Dr. Diana Barnes, Dr. Susan Feingold, Dr. Violet Sherwood, and especially to Dr. Daniela Sieff for paving the way; to the Reproductive Mental Health Forensics group within the International Marcé Society, and to Postpartum Support International, the warm and powerful organizations that relentlessly support mothers.

I am grateful to my women friends who have read pieces of this book and indulged me in conversation for years about Mothers. I appreciate the lawyers who work toward justice for mothers unfairly sentenced. I am deeply indebted to my editor Rebecca Pottenger, whose work has been essential to this entire book. Overwhelmingly, I am indebted to the women who are forced to mother from behind bars. Finally, thank you to Josie and Benny, for your beautiful, spirited lives I get to be a part of, and your patience with me, your mother.

Introduction

I work as a forensic evaluator of infanticidal mothers and as an analytical clinician. I am witness to a raw, ahistorical, and profound experience of motherhood, which I do my best to share in this book through actual accounts from infanticidal mothers. Recognizing their plights as containing the destructive maternal instincts of the archetypal Death Mother, I bring the reader into an encounter with her. Although forced into the shadows in the Western world, she still erupts, insisting on her presence as inherent to motherhood, crucial to recovering the full range of the maternal experience, lost to the pious image of the Virgin Mary as Mother.

Who are these women who murder their babies? Raising their stories scratches at some instinctive horror locked within us. They are easier to dismiss as *mad* than examine them for the universal themes that continue to appear in the conditions surrounding infanticide—conditions we as a society need to grapple with. To work consciously with the Death Mother is to take the archetypal pattern out of unconscious, destructive repetition, attending to her messages in a way that can "activate and strengthen the warm and nourishing inner mother we all need" (Sherwood, 2021, p. 65).

The U.S. has one of the highest maternal child homicide rates of the developed countries, yet little research has been done to identify structural or analytic explanations for infanticide. This is a book about motherhood through the eyes of infanticidal mothers. It is a response to Kristeva's call to engage "a discourse on the complexity of motherhood . . . to sharpen our understanding of this passion, pregnant with madness and sublimity. This is what motherhood lacks today" (2005).

Men and their psychology are largely unacknowledged in this book, although it is clear they are the other half of the story. This book is a phenomenological study of maternal infanticide in which the mother is the speaking subject. I invite readers to stretch into the experience of a mother brought to the brink, and fall over the edge.

In the days leading up to a prison visit with an infanticidal mother, I feel solemn and reverent. I feel curious about meeting this person and honored that I was the

DOI: 10.4324/9781003412809-1

one selected for this meeting. I feel nervous about rising to the occasion, and I am grateful this is where my work has taken me.

References

Kristeva, J. (2005). Motherhood today. *Talk at the Gypsy V. Colloquium*.
Sherwood, V. (2021). *Haunted: The death mother archetype*. Chiron.

Part I

Who She Is

Chapter 1

Infanticide

In pursuit of uncovering who the infanticidal mother is, this chapter begins with an overview of infanticide, filicide, neonaticide, unperceived pregnancy, and postpartum psychosis as they currently exist in Western medical, psychological, and forensic fields. The word *infanticide*—from the old French/Latin *infantium* (unable to speak) and *caedes* (a killing or slaughter)—refers to the killing of a child under a year old. Neonaticide denotes the murder of a newborn within the first 24 hours of life. Both events are most often committed by mothers. Filicide is applied to the killing of one's child who is older than a toddler and is most often committed by fathers (Resnick, 1969). Thus, I use the term *maternal infanticide* as an umbrella term when referring to child death caused by mothers. Maternal infanticide is seen as anti-instinctual and asocial, yet it persists. My work centers on these mothers, their crimes, and their complexities. Their stories are a part of what follows.

Mary's Story

We begin with Mary.[1] Mary was one of the first women I met who had taken her child's life. Mary was a successful woman by many measures: she had advanced degrees, worked as a full-time professional, came from a nuclear family, maintained friendships with high school friends and college friends, met a successful man in her professional world, and married at the 'right time'. Mary had always wanted to be a mother, and within months of her wedding was pregnant. She miscarried that pregnancy, which left her feeling like a failure after all of the successes and sense of control she had had in her life. Mary became pregnant again, but this time had a heightened state of anxiety, "worried all the time, worried she'd do something wrong, eat something wrong, lay the wrong way." Her worries were excessive and obsessive as she was very cautious with how she behaved and what she ate, trying to get "everything right." In her third trimester the doctor found calcium on the fetus' heart, which greatly accelerated Mary's anxiety. After the baby was born, Mary sank into a depression that she initially thought was the "baby blues." She began to have recurring memories of a sexual assault that had happened to her in college, which she had never told anyone about. Mary had been raped in a fraternity house, during which she conceived. Mary had had an abortion,

DOI: 10.4324/9781003412809-3

but again told no one. In her postpartum depression, she was often tearful, describing "waves of emotions coming over her" that felt like "desperation." Mary was preoccupied with the baby's breathing and felt like she needed to watch to see if he would have a seizure, or to make sure her husband didn't drop the baby, or that he didn't roll off the changing table. The baby had trouble with calorie intake; the doctors were concerned about his weight and the pediatrician recommended they have him weighed every two weeks. Mary was then obsessively feeding and weighing the baby, consistently feeling she was failing. Mary tried "everything to make more milk and to make milk more caloric." Every hour Mary noted in her journal the baby's bowel movements, if he ate, how much, the formula type, the sleep, tummy time, awake time, strengthening time, etc. They also saw a pediatric gastrointestinal specialist who endorsed the tracking. By this time Mary was regularly experiencing debilitating hypervigilance and intrusive thoughts, which she tried to share with her husband, to which he said, "it's normal, you'll get over it." Shortly after the baby was born, Mary's husband began openly criticizing her: she was too slow, incompetent, she had a muffin-top body shape, she should exercise, she wasn't not producing enough milk, etc. He established a pattern of verbal and emotional abuse, using menace and control, which began to take all sense of self, autonomy, and worth from Mary. Mary's self-loathing was all-consuming, often leaving her feeling that the baby was "better without me." Memories of her trauma were activated and playing in her mind "like a reel" and she only felt relief from these symptoms when she drank alcohol. Mary was experiencing suicidality but was not sharing her experience, nor was she receiving proper treatment. Mary then fell into a chronic state of numbness while going through the motions of cooking and cleaning and childrearing. She described to me a feeling of being "full of fear, shame, and humiliation," and of "Not feeling like a person." Mary's husband's family lived nearby and were often engaged in all of their activities. Her mother-in-law, much like her husband, was particularly critical of the baby's lack of growth, the lack of milk, and the incompetent feeding. It was during one gathering with her in-laws that Mary felt as if she didn't "know her place," and while all the focus was put on the baby, she had an intense sensation that she needed the baby with her, otherwise something bad would happen. Mary began drinking heavily and in a dazed state she *knew* she needed to escape with her baby. She described feeling outside of herself, and that an internal voice was clearly directing her, promising her death was better than this life. She then put herself and her 8-week-old baby into her car and drove until she came to a bridge, where she increased her speed and drove off into an icy lake. Although Mary survived, her child did not. Mary received 20 years in prison with no possibility of parole for this act.

It may relieve us to think "she is not me," although her story may resonate with many of us. Psychically, we cast out a mother like Mary, the infanticidal mother, as akin to the inhuman character of a fairy tale or a foreigner from a far-off uncivilized land. She is a barbaric monster or an alien beyond our limits of comprehension. She is the Other, the radical counterpart of the Self (Lacan, 1977/1991); the object, the one that is acted upon, the one without power (Cixous, 1976); she emerges, insane from the unconscious—"what is referred and what is unsaid" (Laing, 1961, p. 28). C.G. Jung suggested we project onto the Other our Shadow—unconscious material in ourselves that we cannot see, the inferiority or moral deficiency we deny in ourselves, and that which is instinctive and irrational in us (1948/1969, para. 516). In this way, the infanticidal mother inhabits the shadow of our society; we project our most profound moral deficiencies and anti-life impulses onto the infanticidal mother. It is not me; it is her.

The Evolution of Infanticide

Infanticide has been observed among most mammal species and is recorded in nearly all human cultures (Klerman, 2001). Darwin's naturalist theory and basic evolutionary principles explain infanticide most comprehensively: "Mothering involves anything and everything a female does to ensure her genes make it into subsequent generations" (Hrdy & Sieff, 2015, p. 184). But to achieve that, our ancestors sometimes had to navigate fatalistic obstacles and make difficult choices to maintain survival.

Animal mothers kill or abandon their newborn young when their circumstances are so poor that rearing those young would not be worthwhile or possible. These economical and rational decisions require little deliberation when the mother's reproductive success is threatened by limited access to critical resources—including food, shelter, care, or social position—for her dependent progeny. This general principle carries through to our ancestral human mothers and plays out in modern motherhood. In the human struggle for existence, under certain circumstances, infanticide has served as a nonpathological evolutionary adaptation (Hrdy, 2000). As Sieff noted in "The Death Mother as Nature's Shadow," mothers who shunned favoritism consequently lost all, instead of one, of their children and left no descendants.

A significant difference between humans and other mammals is the extended dependency that human children have on their mothers, making these offspring among nature's most costly to raise. What helps to keep these children alive is social support. Hrdy called women:

> "communal breeders," describing how aid would have come from husbands, teenage children, aunts, and especially from grandmothers . . . because help was so crucial, a mother's feelings for her child would have been subtly affected by the strength of her network. A woman with meager support would probably have felt ambivalent toward her child, because there was a high risk that her solo-nurturing would come to nothing (Hrdy, 1999, 2009).
>
> (Sieff, 2019, p. 23)

In modern Western culture, we erroneously tend to believe that biology has programmed a mother to love and nurture every child. One of Sieff's most significant contributions to this field is her insight that the need for a mother to end the life of or abandon her child is part of a "natural repertoire of behaviors" and an inherent part of our collective unconscious (2019, p. 19).

> . . .the belief that biology has programmed mothers to love and nurture every child they give birth to is a fantasy. Ancestral women mothered their children across a range of environments and circumstances. As a result, a range of maternal emotions and feelings came to be part of our collective human heritage.
>
> (Sieff, 2019, p. 26)

Examples of infanticide can be found throughout history all over the globe. The Aztecs, Mayans, and Incans all practiced child sacrifice to appease their gods, including the Chimú civilization located in what is now Peru, who sacrificed more than 140 children at one time. In the West, infanticide was a commonplace occurrence in the 1st century, when a father's right to murder his children was recognized in Roman law under *patria potestas*—a father as head of the family had complete control over his lineage, including ending their lives. Killing babies was not only sanctioned domestically, but also was a way of punishing or decimating an enemy. In 7 BCE, King Herod the Great of Judea ordered the execution of all male children in the village of Bethlehem to avoid the loss of his throne to a newborn King of the Jews. Generally, infanticide was expected and accepted within the first 3 months of life if the infant was sickly, a bastard, the wrong sex, or unable to contribute to the household. The Roman code of law from c. 449 BCE as written in the Laws of the Twelve Tables stated, "Deformed child shall be killed at birth" (as cited in Netchev, 2023, Table IV).

In medieval times infanticide began to be punishable by the Catholic Church, so the deceased infants had to be hidden. Paintings show infants pulled out of the Tiber and delivered to Pope Innocent in the 1100s, who then issued punishments such as whipping, stocks, or pillory. At the same time advancements in feeding and caring for children decreased the necessity of infanticide, and it began to be generally outlawed in the West.

With the expansion of Christianity, the illegality and punishment of infanticide became more widespread in European cities in the 18th century, thus up to a quarter of all children were reported as abandoned to foundling hospitals, where the probability of surviving to adulthood appears to have been well below a third (Levene, 2005). In 19th-century Victorian England, the business of baby farms became popular, as fathers of illegitimate children were not obligated by law to support their children financially; thus many women had few options and turned to baby farmers who adopted out the unwanted children for a fee. They operated under the ruse that the child would be taken care of, but often the children were mistreated and even killed. Amelia Dyer, an English baby farmer, was convicted of killing over 200 infants, although she had assured clients that children under her care would be given safe and loving homes. Initially, Dyer would let the child die from starvation and neglect. "Mother's Friend," an opium-laced syrup, was given to quiet these children as they suffered through starvation. Among our infanticidal ancestors are not only the mothers but the women who ran baby farms, who killed the feeble and useless babies.

Legal and moral concern for the welfare of unprotected infants was on the rise and infanticide was decreasing (Sherwood, 2021). According to records dating from 1648, infanticide was outlawed in colonial America and often punished by execution. Largely due to the dominance in colonial America of Christianity and its Ten Commandments (Exd.10:2–17) it was understood and adamantly defended that God prohibited murder and human life was to be protected at all costs.

Contemporary Infanticide

The U.S. has the highest rate of child murder among developed nations. In infancy, the U.S. rate of homicide is 8/100,000, several times higher than 4.5 in England, 2.9 in Canada, or Italy at 2.1 per 100,000 (Hatters-Friedman & Sorrentino, 2012; Wilson et al., 2020). Although it is not well reported and difficult to thoroughly analyze due to the archaic ways the U.S. penal system keeps notes, it is surmised that there are about 200 maternal infanticides per year in the U.S., and that the rate of infanticide has remained relatively constant (Hatters-Friedman & Sorrentino, 2012; CDC, 2020). Mothers commit this type of offense more often than fathers. In most convictions, the defendant is charged with manslaughter and sentenced to more than 15 years in prison. The average sentence for this crime in the U.S. is 17 years in prison (Barr & Beck, 2008; Booth et al., 2014; Shelton et al., 2010).

Attorney Michelle Oberman and psychologist Cheryl Meyer have been tracking U.S. maternal filicide cases since the early 1990s. Their research has involved culling and sorting hundreds of contemporary accounts of maternal filicide from the media and legal databases to identify patterns and find answers (Oberman & Meyer, 2008; Meyer et al., 2001). Meyer et al.'s categories are an update of forensic psychiatrist Phillip Resnick's categories, which included infanticide as a result of altruism or love, acute psychosis, an unwanted child, child maltreatment, and spousal revenge (Resnick, 1969, 2016).[2] For decades, Resnick's categories informed a social and clinical understanding of the infanticidal mother but were limited by his failure to account for sociocultural and other external influences and pressures acting on the individual.

An example of the influence of Resnick's categories is the popularization of revenge filicide by clinicians and the media over the past 50 years. Revenge filicide refers to killing her child as revenge against her spouse. It also is referred to as the *Medea method*, after the figure in Greek myth whose infanticide has been interpreted as revenge against their father for abandoning her for another woman. Although the theory of maternal infanticide as spousal revenge has been popularized, in my work with and research on women who have committed filicide, I have found no instances of a woman who killed her child to get back at her husband. As a mythic figure carrying information about maternal infanticide, Medea's motivations are more fully examined in Chapter 2, revealing, rather than simple revenge, the powerful archetypal influences at work in filicide.

Updating Resnick's work, upon reviewing hundreds of cases of maternal infanticide, Oberman and Meyer developed a typology that is predicated on their belief that this crime is not merely about mental illness, but rather arises out of the unique interaction of social, environmental, cultural, and individual variables (Oberman & Meyer, 2008; Meyer et al., 2001). These complex influences and interactions are essential to the discussion of maternal infanticide and are addressed in greater detail in Chapter 5. Their work moves our understanding of the maternal infanticide beyond it being a problem of female hormones or pathology. It suggests that if we are to effectively tend to the dilemma of infanticide, we need to examine it as a comment on and result of sociocultural and systemic, as well as personal, mechanisms. We must look more closely at the personal and political environment that produces a woman who kills a child.

In her research on maternal violence, social psychologist and litigation consultant Julie Blackman identified four categories of infanticidal mothers that I have found applicable to the women I see in my practice: (a) women who were themselves abused as children, whose neglectful or violent acts result in the deaths of their children; (b) women who are victims of domestic violence who kill their children; (c) teenagers who commit neonaticide; and (d) women who kill their babies during the first few days or months due to postpartum psychosis (Blackman, 2004). The following provides a brief discussion of these categories. Throughout the following chapters, the circumstances and motivations related to maternal infanticide are discussed in greater depth.

Infanticidal Women: Domestic Violence and Fatal Maltreatment

In fatal maltreatment filicide, the child's death is not the intended outcome, but rather is the result of a long history of violence, cumulative child abuse, neglect, or medical abuse (i.e., Munchausen syndrome by proxy). Most of the infanticidal women I see are domestic violence victims who, in assisted or coerced infanticides, kill their children in conjunction with their male partners. This phenomenon reflects the common overlap of domestic violence and child abuse. Yet, as discussed further in Chapter 4, in most domestic violence cases in which there is the death of a child, the blame is put on the mother—either the mother is charged with murder with no consideration of the partner's role, or the partner is charged with abuse/manslaughter and the mother is charged with failure to protect.

Cases in which filicide overlaps with domestic violence often involve a single mom with an in-and-out boyfriend who is physically and emotionally abusive, plays no parenting role, and is financially dependent on her. In a case of fatal maltreatment that I worked on recently, a mother had put a pillow over her child's face, but pulled back before the child died and rushed her to the hospital. At the hospital they found the child who had almost died by asphyxiation also had lice and rotted teeth. The mother was detained, interrogated, and arrested within a few days, then put in jail awaiting trial for the next several years, leaving three children under the age of 5 at home.

When I began to review the case, I found reports dating back several years of her partner, the children's father, physically abusing her and the children. Because the boyfriend did not work, they both lived off her disability check, which she received because of a birth injury that left her with a disability. He spent most of their money on his marijuana dependency. With food stamps she purchased for the children inexpensive food that lacked nutritional value, such as powdered juice, which rotted their teeth. When I asked the mother about the lice, she told me she knew the kids had lice as it had been going through the school, but when she went to comb through the youngest one's hair to pull out the lice the baby cried and their father, who could not tolerate the sound of the baby's crying, told her to "make it stop." So, she had not finished combing all the lice out of the child's hair. The day of the near-asphyxiation of the child, the father had already twisted the mother's arm behind her body, almost breaking it. He yelled at the children and stormed out of the house. These are the realities behind fatal maltreatment.

Teenagers, Neonaticide, and Unperceived Pregnancy

About half the incidents of mothers killing their children in the U.S. are identified as neonaticide. Neonaticidal mothers are often young, unmarried women with unplanned pregnancies who receive no prenatal care. These are the teenage pregnancies, the accidental pregnancies, the secret pregnancies; young women like Melissa Drexler, who disposed of her newborn baby in a restroom at her prom (Carmody, 2019). Most of these girls have no psychiatric diagnosis and rarely commit suicide (Hatters-Friedman & Resnick, 2007; Meyer et al., 2001), but they are impoverished, undereducated, and under-supported; their bodies and minds are not capable of ushering in another life. Teen neonaticide might reflect an instinctive choice analogic to black bear mothers who, as a species, are able to prevent an implantation in their womb of a fertilized egg until they have stored enough fat and readied an environment in which they can tenderly care for their cubs. As Sarah Hrdy observed, abandoning a poorly timed infant does not mean she will not be a good mother to those that, when she and her environment are ready, she chooses to raise (2009, p. 110).

Stories of secret pregnancies appear in the media in teenage coming-of-age after-school dramas, but in actuality they tend to end in neonaticides. Teens with secret pregnancies often experience what is referred to as *pregnancy denial*. Pregnancy denial, either partial (1 in 500 pregnancies) or total denial (1 in 2500 pregnancies), refers to the condition in which a woman denies that she is pregnant to her partner, parents, or doctors (Wessel & Buscher, 2002). A few researchers in the field have identified three variations of pregnancy denial: pervasive, affective, and psychotic (Chechko et al., 2023; Friedman et al., 2007; Miller, 2003). Pervasive denial of pregnancy occurs when the physical changes of pregnancy, such as cessation of menstruation, weight gain, fetal movement sensations are unrecognized, and labor contractions are confused with intestinal pains. Women may explain their contractions as having eaten too much or eaten bad food (Silverio et al., 2021). In less pervasive affective denial, the mother knows she is pregnant, but she is emotionally dissociated from and defended against it because it either reminds her of a trauma or portends a future trauma. Finally, psychotic denial often means a woman recognizes the pregnancy, but her awareness is delusional and the fetus is experienced as, for instance, a tumor or an alien (Chase et al., 2021; Galvano & Pugi, 2023; Miller, 2003).

Denial is triggered at least in part by a belief that if she were to disclose her pregnancy, she would be completely cut off from her social support network. Almost always, the girls face their pregnancies alone, as their relationship with the man or boy who impregnated them often ends as soon as the pregnancy is discovered. A variety of factors inhibit the ability of these girls to determine a course of action. First, they usually have a sense of fear, if not terror, surrounding the fact of pregnancy. Their pregnancy evokes terror, and yet, for reasons such as religion, culture, money, and immaturity, these girls are deeply ambivalent about their pregnancy and unaware of, unable, or unwilling to pursue alternatives such abortion or adoption. In addition to the terror it evokes, however, pregnancy represents a child, and a source of unconditional love. The uncertainty and isolation they feel leads these young women to dissociate from their changing bodies, living day to day, disconnected from and making no plans for the inevitable labor and delivery of their baby.

A case of affective denial occurred in the case of a woman I worked with who received a decade sentence in prison for the neonaticide of her daughter. Jana came from a conservative Muslim family, and although they were living in the U.S., the family was immersed in their community and adhered to a strict following of Muslim cultural practices, most notably that men were the leaders. As the first-born child she was a "disappointment" to her father, although he was assuaged by her younger brothers' arrivals. She described a family dynamic of an authoritative father and a submissive mother. When I described the symptoms of battered women syndrome to her, she said it captured her mother. She attended a local college while living at home, during which her parents were seeking an arranged marriage for her. Jana began a relationship with a local young man that she kept secret, and within a short amount of time she was pregnant. Jana was shocked for several reasons: she hadn't understood intercourse enough to expect this pregnancy, as her mother had never discussed sexual health with her; also, she knew it was deeply dishonorable to be pregnant out of wedlock, and she acutely felt she would be disowned or killed. During this same time, in the same community, there had been the case of a woman who had been killed by her father after he discovered her having fled her abusive husband. The concept of honor-killing was within the bounds of Jana's culture and proximity, so even if her family would have had no intention of such a violent response it lived in her psyche. Jana proceeded to hide her pregnancy from others and from herself. Just as explained by 'affective denial', Jana had cognitive awareness; in fact, she had blood results that gave validity to the existence of her pregnancy; but she completely withdrew emotion from this experience and lived as if she was not pregnant. Jana reported to me that she did nothing to acknowledge the pregnancy and would often forget about it. When I inquired if she had ceased menstruating, she reported she had no memory of that, indicating she was likely in periods of dissociation during the pregnancy. When it came time for delivery, she was surprised and confused by the pain and believed she was having a bowel movement. She delivered her child on her bedroom floor, and in a state of shock—she reported no emotions during this time—she disposed of the infant in their outdoor trash bin. Jana emphasized to me that at that moment she was "terrified" because she knew her parents were on their way home from the store, and everything in her existence needed to protect herself from the discovery of these events. It's very possible that Jana's pregnancy denial and neonaticide was an attempt, albeit thwarted, to save her own life.

Unperceived pregnancy is a term first used by psychiatrists Vedat Şar and core-searchers in their work on trauma and dissociation to create a less pejorative, more clinically accurate diagnosis and to account for the limitations of the term *pregnancy denial*. The term *denial* cannot fully encapsulate the traumatic root and variations of disruption to a person's senses (Şar et al., 2016). Denial implies knowledge or consciousness of a situation, whereas "unperceived" implies the mechanism is unconscious, an experience associated with a dissociative disorder, where perception or what is being perceived is disrupted. Dissociation refers to a reaction to a traumatic experience, such as an accident, disaster, or victimization, that enables a person to tolerate what might otherwise be too difficult to bear, mentally escaping from fear, pain, and horror. This may make it difficult to later remember the details of the experience, as reported by many survivors of disaster, accidents, or violence.

An unperceived pregnancy points to a preceding trauma (e.g., rape or a former fetal loss) that has impacted a mother in such a way that her inner mental and physical environment is made unaware of a growing fetus within her. There may be overwhelming fears of pregnancy: solitary and social costs that are unacceptable to her; or layers of religious, cultural, and psychological systems making the existence of a child untenable to the mother's psyche. She may be avoiding abortion, excommunication, or an unforgivable sin. In sum, with her mind and body unconsciously working to solve an inextricable situation, dissociation and an unperceived pregnancy provides a way to comply with the incompatible demands of the fetus, her psychological need to avoid trauma, and her sociocultural world. An unperceived pregnancy can serve as an unconscious holding program aimed at gaining some extra time to solve the conflict.

Without being aware of a pregnancy, a mother is unable to progress to the stages of attachment or attunement to the growing fetus and will be unprepared for delivery and motherhood. This of course sets up significant risks for both the mother and fetus, including emotional disturbance, lack of pre- and antenatal care, precipitous delivery (often into the toilet bowl), and neonaticide. A denied or unperceived pregnancy is most likely to result in death of the infant. One can imagine the acute confusion and disorientation at the time of delivery, the panic after the birth, and the ensuing actions to resolve the unacceptable shock.

Not all unperceived pregnancies end in neonaticide, as a mother may emerge from a dissociated state and discover the pregnancy, whether she is in the later stages of pregnancy or in childbirth, and be able to receive medical care and safely deliver the baby. In some instances, a woman who comes out of dissociation and realizes she has delivered a baby will consciously dispose of it, for the same reasons it was unperceived. But in several cases, I have seen the dissociative state continue after delivery, with the woman unable to perceive her newborn as a reality. For these women, to maintain an ego-syntonic state, the infant must not exist since the fetus never did. She may ignore the infant, disposing of it or leaving it exposed. This sustained post-birth dissociative state is less documented. An acute dissociative reaction may involve disorganized behavior and may turn into a brief psychosis. For example, instead of a mother acknowledging an infant delivered into a toilet bowl she perceives it as an extreme bowel movement, a brown sack, or even a tumor. Her behavior may then follow the logic of the psychosis, she may attempt to flush the material or toss it in a trash bin. She may have no memory or way of describing the events when later asked, as she was in a state of amnesia. Even for women with a diagnosis of acute dissociation, courts are reluctant to acquit defendants under the generally accepted standards of the insanity defense due to the transient nature of the syndrome.

Elena's Story

Elena was born in Guatemala. She struggled in school and barely finished 7th grade, eventually staying home to help raise her siblings and work in a factory. Elena told me she always felt ugly; she was bullied by her peers; and, although she dreamed of having a husband and a family, she felt she was doomed to being alone. At 17 years old she lost her dad, the family provider, to cancer, and she became suicidal. Elena was hospitalized for several weeks. Her family thought it would be best if she went to the United States to start new with better opportunities.

Elena traveled with a small group of strangers, led by men (called *coyotes*) whom they paid to take them from Guatemala to Chicago. The coyotes brandished large guns, regularly pulled her hair, silenced the group with threats, and sexually harassed them. At one point, they were held in a dark room in Texas for several days. One of the men attempted to pull Elena out of the room to rape her but someone stopped him. When Elena arrived in the United States, she stayed with family friends, a brother and sister. To afford to stay with them, Elena began several jobs: working as a nanny, in a factory, and selling tamales on the sidewalks.

Within a month of living there, Elena and the brother entered a relationship. Because Elena was Catholic and didn't believe in having a sex outside of marriage, he promised her repeatedly that they would marry. He pressured her sexually, telling her, "Here in the United States, it's different." He also told Elena that once they got married, he would pay back the money she owed, and they would go to Guatemala together. The brother and sister became mocking and abusive toward Elena, clearly taking advantage of her and demanding extra payments.

One evening, the brother took Elena on what she thought was a date, to a party where there were only men. They gave her a drink and she went to the restroom, but very quickly she was on the floor, falling asleep. Waking up, she found herself on a bed with two men around her, including one who was pulling his pants up. Her boyfriend was there, taking a picture of her in a sexual position. Later, he showed her the picture and threatened her with it. He called her a "whore" and told her, "If you tell anyone you've been raped, I'll show them this picture." He then used that picture to coerce Elena to continue a sexual relationship with him.

It was at this time that Elena became pregnant. However, she thought there was something wrong with her mind because, with no sex education, she didn't think she could be pregnant as she wasn't married and was still menstruating. As the pregnancy progressed, she didn't trust her judgment or understanding of what was happening to her and didn't know what she was feeling move inside her. Elena remembers the sister suggested to her that she had a tumor growing in her belly and she believed her.

When her unperceived pregnancy came to term, Elena felt she had to pee and went to the bathroom. While on the toilet, water and blood came out of her and her stomach became hard and began to hurt. The pain became extreme; she said she felt like she was passing out several times. She didn't know what was happening, but she wanted to clean herself up, so she got into the shower. As she walked from the toilet to the shower, she noticed a cord was attached to her which she thought was her feces. Elena said a "sack" had come out of her, and it was now connected to her with a cord. She believed she had to cut the cord, or she would die. She remembered that the sister had told her she had a tumor. She thought this was the tumor coming out, and she believed she might be dying. Elena reported staying in the shower for a long time, losing track of time. It was as if she lost consciousness and when she again became aware, she found a pair of scissors and attempted to cut the cord. She was cutting what she thought was the cord while the baby was between her legs. Then another sack came out of her. It was then that Elena saw that the first sack was a baby, and she became paralyzed. When she first saw the baby, she thought it was dead. She said that then she wanted to die. Her first thought was to jump out the bathroom window with the baby, so she first threw the baby out the window and as she attempted to climb out the window, she slipped and fell, hit her head on the bathroom floor, and passed out. When she came to, she attempted again to jump out the window, but failed again. At one point the brother opened the door, saw her on the floor in a pool of blood, and left, closing the door. Then the sister came into the bathroom, picked up the placenta and threw it away. Elena, in shock, had forgotten she threw the baby out the window. She continued to believe she was going to die. Eventually Elena was taken to the hospital and subsequently arrested.

By the time I met her, she had been in prison for over 15 years.[3] A new lawyer on her case was working on a clemency plea and hired me to do an evaluation. I found that Elena had experienced a *non-psychotic affective and persistent denial of pregnancy*, comorbid with lifelong major depressive disorder. Elena had an inability to acknowledge or become aware of the pregnancy as she was protecting herself from emotional conflict and extreme stress. The pregnancy presented a life-threatening element in the dangerous situation in which she was trapped—living with a physical, emotional, and sexual abuser, financial debt, isolation, and the threat of being turned in to the authorities/police. Elena may have been at times intellectually aware of the possibility that she was pregnant, but her inability to trust herself, fear, and denial were aided and abetted by the sister and brother. Thus, she made no emotional or physical preparation for the birth. This affective and persistent denial of pregnancy put her at risk for neonaticide.

During her pregnancy, Elena was experiencing a dissociative disorder that consists of persistent or recurrent depersonalization and derealization. The disorder is often triggered by severe stress. It was not as if she knew she was pregnant but did not want to believe it; for most of the pregnancy, it was unperceived—she did not *know* of its existence. This dissociative state diminished her capacity to discern right from wrong, having no awareness of the actual nature of what was occurring. Moreover, Elena had no intention of violence on the day of her offense. Barnes, who has worked extensively with pregnancy denial, states, "When babies succumb at birth, it is not to be assumed that it is a woman's intention to harm the newborn, but instead, it is her inability to manage her own actions as a consequence of the dissociative episode" (2022, p. 57). Elena's dissociation continued into the immediate postpartum period. For her reality to remain ego-syntonic with her thought that she was not pregnant but had a tumor, she could not perceive the "sack" as a baby. The baby arrived as if it was a tumor, and then when perceived it appeared "dead" to Elena. In her fear, distress, confusion, and her shame from her Catholic background, she needed it and herself to disappear. Without premeditation but a form of rudimentary and detached thinking, she threw the baby out the window, intending to follow it. Overwhelmed and distraught, with no sense of a way forward, and going in and out of consciousness, Elena wanted to die. But again, without premeditation or logical thinking, she was not able to complete the task of jumping out the window herself. Despite the accusations of "baby killer" in court and in the media, Elena's full story sheds light on an entire set of circumstances unbearable to most people. Elena is expected to remain in prison for 10 more years.

Infanticide, Postpartum, and Psychosis

Most maternal infanticides occur while the mother is in a psychotic state (Resnick, 1969, 2016). Postpartum psychosis can take on various forms, one of the most common of which is altruistic filicide, when a mother kills her child out of love, or the belief death is in the child's best interest. For example, a suicidal mother may not wish to leave her motherless child to face an intolerable world, or a psychotic mother may believe that she is saving her child from a fate worse than death. In acute psychosis, filicide can be a response to a hallucinatory, overpowering command to kill.

In the contemporary Western world, we have several ways of referring to the experience of a mother after birth that we perceive as "off" or not quite as expected.

Because the signs are often nebulous and we generally do not want to reproach a new mother, we may rationalize odd behavior as the baby blues or describe it with the mysterious phrase, *she has postpartum*, with the understanding that what that means is not to be pursued. Within the field of psychology, symptoms during the postpartum period are categorized within a continuum of diagnoses ranging from postpartum depression to anxiety, obsessive compulsive disorder, panic, posttraumatic stress disorder, bipolar disorder, and postpartum psychosis. Most often the symptoms for these conditions show up within a few weeks after delivery, but they can certainly manifest as early as during pregnancy or as late as in the 2nd year postpartum. Postpartum depression affects between 10% and 22% of mothers before the infant's first birthday; psychosis occurs in postpartum women at a rate of about 1–2 cases per 1000 births, or .15% (Stowe et al., 2001).

The period after delivery is a uniquely vulnerable state for a mother. The hormone changes that occur during pregnancy and after a baby is born are the most dramatic a woman experiences in her lifetime. The levels of progesterone and allopregnanolone rise during pregnancy and plummet after childbirth. This drop significantly contributes to emotional dysregulation. Most often, this includes the "baby blues" (mood swings, anxiety, sadness, or irritability, which resolve within a week or so of birth) or postpartum depression (similar symptoms that are more intense, last longer, and interfere with the mother's daily life). Meanwhile, oxytocin—the bonding hormone—floods the system right after delivery. Often, when oxytocin goes up, so can anxiety. These hormones influence one another in a complex way that affects energy and mood. Progesterone, a natural anti-anxiety substance, is especially low after birth—right when a mom could use more of it.

The possibility of things going physically or psychologically wrong for a mom is heightened in the perinatal period. Ectopic pregnancies, miscarriages, preeclampsia, and placental complications are not uncommon. Issues such as hemorrhaging, postpartum infections in the urinary tract and uterus, incision infections, and sepsis can extend a mother's stay in the hospital or bring her to the ER, increasing her experience of stress and contributing to anxiety and depression. Additionally, mothers of premature infants generally show higher rates of postpartum depression than mothers of full-term infants. The rates of postpartum depression are doubled for mothers while their newborn is in the neonatal intensive care unit (NICU).

Postpartum depression is distinct from what people refer to as the "baby blues," which represent a normal adjustment period after giving birth. About 80% of new mothers experience mood swings and weepiness during the first 2–3 weeks after giving birth, but these baby blues resolve without any medical assistance. On the other hand, about 20% of women experience postpartum depression, a diagnosis denoting a disturbing emotional state that lasts beyond 2–4 weeks and interrupts the mother's ability to function. The Massachusetts General Hospital Center for Women's Mental Health (MGH) is the epicenter of treatment and research on reproductive psychiatry in the U.S. and has found high occurrences of anxiety and obsessiveness in women with postpartum depression, including symptoms of obsessive-compulsive disorder (OCD)—intrusive, anxious thoughts or obsessions followed by compulsive behaviors aimed at relieving the anxiety. In the therapy room, I have found anxiety and OCD are largely what women are in despair about. MGH found the most common obsessions were about aggression and contamination, and the most common compulsions were cleaning/washing and checking. Intrusive thoughts generally hover around a preoccupation with harm coming to the baby or harm coming to the baby by the mother (Miller et al., 2015a, 2015b).

Mothers, especially first-time mothers, enter a heightened state of vigilance when the baby comes home from the hospital. Even if they had not previously suffered from anxiety, they are now checking the baby monitor several times per hour, leaning in to hear their baby breathing, regularly checking door locks, and pursuing information on the internet regarding the safety of car seats, cribs, and highchairs. Danger has suddenly become foremost in their awareness and a preoccupation.

Because it is such a pervasive life transition and time of flux, physically and mentally, previously dormant conditions such as posttraumatic stress disorder (PTSD) or bipolar disorder tend to emerge postpartum. If a mother has suffered a trauma in her past that has been unacknowledged or untreated, it is almost sure to cause some havoc during the postpartum period. I have seen many new mothers who had sexual trauma from their past that they had repressed or never discussed suddenly be unable to leave their homes with their new baby for fear of a predatory world. Symptoms of hypervigilance or flashbacks may surprise new mothers and detrimentally affect the baby, requiring treatment that focuses on the trauma.

Postpartum psychosis is at the extreme end of the continuum, and when it occurs it is a psychiatric emergency. Clinical features of postpartum psychosis include elated, dysphoric, or labile mood; agitation; bizarre or disorganized behavior and thought processes; and insomnia. The psychotic symptoms are mood-incongruent delusions, hallucinations, or delusions of control, with content often related to harm to the infant or self. The onset usually appears within days to 2 months of childbirth, coming "on suddenly, . . . around the time of weaning, or following a period of extreme sleep deprivation . . . A woman experiencing postpartum psychosis may, for stretches of time, appear to be perfectly normal" (Winter, 2023, para. 5).

Because untreated postpartum psychosis has an estimated 4% risk of infanticide and a 5% risk of suicide (Hatters-Friedman & Sorrentino, 2012), psychiatric hospitalization—not just a good night's sleep or a better diet, but safe monitoring and medication—is required to protect the mother and her baby. Nearly 75% of mothers with postpartum psychosis have bipolar disorder. Mothers with a history of bipolar disorder have a 100-fold increase in rates of psychiatric hospitalization in the postpartum period. This suggests that postpartum psychosis is an overt presentation of bipolar disorder that coincides with the tremendous hormonal shifts after delivery.

Postpartum psychosis has been noted since antiquity. In 400 BCE, Hippocrates recorded the first case found in medical literature. His patient was delusional, confused, and insomniac within 6 days of a twin birth. A medieval gynecologist attributed the disorder to "too much moisture in the womb, causing the brain to fill with water" (Spinelli, 2008, p. 455). In 1858, French psychiatrist Louis Victor Marcé published his treatise in which, having carefully observed postpartum mothers, he identified the same symptoms we see in mothers today. Marcé made early conjectures about the role of the immune response and the endocrine system. Recent medical research has shown that inflammatory immune response in the maternal brain (Dye et al., 2022), and it is widely acknowledged that a dramatic decrease in estrogen and progesterone hormones contribute to postpartum mental illness (McCoy et al., 2003).

Margaret Spinelli, founder and former director of the Women's Program in Psychiatry at Columbia University, has spent decades researching postpartum psychosis. In her work she suggests, and I agree, that postpartum psychosis is distinct from psychosis that occurs at any other time in any other individual's life. This is for several reasons:

> First, it has unique precipitants, namely pregnancy and childbirth. Second, it is triggered by a significant neuroendocrine event. Third, the literature consistently describes affective (likely bipolar) psychotic phenomena associated with organic delirium (amnesia, impaired sensorium, and cognitive dysfunction). Fourth, cognitive disorganization is reliably reported and demonstrated by systematic investigation and objective neuropsychiatric testing.
>
> (Spinelli, 2004, p. 1551)

A further distinction is in its severity. Postpartum psychosis has been found to appear more delusional, disoriented, and agitated than in psychosis unrelated to childbirth. "Symptoms of confusion and disorientation are distinct from other psychoses and can resemble delirium in the fluctuating severity of symptoms" (Ayers, 2007, p. 469).

Katherine Wisner, an expert in postpartum psychosis with whom I have regularly discussed this material, has documented the distinct nature and increased severity of psychosis postpartum, characterized by extreme confusion, loss of touch with reality, paranoia, delusions, disorganized thought process, and hallucinations (Wisner et al., 1994). Wisner and coresearchers reported that women with childbearing-related onset of psychosis experience more frequent and severe cognitive disorganization and more unusual psychotic symptoms. These were often mood-incongruent delusions of reference, persecution, jealousy, and grandiosity, along with visual, tactile, or olfactory hallucinations that suggest an organic syndrome (Sit et al., 2006). There is often a conviction of the baby's altered identity or a sense of persecution from the baby/changeling (Brockington, 1996). It is as if the content and structure of the madness/psychosis itself is constellated around the transition to motherhood.

Postpartum psychosis can be a difficult condition to diagnose initially, which is often why it evades alarm and intervention from family members. It appears that in most cases, postpartum psychosis presents as an episode of bipolar illness, mimicking a rapidly evolving manic (or mixed) episode. The earliest signs are restlessness, irritability, and insomnia. Psychotic features tend to wax and wane with some frequency, meaning that at one moment, a mother may seem coherent and organized and in the next moment she may be frantically quoting the Bible. A mother may say that she sees her dead father in the room, or she may be terrified that the police are coming to take her child or that her in-laws have a conspiracy to kill her. She may fixate on a small feature on her baby and obsess over fictionalized health issues. While a mother experiencing postpartum anxiety may have intrusive thoughts such as putting the baby in the oven or dropping it from an elevated surface, she will find these thoughts incredibly disturbing (ego dystonic), but the mother in postpartum psychosis identifies with her obsessive and violent intrusive thoughts (they are ego syntonic), often leading her to fatal actions.

Psychosis in the Absence of a Diagnosis

Postpartum psychosis as a diagnosis is not included in the American Psychiatric Association's current *Diagnostic and Statistical Manual* (5th ed.; DSM-5; American Psychiatric Association, 2013).[4] Dr. Veerle Bergink, director of the Women's Mental Health Program at Mount Sinai, explained,

> Postpartum psychosis has been around for thousands of years, and yet it is not an official disease category in the DSM-5 . . . There is no money for it, not for research, not for treatment. There are no guidelines. This is one of the most severe conditions in psychiatry, one that has huge impacts on the mother and potentially on the child, and there's nothing.
>
> (As cited in Winter, 2023, para. 8)

Postpartum psychosis is one of the only disorders associated with homicide. Its inclusion in the DSM as a credible psychiatric disorder would support its identification and the evolution of its treatment, saving the lives of women and babies. For example, the floridly psychotic Andrea Yates was misdiagnosed and discharged from two hospitalizations (O'Malley, 2002). A few days before she killed her children, she was taken off her antipsychotic medications because her catatonia was misdiagnosed as "akinesia," the inability to execute perceivable movement (Spinelli, 2021).

> Psychosis is the perpetrator of the criminal act, and the new mother is a victim of this insidious illness that strips her of the capacity to exercise rational and logical thought and to determine right from wrong. By its very nature, postpartum psychosis renders a woman insane; delusions are fixed and cannot be willed away.
>
> (Barnes, 2021, p. 146)

In the courtroom, postpartum psychosis is difficult for defense lawyers to put forth without the ability to refer to a formal diagnosis. A lack of DSM diagnostic criteria leaves postpartum psychosis vulnerable to misdiagnosis and treatment failure, and a missed opportunity for an accurate and effective criminal defense. For example, I recently received a call from a lawyer who had a client who had attempted to end the life of her 1-year-old while screaming, "I'm getting the demons out of her." Although he had identified domestic violence and had a mitigation report done by a social worker, it was only after he spotted a *Time Magazine* headline that it occurred to him that his client had postpartum psychosis. The article referred to Lindsay Clancy, a mother who had jumped out of her second-story window after killing her three children. Lindsay was a wealthy young woman who had a social media presence as a loving and dedicated mother. Lindsay survived the jump but will be paralyzed for the rest of her life. In its shocking bleakness her story made national news, bringing the phenomenon of postpartum psychosis further into public consciousness.

Even with an identification of psychosis in a convicted mother, her legal team is hard-pressed to succeed with an insanity defense. In roughly half of U.S. states, an insanity defense must conform to versions of the M'Naghten Rule, which originated in mid-19th-century England (Manchester, 2002; West & Lichtenstein, 2006). According to M'Naghten, a defendant must prove either that she did not know what she was doing when she committed a crime or that she did not know it was wrong. M'Naghten is a standard that does not apply to most cases of maternal filicide involving postpartum psychosis, due to the waxing-and-waning nature of the disorder.

> It's difficult on a bunch of levels when someone is in and out of psychosis, because, when they're "out," there's a tendency to believe that they have the ability to control when they're "in." It starts to look more volitional, and volition is one of the key components of M'Naghten . . . . The legal system is predicated on a binary of sanity/insanity.
>
> (Oberman, as cited in Winter, 2023, para. 14)

Treating Postpartum Psychosis

Treatment for postpartum psychosis is largely in the hands of psychopharmaceuticals, namely antipsychotic medications and mood stabilizers. The goals of treatment are generally to maintain medication, control the symptoms, remove the psychosis, and stabilize anxiety and depression. Managing life stress and seeking supportive therapy are also recommended. Charlotte Perkins Gilman, in her book *The Yellow Wallpaper* (2018), gave a riveting description of her own experience. She described being released from the hospital after giving birth, with the following instructions from her doctor:

> Live as domestic a life as possible. Have your child with you all the time . . . . Lie down an hour after each meal. Have but two hours intellectual life a day. And never touch pen, brush, or pencil as long as you live.
>
> (Gilman, 1991, p. 96)

The same framework of hollow advice exists today. What is not typically encouraged is to explore the actual event or potentialities of the mother's psychosis; very rarely do I hear clinicians or clients ask: Why does psychosis happen? What does it mean if it does?

In the groups I run for women who have experienced postpartum psychosis,[5] none of the participants have committed crimes during their episodes but the specter of infanticide often feels present in their narratives. There are several topics that regularly get covered in these groups, including the fragility and depression a mother feels in the aftermath of experiencing psychosis. The women who attend these weekly drop-in groups have not lost a child's life, but some have lost their children in a subsequent custody battle. They grieve the loss of what they see as a normal birth experience, of early bonding with their infant, and the rite of passage of becoming a mother that they believed they would receive. Instead, they experience PTSD from being hospitalized, from being dramatically separated from their newborn, and from the sometimes-violent events that have occurred. They mourn their inability to breastfeed, as trauma interrupted that process. They fear for their future, worrying that psychosis will overwhelm them again. They wonder if there is any hope of having another child.

Most of these women suffered a debilitating episode of depression after the psychotic symptoms abated. This is rarely talked about. Sometimes they had plans to end their lives, sometimes they believed they already had. The women tend to stay away from discussing the actual psychosis they experienced, although many will describe the beginning stages of mania or the days when they felt paranoid and no one around them knew they were scanning the walls for hidden cameras. While treading lightly so as not to destabilize another group member, we do get into the psychotic content, but when stories do emerge, they often carry themes of spiritual warfare—good versus evil, possession, sacrifice, aliens, life after death, or a destined union with Christ.[6]

A Study

As there has been a dearth of research done on spiritual themes in postpartum psychosis, I began a qualitative phenomenological study on postpartum psychosis in which I interviewed about 20 women who have experienced postpartum psychosis. The data from this study, not yet published, has informed this book. In the study, my research assistant and I discerned and coded for 11 categories: history of trauma, relationship with partner, relationship with mother and father, obsessive thoughts about infant, length of psychosis, religious history, religious preoccupation, paranoia, perceived stress prior to birth, and history of mental illness and diagnosis. Emergent themes from the interviews reflected data found in the literature: psychotic symptoms usually lasting no longer than 6 months, no history of psychosis, a new diagnosis of bipolar, a stressful relationship with their partner and with their mother. Notably, most of the participant women are first-born or only daughters, have type-A personalities, and are high-functioning. As first-time mothers, they spiraled with an inability to maintain control and self-sufficiency, and they pleaded for help from their spouses and mothers, eventually finding sterile support in a psychiatric ward.

At the end of the interviews, I asked each participant if the experience of psychosis had changed their lives in a positive way. Most of the participants said yes, noting, for example, that "now I know how to take care of myself, make boundaries, meet my needs, and ask for help from the right people."

Through the study and in my individual and group work with mothers, I've come to some interpretations regarding the continuum of postpartum psychiatric disorders: Sometimes pregnant mothers or new mothers report dreams that are feverish and baby-centered. Because of the vulnerability of a porous emotional, spiritual, and physical membrane during the perinatal period, the same images in the dream brought forth from the unconscious may emerge in the waking day as intrusive thoughts. With the right amount of internal and external duress, these intrusive thoughts can build momentum and gain traction such that the mind may align with them to become ego syntonic; as a result, they blossom into delusions. The psychosis takes on a life of its own and should now be signaling to those around her that she and the baby are in great danger. Like a possession by an archetype—in this case, the Death Mother—psychosis takes over and the mother is its vehicle. Some mothers are more vulnerable and available for this dark inhabitation, depending on the complex web of oppressive dynamics in which they live. The chapters that follow investigate the nature of this possession, the sociocultural and personal dynamics that contribute to it, and ways in which maternal infanticide might more effectively be addressed.

Notes

1 All names are changed in this book, and although the stories are accurate as told to me, their details are disidentified.

2 Men are likely to be unemployed, to be facing spousal separation, abusing alcohol or drugs, questioning their paternity, or viewing the child as an impediment to their career (Resnick, 1969; Resnick & Friedman, 2016).

3 If I meet a mother years after the infanticidal event, she often has come to a state of acceptance and reconciliation. She has a sense of honesty with herself and in our conversation. If I meet her soon after the incident she is often in shock, unable to articulate her experience and often in a state of dissociation, anger, or depression.

4 Because postpartum psychosis is not a diagnosis in the DSM-5, I use as other diagnoses (e.g., major depression with psychosis or bipolar disorder) with peripartum onset.

5 At Postpartum Support International we use the term *perinatal psychosis* because for many women psychotic symptoms began during pregnancy or during labor. Some colleagues in the field are opposed to identifying postpartum psychosis as perinatal, as it detracts from the distinct experience of post-birth psychosis when the hormonal state is in high flux. They argue psychosis during pregnancy can be considered part of a bipolar or depressive disorder with peripartum onset.

6 One of the first examinations of psychosis during postpartum is in a 1420 autobiography by Margery Kempe, an English Christian mystic. Kempe depicted her spiritual, physical, and mental suffering after the birth of her first child, which became a catalyst for her experience of merging with Christ. Kempe indicated that in her "sickness" she found relief because Christ's pain displaced hers.

References

American Psychiatric Association, DSM-5 Task Force. (2013). Diagnostic and statistical manual of mental disorders: DSM-5™ (5th ed.). *American Psychiatric Publishing, Inc.* https://doi.org/10.1176/appi.books.9780890425596

Ayers, S. (2007). Childbirth and stress. In G. Fink (Ed.), *Encyclopedia of stress* (2nd ed., pp. 467–471). Academic Press.

Barnes, D. (2021). Altruistic filicide: A trauma-informed perspective. In G. Wong & G. Parnham (Eds.), *Infanticide and filicide: Foundations in maternal mental health* (pp. 133–152). American Psychiatric Association.

Barnes, D. (2022). Towards a new understanding of pregnancy denial: The misunderstood dissociative disorder. *Archives of Women's Mental Health, 25*, 51–59.

Barr, J., & Beck, C. (2008). Infanticide secrets: Qualitative study on postpartum depression. *Canadian Family Physician, 54*, 1716–1717.

Blackman, J. (2004). Maternal violence: The social psychology of mothers who kill. In B. J. Cling (Ed.), *Sexualized violence against women and children: A psychology and law perspective* (pp. 261–291). The Guilford Press.

Booth, B., Friedman, S., Curry, S., Ward, H., & Stewart, S. (2014). Obsessions of child murder: Underrecognized manifestations of obsessive-compulsive disorder. *Journal of the American Academy of Psychiatry and Law, 42*, 66–74.

Brockington, I. (1996). *Motherhood and mental health*. Oxford University Press.

Carmody, D. P. (2019, April 6). *"Prom mom" case recalled*. Asbury Park Press.

CDC. (2020). *WISQARS: Leading causes of death reports, 1981–2018*. https://wisqars.cdc.gov/fatal-leading/

Chase, T., Shah, A., Maines, J., & Fusick, A. (2021). Psychotic pregnancy denial: A review of the literature and its clinical considerations. *Journal of Psychosomatic Obstetrics & Gynecology, 42*, 253–257.

Chechko, N., Losse, E., & Nehls, S. (2023). Pregnancy denial: Toward a new understanding of the underlying mechanisms. *Current Psychiatry Reports, 25*, 493–500.

Cixous, H. (1976). *The laugh of the Medusa*. University of Chicago Press. http://www2.csudh.edu/ccauthen/576F10/cixous.pdf

Dye, C., Lenz, K., & Leuner, B. (2022). Immune system alterations and postpartum mental illness: Evidence from basic and clinical research. *Frontiers in Global Women's Health, 2*, article 758748, 1–13.

Friedman, S., Cavney, J., & Resnick, P. (2012). Mothers who kill: Evolutionary underpinnings and infanticide law. *Behavioral Sciences & the Law, 30*, 585–597.

Friedman, S., Heneghan, A., & Rosenthal, M. (2007). Characteristics of women who deny or conceal pregnancy. *Psychosomatics, 48*, 117–122.

Friedman, S., & Sorrentino, R. (2012). Commentary: Postpartum psychosis, infanticide, and insanity—implications for forensic psychiatry. *Journal of the American Academy of Psychiatry and the Law, 40*(3), 326–332.

Galvano, F., & Pugi, P. (2023). *The dark side of motherhood—understanding perinatal psychopathologies and extreme behavioral reactions of mothers toward their children and themselves*. www.researchgate.net/publication/370654325_The_dark_side_of_Motherhood_-_Understanding_perinatal_psychopathologies_and_extreme_behavioral_reactions_of_mothers_toward_their_Children_and_themselves

Gilman, C. P. (1991). *The living of Charlotte Perkins Gilman: An autobiography*. University of Wisconsin Press.

Gilman, C. P. (2018). *The yellow wallpaper*. Martino Fine Books.

Hatters-Friedman, S., & Resnick, P. J. (2007). Child murder by mothers: Patterns and prevention. *World Psychiatry, 6*(3), 137–141.

Hatters-Friedman, S., & Sorrentino, R. (2012). Commentary: Postpartum psychosis, infanticide, and insanity-implications for forensic psychiatry. *Journal of the American Academy of Psychiatry and the Law*, *40*(3), 326–332. PMID: 22960914.

Hrdy, S. (1999). *Mother nature: Natural selection and the female of the species*. Chatto & Windus.

Hrdy, S. (2000). *Mother nature: Maternal instincts and how they shape the human species*. Ballantine.

Hrdy, S. (2009). *Mothers and others: The evolutionary origins of mutual understanding*. Belknap Press.

Hrdy, S., & Sieff, D. (2015). The natural history of mothers and infants. In D. Sieff (Ed.), *Understanding and healing emotional trauma* (pp. 182–202). Routledge.

Jung, C. G. (1969). General aspects of dream psychology (R. F. C. Hull, Trans.). In H. Read, M. Fordham, & G. Adler (Eds.), *The collected works of C. G. Jung: Vol. 8. Structure and dynamics of the psyche* (2nd ed., pp. 237–280). Princeton University Press. (Original work published 1948). https://doi.org/10.1515/9781400850952.237

Kempe, M. (2000). *The book of Margery Kempe* (B. Windeatt, Trans.). Penguin Classics. (Original work published 1420)

Klerman, J. A. (2001). Infanticide and induced abortion. In N. Smelser & P. Baltes (Eds.), *International encyclopedia of social and behavioral sciences*. Elsevier. www.sciencedirect.com/topics/social-sciences/infanticide

Lacan, J. (1991). *The seminar of Jacques Lacan: Book II: The ego in Freud's theory and in the technique of psychoanalysis 1954–1955* (J.-A. Miller, Ed., S. Tomeaselli, Trans). W. W. Norton. (Original work published 1977)

Laing, R. D. (1961). *Self and others*. Pantheon Books.

Levene, A. (2005). The estimation of mortality at the London foundling hospital, 1741–1799. *Population Studies*, *59*(1), 87–97. www.jstor.org/stable/30040438

Manchester, J. (2002). Beyond accommodation: Reconstructing the insanity defense to provide an adequate remedy for postpartum psychotic women. *Journal of Criminal Law & Criminology*, *93*, 713.

Marcé, L.-V. (1858). *Traité de la folie des femmes enceintes, des nouvelles accouchées, et des nourrices*. J. B. Ballière.

McCoy, S. B., Beal, J. M., & Watson, G. (2003). Endocrine factors and postpartum depression: A selected review. *Journal of Reproductive Medicine*, *48*(6), 402–408.

Meyer, C. L., Oberman, M., & White, K. (2001). *Mothers who kill their children: Understanding the acts of moms from Susan Smith to the "prom mom"*. New York University Press.

Miller, E., Hoxha, D., Wisner, K., & Gossett, D. (2015a). The impact of perinatal depression on the evolution of anxiety and obsessive-compulsive symptoms. *Archives of Women's Mental Health*, *18*(3), 457–461.

Miller, E., Hoxha, D., Wisner, K., & Gossett, D. (2015b). Obsessions and compulsions in postpartum women without obsessive compulsive disorder. *Journal of Women's Mental Health*, *24*(10), 825–830.

Miller, L. J. (2003). Denial of pregnancy. In M. G. Spinelli (Ed.), *Infanticide: Psychosocial and legal perspectives on mothers who kill* (pp. 81–104). American Psychiatric Publishing.

Netchev, S. (2023, June 2). The Roman laws of the twelve tables, c 490. BCE. *World History Encyclopedia*. www.worldhistory.org/image/17482/the-roman-laws-of-the-twelve-tables-c-449-bce/

Oberman, M., & Meyer, C. L. (2008). *When mothers kill: Interviews from prison*. New York University Press.

O'Malley, S. (2002, February). A cry in the dark. *Oprah Magazine*. www.oprah.com/omagazine/andrea-yates-a-cry-in-the-dark/all

Resnick, P. J. (1969). Child murder by parents: A psychiatric review of filicide. *American Journal of Psychiatry, 126*(3), 325–334.

Resnick, P. J. (2016). Filicide in the United States. *Indian Journal of Psychiatry, 58*(suppl. 2), 203–209.

Şar, V., Aydın, N., van der Hart, O., Frankel, A., Şar, M., & Omay, O. (2016). Acute dissociative reaction to spontaneous delivery in a case of total denial of pregnancy: Diagnostic and forensic aspects. *Journal of Trauma & Dissociation, 18*(5), 710–719.

Shelton, J. L. E., Muirhead, Y., & Canning, K. E. (2010). Ambivalence toward mothers who kill: An examination of 45 US cases of maternal neonaticide. *Behavioral Sciences & the Law, 28*(6), 812–831.

Sherwood, V. (2021). *Haunted: The death mother archetype.* Chiron.

Sieff, D. F. (2019). The death mother as nature's shadow: Infanticide, abandonment, and the collective unconscious. *Psychological Perspectives, 62*(1), 15–34.

Silverio, S. A., Wilkinson, C., Fallon, V., Bramante, A., & Staneva, A. A. (2021). When a mother's love is not enough: A cross-cultural critical review of anxiety, attachment, maternal ambivalence, abandonment, and infanticide. In C.-H. Mayer & E. Vanderheiden (Eds.), *International handbook of love: Transcultural and transdisciplinary perspectives* (pp. 291–315). Springer.

Sit, D., Rothschild, A. J., & Wisner, K. L. (2006). A review of postpartum psychosis. *Journal of Women's Health, 15*(4), 352–368.

Spinelli, M. G. (2004). Maternal infanticide associated with mental illness: Prevention and the promise of saved lives. *American Journal of Psychiatry, 161*(9), 1548–1557.

Spinelli, M. G. (2008). *Infanticide: Psychosocial and legal perspectives on mothers who kill.* American Psychiatric Association.

Spinelli, M. G. (2021). Postpartum psychosis: A diagnosis for the DSM-V. *Archives of Women's Mental Health, 5*, 817–822.

Stowe, Z. N., Calhoun, K., Ramsey, C., Sadek, N., & Newport, J. (2001). Mood disorders during pregnancy and lactation: Defining issues of exposure and treatment. *CNS Spectrums, 6*(2), 150–166.

Wessel, J., & Buscher, U. (2002). Denial of pregnancy: Population based study. *BMJ, 324*, 458.

West, D. A., & Lichtenstein, B. (2006). Andrea Yates and the criminalization of the filicidal maternal body. *Feminist Criminology, 1*(3), 173–187.

Wilson, R. F., Klevens, J., Williams, D., & Xu, L. (2020). Infant homicides within the context of safe haven laws—United States, 2008–2017. *Morbidity, Mortality Weekly Report, 69*, 1385–1390.

Winter, J. (2023, March 14). What we still don't understand about postpartum psychosis. *New Yorker Magazine.* www.newyorker.com/science/annals-of-medicine/what-we-still-dont-understand-about-postpartum-psychosis

Wisner, K., Peindl, K., & Hanusa, B. (1994). Symptomatology of affective and psychotic illnesses related to childbearing. *Journal of Affective Disorders, 30*, 77–87.

Chapter 2

The Death Mother Archetype

The modern infanticidal mother, in her ineffable and brutal manner, may be better captured by an archetypal language as opposed to a clinical or anthropological one. Rather than searching for diagnostic criteria or symptoms that tend to miss the forest for the trees, the drastic intensity of infanticide is better understood by use of metaphor, symbol, and imagination—containers better able to carry her weight. I have encountered the Death Mother archetype while listening to the stories of mothers who have ended the lives of their children. It emerges as the unfiltered energy of a wounded mother's need to destroy what she cannot bear as part of life. The Death Mother archetype is akin to what Jung referred to as the *Terrible Mother* (1952/1967b, para. 567). Although he identified this side of the Great Mother as relegated to the shadow in modern Western culture, he left much unsaid as to her force.

Archetypal Theory Briefly

Early in his work, Jung noticed a pattern of stories and images throughout various cultures that he saw as specifically meaningful. He saw these repeated in patients' dreams and wrote:

> For years I have been observing and investigating the products of the unconscious in the widest sense of the word, namely dreams, fantasies, visions, and delusions of the insane. I have not been able to avoid recognizing certain regularities, that is, types . . . . [These] repeat themselves frequently and have a corresponding meaning. I therefore employ the term "motif" to designate these repetitions . . . . [These] can be arranged under a series of archetypes, the chief of them being . . . the shadow, the wise old man, the child (including the child hero), the mother ("Primordial Mother" and "Earth Mother") as a supraordinate personality ("daemonic" because supraordinate), and her counterpart the maiden.
>
> (1954/1969c, para. 309)

Archetypes are primordial, structural elements of the human psyche reborn in the deepest collective layer of the unconscious in every individual. Inherited across

DOI: 10.4324/9781003412809-4

time and derived from the natural world, the archetypal image both "signifies and at the same time evokes the instinct" (1954/1969c, para. 414). In citing the archetypal Mother as demonic, Jung is referencing her as mediating between and partaking of the divine (or that which transcends human life) and humans. Deeply unconscious, archetypes are influences common to us all, but we are often unaware of them. Carrying energy that is instinctual, collective, and transcendent of consciousness, they tend to have an emotionally possessive effect, capturing consciousness so that it is blind to its own archetypal stance (Hillman, 1975).

James Hillman, founder of archetypal psychology, suggested the archetypal perspective offers the advantage of organizing into clusters or constellations a host of events from different areas of life. As the primordial elements that structure the human psyche, archetypes are also "Gods who cannot be encompassed by anyone's individual soul" (1975, p. 134). They form the gravitational center around which our experiences cluster in the unconscious as groups of affect- and meaning-laden images, or *complexes* (Jung, 1948/1969b, para. 204). For example, one's experiences of mothering (whether positive or negative) creates a mother complex. At the core of the complex resides the Great Mother archetype. This archetype, arising from the deepest collective layer of our unconscious, carries with it all the potential ideas and behaviors related to the natural rounds of birth, life, death, and rebirth—symbolized in the image across time and cultures of the Great Mother. Archetypes manifest both on a personal level, through complexes, and collectively, as characteristics of whole cultures.

> The archetype of the hero, for example, appears first in behavior, the drive to activity, outward exploration, response to challenge, seizing and grasping and extending. It appears second in the images of Hercules, Achilles, Samson (or their cinema counterparts) doing their specific tasks; and third, in a style of consciousness, in feelings of independence, strength, and achievement, in ideas of decisive action, coping, planning, virtue, conquest (over animality), and in psychopathologies of battle, overpowering masculinity, and single-mindedness.
>
> (Hillman, 1975, xx)

As an aspect of the Great Mother, the Death Mother is present in every woman as an archetypal inheritance of possible ideas and instinctual energies.

The Mother Archetype

In "Symbols of the Mother and Rebirth" (1952/1967b) Jung provided poetic descriptions of the Great Mother's iconography and archetypal attributes. He considered the Mother the most important archetype, symbolizing the source of life and the primordial unconscious. The Great Mother appears under an almost infinite variety of guises, from the Hindu Mother goddess Durga who as protection and strength slew the demon king Mahishasura to Demeter and Persephone, Greek goddesses of fecundity and the birth–death cycles of nature. As Gaia, or Mother

Earth, she is associated with the ecological (interconnected, relational) nature of life. "Her commitment to the continuation of life is central, but the commitment to any specific life is nonexistent; there is an unconflicted acceptance of the value and necessity of death as an integral part of life" (Stevens, 1982, p. 17). The Great Mother symbolizes the range of mothering from cherishing and nourishing to orgiastic emotionality, her Stygian depths—from plentiful harvests to plagues of locusts.

The procreative, life-sustaining, and deadly power of the archetypal Mother is humanized in the personal mother, her ancestral mothers, and women related to caregiving. Within and beyond the personal mother and our relationships with mothering is the archetype of the Great Mother—the force that drives creation *and* destruction, fecundity but *also* the barren womb.

In the lineage of Christian mythology, she is Eve who, eating of the tree of knowledge, birthed consciousness and humanity, the Gnostic Sophia or Divine Wisdom, and later Mary, Mother of God. Over the course of the evolution of Western culture, her archetypal purview has been sequestered into images of the Good Mother that stand for purity and fruitfulness, such as the cornucopia, a plowed field, or a garden. The Good Mother offers the protection, devotion, sympathy, and love that inhabits the home, Paradise, the Church, the country, the Earth, the woods, the sea, and the moon. In the West, the Virgin Mary has come to encapsulate the energies of the Good Mother, dissociating the feminine and mother from sexuality, menstruation, and the natural cycles of life. This has largely split the culture consciousness and female identity in the West off from the natural wholeness of the Great Mother, which includes her sexuality and, through the blood of her barren womb, her cyclical relationship with death.

Split off from the Good Mother and relegated to shadow is the negative or Terrible Mother, which Jung described as denoting, "anything secret, hidden, dark; the abyss, the world of the dead, anything that devours, seduces, and poisons, that is terrifying and inescapable like fate" (1954/1969c, p. 82). Denied her place and power in Western culture's drive to govern rather than be governed by nature, the Death Mother's energies have been driven into the shadow as feminine evil in images of the witch (hunted and burned at the stake); devouring and entwining animals, such the snake or serpent; the grave or sarcophagus; and deep water. In the Book of Revelations, she has been made into the Whore of Babylon, a devouring bestial woman who is also the place of hell and abomination. She is also the Echidna—half-woman, half-snake, the mother of monsters—and Medusa, who had snakes for hair.

Jungian scholar Louise Marie von Franz coined the term *Death Mother* to refer to the deep shadow expression in fairy tales of the archetypal feminine portrayed as a possessively devouring mother, literally and intra-psychically. Von Franz identified the ensnaring, depriving, and rejecting creatures in fairytales as aspects of the negative mother. They are repeatedly depicted as a stepmother, witch, serpent, spider, or female ogre who eats, imprisons, chases, and punishes children. "The animal form of the spider characterizes an *evil mother* because the spider is treacherous and a manifestation of blood-sucking night spirits" (2020, p. 203).

Erich Neumann, a close student of Jung's, furthered the examination of the Terrible Mother archetype:

> The maternal womb becomes the deadly devouring maw of the underworld . . . the abyss of hell, the dark hole or the depths, the devouring womb of the grave and of death, of darkness without light, of nothingness. For this woman who generates life and all living things on earth is the same who takes them back into herself, who pursues her victims and captures them with snare and net.
>
> (1955/1963, p. 149)

Neumann offered a schema that presents the feminine as a circle, the "Great Round or the Great Container," which "tends to hold fast to everything that springs from it and to surround it like an eternal substance. Everything born of it belongs to it and remains subject to it" (1955/1963, p. 25; see Figure 2.1).

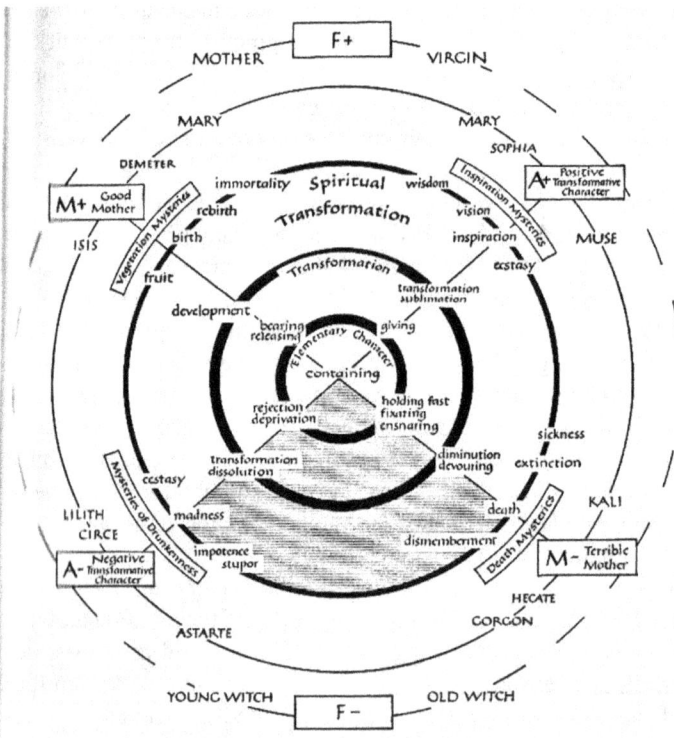

Figure 2.1 Schema III. Erich Neumann (1955/1963, p. 82 facing page). © Bollingen Foundation.

In Neumann's schema, the upper portion of the circle (F+) shows the Great Mother's positive side, which is protective and comforting, whereas the lower, negative pole (F-) is shaded, held in shadow, and like quicksand or a spider web that entraps and smothers. In sum, the Great Mother is both savage and protective, having an intimate relationship to the underworld. There is nothing coy or sexual about her; although she unabashedly gives birth to all creatures, including anima figures (inner images of the feminine), from the depths of her body. She is Life and Death, does not seek immortality, and destroys those who defy or threaten her.

Neumann and Jung purported that the ego is the center of consciousness, and as a human develops the ego must separate itself from the unconscious or the Great Mother archetype, the great round container, to become a separate conscious individual. In its attempt to individuate and separate from the gravitational force of the Mother archetype, it may encounter the energy of the devouring Terrible Mother. This is the Great Mother's shadow, the shaded area of Neumann's schema, where containment is experienced as ensnaring and fixating, and "the mother becomes the devourer, giving sickness, death and extinction" (Harding, 1935, p. 99). Both Jung and Neumann were likely speaking to their own tension of separation from their mothers, a developmental need Jung repeatedly referred to; one that is harrowing but essential to becoming a man. Jung's preoccupation with the devouring mother is evident in his cry, "The Battle for Deliverance from Mother" (1952/1967a).

Jung's theories have long been criticized for essentializing the masculine and feminine, asserting that the true nature of the feminine is to be nurturing. Jung suggested the receptive and relational archetypal energy is dominant in women and dormant in men, whereas creative and cognitive archetypal energy is dominant in men and dormant in women. Her access to Logos (the archetypal masculine quality of logic) manifests negatively and unconsciously and places her "in danger of losing her femininity" (1928/1966, para. 337). A feminist critique of this divide is apt, as the danger of continuing to trap women in a patriarchal standard that devalues their intellect and controls their expression of feminine energy while denying men access to their own feminine energies is dangerous for all of us.

"There is a seed within [Jung's] theory which contains the possibility of freeing women and the feminine from the very patriarchal formulations that surround them" (Douglas, 1989, p. x). To find this seed and more fully access the Great Mother, it's invaluable to hear from the women themselves who have been caught in the Death Mother archetype.

The Death Mother

Marion Woodman elaborated on the concept of the Death Mother archetype as the strong negative energy of the mother whose end is the killing, smothering, or annihilation of her child. Woodman described what happens when the Death Mother's energies are "released from someone's unconscious":

> The Death Mother wields a cold, fierce, violent, and corrosive power. She is rampant in our society right now. When Death Mother's gaze is directed at us,

it penetrates both psyche and body, turning us into stone. It kills hope. It cuts us dead. We collapse. Our life-energy drains from us and we sink into chthonic darkness. In this state we find ourselves yearning for the oblivion of death. Eventually this yearning for death permeates our cells, causing our body to turn against itself. We may become physically ill. This energy is most destructive when it comes from somebody that we love and trust. It's the archetypal Death MOTHER, . . . It's what happened in the original trauma; we trusted our beloved mother and suddenly we were hit with the realization that we were not acceptable. We realized that our mother wished that we, or some part of us, was dead.

(Woodman & Sieff, 2015, p. 70)

Sieff defined the archetypal Death Mother as:

harmful and traumatizing energy which comes to us from a person, institution, culture, or nation-state that we would naturally expect to nurture, protect, and support us. In its most extreme form, she might consciously or unconsciously want us dead; in a less extreme form, she feels ambivalent or indifferent about our existence and wants a part of us dead.

(Sieff, 2022)

In her discussion of the Death Mother, Woodman's focus tended to be on the effects of the archetype on the child. Medusa's gaze freezes a child in toxic shame, who then contends with the traumatized remnants of this in their adulthood, often, as Woodman points out, through addiction. This is important work, which Sieff has stalwartly taken up in her work on maternal hostility and shame.

Alternatively, my focus lies with the human mother who has become possessed by the Death Mother. She can be difficult to access, "buried deep in the shadow and surrounded with shame" (2019, p. 15). It is difficult for a woman to admit and work consciously to mediate her relationship with the instinctive energies of the Death Mother when they arise from the inherited depths of her unconscious on the tide of overwhelming and distressing emotions.

The energy of the Death Mother archetype is more than the drive to kill a child, it is a dynamic of energies, vexing to the intellect, almost impossible to contain in a description. The Death Mother archetype is a fury of the betrayed, a fear of the entrapped, a movement of liberation, and a blind white rage of action. It is the catalyzing of a movement from the mundane to the *mysterium tremendum* in the activation of the sacred, deadly force of the Great Mother that transcends human life. Specifically, these archetypal energies arise in a mother whose children are still close to her womb and who has experienced a deep constitutional wrong that has injured her integrity as a mother to such a degree that a wire is tripped and an electricity released. We know from neuroscience that the trip wire of a trauma reaction bypasses the executive, decision-making functions of the brain. Moreover, in the frame of archetypal and Jungian psychology, the quality of this electrical surge that floods the maternal psyche in reaction to trauma is that of the Death Mother archetype.

Images of the Mother Archetype

As deeply chthonic in nature, "archetypes are irrepresentable in themselves, but their effects are discernible in archetypal images and motifs" (Sharp & Jung, 1991, p. 27). Arising from the unconscious, archetypal images and motifs are found in myths, legends, religions, and fairytales. These images are imbued with power because they arise from the instinctual level of the unconscious and carry the "dynamism of instinct . . . which makes itself felt in the numinosity and fascinating power of the archetypal image" (Jung, 1954/1969c, para. 414). Archetypal images offer a way for us to access the energy of an archetype.

In Fairytales

Fairytales provide a remarkable cultural backdrop for the human imagination and a showpiece of the emergence of repressed instincts that help narrate the archetypal meaning of events, including filicide. Fairytales "have the great advantage of being naive (not literary) and of having been worked out in collective groups, with the result that they contain purely archetypal material unobscured by personal problems" (Franz, 1993, p. 1).

Filicide is one of the most common features in fairytales: the Wolf's consumption of Little Red Riding Hood; the old woman's attempt to bake and eat young Hansel and Gretel; the insistence of the Evil Witch on killing Snow White, not once but twice, for her pure white beauty; and a desperate mother's need to stay young forever, which she can only do by feeding on Rapunzel's lustrous hair. The character of the wicked stepmother has gained notoriety as one of the evilest villains to be found in fairytales, frequently set up as a foil to the innocent and virtuous stepdaughter whom she mistreats and who ultimately gains victory over her.

Early in a fairytale, a death of the Good Mother, often piously in childbirth, signals to us we are in the territory of the Death Mother. The father has quickly remarried another queen with a slightly sterner complexion or brash style, who quickly becomes jealous of the king's daughter because the daughter is kinder and fairer than the queen.

Freudian psychologist Bruno Bettelheim suggested, "The fantasy of the wicked stepmother not only preserves the good mother intact, it also prevents having to feel guilty about one's angry wishes about her" (1976, p. 69). However, I would contend that splitting off the biological mother (imagined as naturally all-good) from the unnaturally wicked stepmother represents the repression of the inherent presence of the Death Mother and our collective great difficulty in tolerating both the good and bad in motherhood. In other words, the mother becoming the stepmother is a personification of the murderous impulses in mother.

In the fairytale "Hansel and Gretel," it was originally the mother, not the step-mother, who kicked the children out of the home (Marchiano, 2021). If we knew it was Hansel and Gretel's biological mother who forced them out and into an even worse (grand)mother's house, it would be hard to bear the endless maternal wickedness. The Death Mother is intolerable as the totality of the *actual* mother; it's easier to distantly know her as the stepmother, the mother-in-law, the witch, the hag, the nag. "Female monsters represent the bedtime stories patriarchy tells itself" (Zimmerman, 2021, p. 80).

Von Franz suggested that because there is a notable lack of Goddess images in Christian religion, fairytales hold the feminine images that complement this lack, although they are thrust into patriarchal roles.

> The shift from mother to stepmother as seen through a patriarchal lens also becomes more profound: evil, destructive mothers presented a challenge to patriarchal family values, whereas stepmothers were outsiders and could there-fore act as a warning to other women without completely defying patriarchal structures. These depictions of stepmothers were so powerful that even today, we have internalized the narrative of a powerful woman equating to an evil woman.
>
> (Behrooz, 2016, para. 9)

The large-scale witch hunts and trials that took place throughout Europe in the 16th and 17th centuries illuminate this fear of the evil nature of the feminine and need to oppress women who, if allowed any agency, became figures of great terror and misfortune (Lewis, 2020). Like the witches in fairytales, the women accused of witchcraft were seen as having uncanny and unholy powers and were ostracized because their ways stood in opposition to accepted values.

> The witch figure presents an awesome image of the primordial feminine con-cern with herself. Maternal life spends itself like life's blood flowing outward to nourish the sounds and bodies of loved ones. In the witch figure, life flows inward and downward to fuel the dark recesses of a woman's psyche or a man's anima.
>
> (Ulanov & Ulanov, 1987, p. 33)

The uncanny feminine threatens the established order and is demonized to silence her challenge to our own impulse to conform. In the Rapunzel story the stepmother is described as "a witch with great power who was feared by all the world" (Behrooz, 2016, para. 4). Witch-like characters are often the most powerful in fairytales. They provide much of the narrative drive of the tales and possess a considerable amount of agency in their actions. In these tales, the men are almost always nonexistent; the fathers, if alive, are passive and complicit or ineffective. Even the father of Sleeping Beauty could not manage to hide the spinning wheel.

Devouring or eating the children is a hallmark Death Mother act, as it perfectly defies the nurturing and protective characteristics normally associated with a maternal figure. "Cannibalistic female villains withhold food and threaten to turn children into their own source of nourishment, reincorporating them into the bodies that gave birth to them" (Tatar, 1987, p. 140). Thus, by going against their intended maternal natures in a culture that sees the natural mother as all-loving, these women transform into something monstrous and ogre-like.

We are consistently exposed to these stories but with very little sympathy for or understanding of the female villain. Where did the witch come from? How did the negative mother complex come to inhabit her? Perhaps the old hag who kidnapped Hansel and Gretel was once a shining young girl who was raped and impregnated, then lost her baby and in shame and devastation isolated herself in the woods, longing for children.

> We just assume that [the stepmother or witch] was always that way—mean, cruel, withholding, manipulative, jealous, and greedy. We never get to hear her side of the story about the whining, disobedient, manipulative child who is the apple of her father's eye. The wicked stepmother represents the disappointments each child carries at not having the perfect mother, that illusory mother next door who is ever present, ever understanding and unconditionally loving.
>
> (Murdock, 2020, p. 155)

In fairytales, mothers like the Evil Queen in "Snow White" or Mother Gothel in "Rapunzel" carry a strong negative energy of vanity, narcissism, and envy that drives them to devour, smother, abuse, or annihilate their child. These mothers are not different from modern mothers who obsessively use medical interventions and fad diets to stay thin and young-looking forever while constantly making small verbal assaults and criticisms of their daughters. Though these mothers are not actively infanticidal, they slowly kill their children by burdening them with their narcissistic needs, seeking in the mirror to see the most desirable woman of all.

In "Cinderella," we also see the dark side of this beauty ideal, where the stepmother encourages her daughters to mutilate their feet to fit into the slipper and trick the prince. Behrooz observed this to

> be uncomfortably reminiscent of the present-day beauty industry, of the plastic-surgery, Photoshop and eating disorders which twist and conform women into the requisite beauty ideal. If this is the world the stepmother is forced into, where she must viciously compete with other women in order to attract and keep men, and therefore status, stability and significance, her resorting to evil in order to maintain her position becomes, if not justifiable, at least understandable. By seeing the stepmother as a victim of patriarchal values, much in the same way the heroines are a victim of her, . . . [she] becomes . . . a complex character deserving of the reader's consideration and sympathy.
>
> (2016, para. 10)

Playwright Irma Mayorga stressed, "Myths are human stories that contain meta-phoric truths to reveal healing potential whether modern or ancient in their origins by bringing opposing forces together" (2001, p. 160). Myths help us hold the tension of the Great Mother—that she abundantly gives and nourishes, but she *also* mercilessly destroys to bring renewal. Fairytales reveal her presence despite patri-archal culture's attempt to banish her. In real life she can be seen in variations of loss and justice, protection and destruction, and rage and empowerment.

Kali, Oshun, Lamia, Lilith, and La Llorona

There are many archetypal images that hold the Death Mother energy, which reflects not only its existence but its need to come forward. There are archetypal images that hold the duality of the mother both nurturing and terrifying, and there are a few that lean more toward evil. Images from Latin or Eastern countries tend to have archetypes that hold opposites, whereas in the United States, largely due to puritanism and Protestantism, our images are split between Mother Mary and the serpent Lilith, posing an either–or divide between good and bad, virgin and whore, saint and demon.

Almost every ancient culture and religion acknowledges the Death Mother. She is symbolized in Lilith or Malkah-ha-Shadim in the (pre-)Jewish and Christian religions, Maha-Kali in Indo-Germanic spirituality, and the Mórrigan in the Celtic tradition the Harbinger of Doom, and Angrbodha in the Germanic. The Egyptian goddess Anuket/Anukhet was the giver of life and later merged with Mother God-dess Nephtys, the devourer. The Death Mother also makes an appearance as the vile Hel, who rules the Norse underworld, and as the demon goddess Tiamat from Sumerian mythology, who is often depicted as a serpent or dragon, but is consid-ered both a creator goddess and the monstrous embodiment of primordial chaos. These traditions carry the wisdom that life comes with the price of death; the Divine Feminine is abundantly giving and nourishing but also merciless in the destruction needed to bring renewal. She is the Mother of necessary painful change and knows duty to the higher good instead of motherly love for love's sake. The discussion that follows highlights her relationship to the need for death and destruction and her repression in Western culture.

The Hindu goddess Kali—*Kali Ma*, meaning *Kali Mother*—has both nurturing and devouring aspects. Hindus worship her as the universal mother of all beings; while simultaneously giving birth to all humanity, she devours her own children and wears a bloody belt of severed heads around her waist and a necklace of sev-ered arms. Kali is an energetic form that exists in our collective unconscious, which "contains the whole spiritual heritage of [hu]mankind's evolution" (Jung, 1931/1969a, para. 342). Millions of Hindus, particularly in eastern and southern India, worship her regularly and ritualistically; she is as integrated and essential as the Holy Trinity is in the West. Yet, unlike any entity accessible in the West, Kali is "simultaneously womb and tomb"—both giving life to her children and taking it away.

Figure 2.2 Goddess Kali. Religious painting showing Kali standing on Shiva (1883). Calcutta Art Studio. Public domain.

Kali was born of rage, bursting from a warrior's forehead. Once born, the black goddess went wild and ate all the demons she came across, stringing their heads on a chain that she wore around her neck. It is understood that Kali Ma is willing and able to do the necessary deeds that others are not capable of doing, including destroying the ego. She destroys our attachment to the temporary body and reminds us to enjoy the beauty of life because death is certainly coming. The garland of severed heads she wears represents her children, whom she has liberated from the illusion of the ego.

> Every woman has a Kali side; every mother has a secret devourer, a baby killer in her soul. When contemporary women write honestly out of their own lived lives, they wrestle with the shadows of their actions and their fates. They wrestle with their Kali natures; they dare to name the terrible taboos of motherhood. Some write about their murderous impulses toward their own children.
>
> (Lowinsky, 1992, p. 195)

It is a difficult maternal struggle to navigate the conflicts between one's own and one's children's needs, especially in the face of the cultural ideal of mother love. Most mothers do not always feel joy in, at peace with, or kindly toward their children. In our modern lives, Kali's power to free one from the ego's attachment to an idealized self has been forced underground. Women's strengths and agency are suppressed in acquiescence to domestic and domesticated roles. Kali's Death Mother energy festers in the unconscious, and without release it toxifies into depression, suicidality, and murderous Kali rage. Unchanneled into creative forms, it becomes "the dark devouring stagnation of life unlived" (Murdock, 2020, p. 23). Kali then takes other forms: self-destruction, ruined lives, neglected and abused children or, in the case of many of the women with whom I work, infanticide.

Oshun is both a spirit and a goddess in the Yoruba religion of West Africa. She presides over fertility, love, and freshwater, and is one of the 400+ *Orishas* who are avatars of the supreme deity Olodumare, who is neither male nor female, is referred to as *they* or sometimes *it*, and who created and is the universe. According to some accounts, Oshun is the favorite of Olodumare and is the only one who is welcomed and can deliver messages to the realm of Orun, Olodumare's sphere. Oshu is invoked by women and men for luck, health, strength during times of change, and prosperity. Oshun is both a creative and destructive force—a Great Mother who participated in the creation of the world and has saved it from distinction, but who is also known in her Death Mother aspect, destroying life when humans offend her through their carelessness, cruelty, and lack of respect for the divine and the natural world.

The Death Mother appears in the Greco-Roman mythological world first as Lamia, a female spirit of evil with a human body from the waist up and a serpentine body from the waist down. Lamia is often regarded as the Queen of the Damned—the mother of vampires and succubi—with an insatiable sexual appetite and an unquenchable thirst for blood. Despite this, Lamia is sometimes seen as a figure deserving sympathy as she was turned into a monster by her grief at the discovery of her dead children, who had been killed by the goddess Hera in revenge for Lamia sleeping with *her* husband, Zeus. Since then, raging Lamia haunts pregnant women, kidnaps newborn infants, and persecutes and destroys children. Lamia characters, such as the witch in "Hansel and Gretel," appear in the lineage of Western fairytales.

Similar in spirit is Lilith from the Christian, Judaic, and Islamic texts, where she is generally referred to as the mother of demons. She is commonly believed to have been Adam's first wife. In her story, Lilith left Adam and the Garden of Eden after she refused to become subservient to him. Primary characteristics seen in the legends about Lilith are that she is the incarnation of lust, causing men to be led astray, and as an enemy of faithful, fruitful women, she kidnaps and kills children. A demonizing female agent, she is seen as the serpent who tempted Eve to eat from the tree of knowledge—an act of feminine disobedience that births human consciousness from the primordial state of unconscious oneness.

In Latin American folklore, La Llorona, "The Weeping Woman," is a mother who drowned her children. She drowned herself as well, but she was not allowed through the gates of heaven and was forced to remain in purgatory, roaming and wailing while looking for her children. The most popular version of the story tells of La Llorona as a young mother whose betrayal by her husband drives her mad. In her madness, she takes her toddlers down to the river and drowns them, one after another. When she comes to her senses and realizes what she has done, she also drowns herself. Stuck in purgatory, La Llorona steals children who wander outside after dark; thus, generations of mothers have used her specter to frighten their own children away from dangerous places. "She killed her own children when she was alive, imagine what she'll do to you now that she's dead" (Elbein, 2015, para. 12). Maybe due to her roots in Aztec mythology and Christian morality, La Llorona, like Lamia, is both monster and victim, never settled in either role, but dependent on the reader's perspective.

La Llorona, Medea, Kali, Lilith, and Lamia—among many others—are not time travelers, nor are they physically or geographically linked. Rather, they are representations of the energetic states/archetypes that exist in the collective unconscious of modern mothers. La Llorona was brought to my attention by a woman who had recovered from postpartum psychosis. As a child of Mexican parents, she had often heard La Llorona's story. It is possible that because she grew up with the story, she had a reference for the madness she experienced as a new mother that allowed her to contain her infanticidal feeling so that both she and her child survived.

In 1986 Juana Leija, a Texan mother of seven, took her children to a nearby river and threw six of them in, intending to follow before she was stopped. Two children died and four were rescued. Later it was said she "had not eaten well in days after repeated abuse from her husband . . . she had no appetite . . . He had badly beaten her the night before" (Ruiz, 2001, para. 4). At trial she said, "I saw no way out for us . . . I saw that the best thing was to end my life and their lives and that would end all of our suffering," and in an interview she later said, "Yo soy La Llorona" (as cited in Elbein, 2015, para. 17).

> Leija's identification with La Llorona points to a theme not of madness, but of desperation. A poor woman with no means of support and illegitimate children, as in the original folktale, would be in deep trouble whether she lived in colonial Mexico or modern San Antonio. Perhaps the homeless, starving La Llorona chooses to kill her children out of love . . . to save them the suffering of wasting away.
>
> (Elbein, 2015, para. 35)

Denise's Story

Denise was raised by a single mother, who was protective and abusive, using ridicule to scold. Denise had a stepfather who sexually assaulted her when she was in middle school. Within a year, she began to run away from home. During that time, a gang "pulled a train on her," which meant she experienced the violent, prolonged assault of *gang rape*, being raped by several men one after another. Denise never reported the crime. After this incident, and while growing up, she was bullied and called names like "slut" and "whore." When Denise was a teenager, she became pregnant and hid the pregnancy from her mother until one evening, while taking a bath, her mother walked in and saw her protruding 6-month-pregnant belly. Her mother insisted Denise abort the child. Denise resisted; she was excited to have something to love within her abusive home. Her mother forced Denise to have a late-term abortion, which at that time was a 3-day procedure: day 1, feticide; day 2, intact dilation and evacuation; and day 3, recovery. Denise was despondent after this. For years, this event informed her life of mothering.

Between the ages of 19 and 26, Denise had five children, which means she was either pregnant or tending to a newborn for seven consecutive years, during which she endured an extended state of postpartum depression. The father of three of her children was severely abusive. As Denise reported, he "practiced his boxing skills on me," brandished guns, and trained fighting dogs in the home. Denise stayed in the relationship because she wanted her children to have a father in their lives, "unlike the way I grew up."

Because she wanted to "keep a roof over my children's heads," and the family was destitute, Denise had been engaging in transactional sex with the apartment building landlord to keep the apartment. After she had her fifth child, she no longer wanted to continue the arrangement. Denise reported to me that one day when she had her newborn with her, he attempted to assault her again. She said, "No." When he pushed her and became violent, Denise described feeling overwhelmed and confused. She reported, "At that moment the landlord and my boyfriend and my stepdad were the same person. I lost myself." But she was distinctly aware of her 8-week-old baby next to her; her maternal instincts were hypervigilant. Her nervous system was in fight mode when she grabbed a weapon to stop further harm coming to herself and her baby. Denise's Kali rage, the pain and anger that had been forced underground, erupted exponentially, and she shot the landlord point-blank. Denise was executing justice, as Kali does, as Oshun does, as von Franz suggested Mother Earth does, and as Medea did. In this way, the Divine comes through the dark mother to right a wrong.

Denise and the first infant she carried in her womb are victims of Denise's mother's compromised maternal instincts, the instincts that failed to protect Denise from her stepfather but overprotected Denise from an unborn child. Unmitigated was this Death Mother energy which was then taken up by Denise at her moment of need.

Medea

Medea anchors my understanding of the Death Mother archetype. She is past and present. The women's chorus in a contemporary play about Medea expresses her presence in modern mothers: "In every quiet suburban wife/dissatisfied with married life/is Medea raging" (Harrison, as cited in Van Zyl Smit, 2002, p. 112).

As an archetypal image, Medea speaks to what happens when the entrapment, fury, and pain women experience because of the collective fear and oppression of the feminine leads to female violence, including maternal infanticide.

There are many versions of Medea: in Ovid's *Metamorphoses*, she is revered as a powerful sorcerer who can invoke the powers of darkness, and in Seneca's *Medea* (50 CE/2014), she is presented as a witch with demonic subordinates. In Euripides's 480 BCE play, a young Medea falls in love with Jason, the leader of the Argonauts, and helps him obtain the Golden Fleece, but then kills their children after.

> Medea has always been multiple, existing in many different versions simultaneously. She is never simply a literary construction, a stratified intertextual ensemble made up of all the other literary Medeas that came before her, but a product of the values and fears of each culture that imagines her, recreates her, and uses her to represent meaning.
>
> (McElduff, 2012, p. 190)

Archaic stories such as Medea's are integral to the history and systems of Western psychological theory and practice. The enduring interest today in Medea reveals the fact that her story has a certain resonance with the modern world that lies in the cry of an incensed woman. Medea is many things: She is an outsider in the Greek world, a woman of power and means, a woman dishonored by her husband, an ordinary woman, a mother, the murderer of her children. In modern works of art, Medea is often explored in terms of the subjugation of women by men but more often as a symbol of threatening power. Betine van Zyl Smit wrote, "Medea has become a symbol for women and an icon of feminism" (2002, p. 102), fascinating "because of the power of her love and the power of her hatred, because she refuses to become a victim" (112–113).

Whether Medea is a victim, a feminist agent, or a baby killer, it is clear we often understand her out of context—the same way the media understands the infanticidal mother out of context. Situated within her sociocultural context, Medea lives on now not only because she embodies the archetypal Death Mother but also because she lived in the context of Western patriarchal structures that we still inhabit. I turn to Euripides's version of Medea as it is the one most often recalled—giving us the image of a stoic or maddened woman holding the corpse of her children while wielding a sword. For Medea, who was lovestruck for Jason, to help him attain the Golden Fleece she had to betray her family, decapitating her brother, who in some versions of the story is the closest person to her. Medea did this with ingenuity and magic, using herbs and poison, as instructed by her aunt Circe in powers that came from Hecate, goddess of magic arts. With Jason, Medea left her home country and settled in Corinth, where she had their two sons. Jason then announced his intention to marry a Corinthian princess, leaving Medea, a foreigner, with little chance of surviving in the absence of the identity and economic support that had come from Jason. She was told to leave Corinth, but she had nowhere to go. Facing a hopeless fate for herself and her children, Medea kills her two boys in the potent scene that gets extracted from the whole, turned into a story of simple revenge, and persistently referenced today.

During the time of Medea's story, Athenian law codified a woman's primary civic role as the (present or future) mother of citizen children. Legally a daughter, then a wife, then a mother, all authority in the household rested in its male head, the *kurios*. A nubile woman passed from the kurial authority of her father to that of her husband. In the event of divorce, a woman returned to her father's authority. In the event of a husband's death, she passed into the authority of her husband's male relatives.

One of the most striking aspects of Euripides's drama is that he made Medea credible as a woman. She is portrayed as a woman accepted as a peer by other women and supported by their solidarity with her cause. Even Jason's treatment of her—his planning of her future without consulting her, his deception, and his betrayal of her—mark her as an ordinary woman. Medea knows this is the position of an ordinary woman, as is apparent in her central "Women of Corinth" speech:

> Of all creatures that have breath and sensation, we women are the most unfortunate. First at an exorbitant price we must buy a husband and master of our bodies. [This misfortune is more painful than misfortune.] And the outcome of our life's striving hangs on this, whether we take a bad or a good husband. For divorce is discreditable for women and it is not possible to refuse wedlock. And when a woman comes into the new customs and practices of her husband's house, she must somehow divine, since she has not learned it at home, how she shall best deal with her husband. If after we have spent great efforts on these tasks our husbands live with us without resenting the marriage-yoke, our life is enviable. Otherwise, death is preferable. A man, whenever he is annoyed with the company of those in the house, goes elsewhere and thus rids his soul of its boredom [turning to some male friend or age-mate]. But we must fix our gaze on one person only. Men say that we live a life free from danger at home while they fight with the spear. How wrong they are! I would rather stand three times with a shield in battle than give birth once.
>
> (Euripides, 451 BCE/1994, lines 235–250)

Not long after this, Medea killed her two children with a sword. In one of her final speeches, we are at the heart of her infanticidal position:

> Ah me, I groan at what a deed I must do next. I shall kill my children: there is no one who can rescue them. When I have utterly confounded the whole house of Jason, I shall leave the land, in flight from the murder of my own dear sons, having committed a most unholy deed. The laughter of one's enemies is unendurable, my friends. Let that be as it will. What do I gain by living? I have no fatherland, no house, no refuge from calamity . . . . Let no one think of me as weak and submissive . . . but as a woman of a very different kind, dangerous to my enemies and good to my friends. To such a life glory belongs.
>
> (lines 795f)

Figure 2.3 Medea. Giovanni Benedetto Castiglione detto il Grechetto—collezione privata, 17th century. Public domain.

From Jason, King of Corinth, we hear, "No Greek woman would have dared to do this, . . . You are a lioness, not a woman, with a nature more savage than Tyrrhenian Scylla." Medea responds, "Call me a lioness, then, if you wish, and Scylla who lives on the Tuscan cliff; for I have touched your heart in the vital spot" (lines 1339f).

At the end of Euripides's play, Medea escapes to Athens on a chariot drawn by winged Dragon-Serpents, which she had received from her grandfather, the sun God Helios. Received by the Gods, Medea takes on the role of *deus ex machina*, an unexpected power or event that dramatically upends the entire storyline and what had been believed to be the natural course of events. She reflects the way in which every infanticide is a deus ex machina, in which an unsolvable problem in a story is suddenly or abruptly resolved. Having wielded the power of the Death Mother in revolt against the established order, her deus ex machina, she is granted a victory few other heroes have held in mythology. Unlike Achilles, Ajax, or Antigone, Medea is not dead by the end, but triumphant: "She, unlike them, does not feel herself abandoned by the gods but supported by them" (Kovacs, 1993, p. 48).

The chariot in which Medea escapes is an ancient symbol of the balance between intellectual and emotional powers in the convergence upon an ideal goal (Gad,

1994). As her transport, the chariot emphasizes the uniqueness of Medea's role as an enforcer of justice; in a strange twist, Medea fulfills both her and the Chorus's wish for divine vengeance upon Jason as an embodiment of an oppressive order by becoming a goddess.

However, this is not the whole story, for Medea's justice is also the source of her own punishment in her self-inflicted human suffering with the deaths of her children. In moments of myth meeting reality, of Leija's identification with La Llorona, of Medea's rage erupting through Denise, the Death Mother archetype lives through human mothers. That in Medea's story of tragic rebellion she is saved by the Gods, elevated to a semi-divine status at the end of the play, places her in the position of a symbol of transcendent energies that remain alive in the collective unconscious. These stories of the mythic nature of infanticide offer psychological containment for the shadow of the modern mother. They also suggest we look more deeply at the sociocultural forces that surround her.

References

Behrooz, A. (2016). Wicked women: The stepmother as a figure of evil in the Grimms' fairy tales. *Retrospective Journal of Legend & Folklore, 18*, 5–6.

Bettelheim, B. (1976). *The Uses of enchantment: The importance and meaning of fairy tales*. Thames and Hudson.

Douglas, C. (1989). *The woman in the mirror: Analytical psychology and the feminine*. Sigo Press.

Elbein, A. (2015, February 23). The return of La Llorona. *Texas Observer*.

Euripides. (451 BCE/1994). *Euripides: Ion, Hippolytus, Medea, Alcestis* (D. Kovacs, Ed., J. F. Nims, Trans.). Forgotten Books.

Franz, M.-L. V. (1993). *The feminine in fairy tales* (Rev. 1st ed.). Shambhala.

Franz, M.-L. V. (2020). *Archetypal symbols in fairytales*. Chiron.

Gad, I. (1994). *Tarot and individuation: Correspondences with Cabala and alchemy*. Nicolas-Hayes.

Harding, E. (1935). *Woman's mysteries; ancient and modern*. Longmans, Green.

Hillman, J. (1975). *Re-visioning psychology*. HarperPerennial.

Jung, C. G. (1966). The relations between the ego and the unconscious (R. F. C. Hull, Trans.). In H. Read, M. Fordham, & G. Adler (Eds.), *The collected works of C. G. Jung: Vol. 7. Two essays on analytical psychology* (2nd ed., pp. 121–241). Princeton University Press. (Original work published 1928). https://doi.org/10.1515/9781400850891.121

Jung, C. G. (1967a). The battle for deliverance from the mother (R. F. C. Hull, Trans.). In H. Read, M. Fordham, & G. Adler (Eds.), *The collected works of C. G. Jung: Vol. 5. Symbols of transformation* (pp. 274–305). Princeton University Press. (Original work published 1952). https://doi.org/10.1515/9781400850945

Jung, C. G. (1967b). Symbols of the mother and rebirth (R. F. C. Hull, Trans.). In H. Read, M. Fordham, & G. Adler (Eds.), *The collected works of C. G. Jung: Vol. 5. Symbols of transformation* (pp. 207–273). Princeton University Press. (Original work published 1952). https://doi.org/10.1515/9781400850945

Jung, C. G. (1969a). The structure of the psyche (R. F. C. Hull, Trans.). In H. Read, M. Fordham, & G. Adler (Eds.), *The collected works of C. G. Jung: Vol. 8. Structure and dynamics of the psyche* (2nd ed., pp. 139–158). Princeton University Press. (Original work published 1931). https://doi.org/10.1515/9781400850952.139

Jung, C. G. (1969b). A review of the complex theory (R. F. C. Hull, Trans.). In H. Read, M. Fordham, & G. Adler (Eds.), *The collected works of C. G. Jung: Vol. 8. Structure and dynamics of the psyche* (2nd ed., pp. 92–104). Princeton University Press. (Original work published 1948). https://doi.org/10.1515/9781400850952.92

Jung, C. G. (1969c). On the nature of the psyche (R. F. C. Hull, Trans.). In H. Read, M. Fordham, & G. Adler (Eds.), *The collected works of C. G. Jung: Vol. 8. Structure and dynamics of the psyche* (2nd ed., pp. 159–234). Princeton University Press. (Original work published 1954). https://doi.org/10.1515/9781400850952.159

Kovacs, D. (1993). Zeus in Euripides' Medea. *American Journal of Philosophy*, *114*(1), 45–70.

Lewis, J. (2020, February 20). *A timeline of witch hunts in Europe.* www.thoughtco.com/european-witch-hunts-timeline-3530786

Lowinsky, N. (1992). *The motherline: Every woman's journey to find her female roots.* J. P. Tarcher.

Marchiano, L. (2021). *Motherhood: Facing and finding yourself.* Sounds True.

Mayorga, I. (2001). Homecoming: The politics of myth and location. In C. Moraga (Ed.), *The hungry woman: A Mexican Medea* (pp. 155f). West End Press.

McElduff, S. (2012). Epilogue: The multiple Medeas of the middle ages. *Ramus*, *41*(1–2), 190–205.

Murdock, M. (2020). *The heroine's journey: Woman's quest for wholeness.* Shambhala.

Neumann, E. (1963). *The great mother: An analysis of the archetype.* Princeton University Press. (Original work published 1955)

Ovid. (1 BCE/n.d.). *Metamorphoses* (S. Garth et al., Trans.) http://classics.mit.edu/Ovid/metam.html

Ruiz, R. (2001, July 3). Woman recalls drowning kids in 1986. *Houston Chronicle*.

Seneca, L. A. (50CE/2014). *Two tragedies of Seneca: Medea and the daughters of Troy* (E. I. Harris, Trans.). Houghton, Mifflin.

Sharp, D., & Jung, C. G. (1991). *Jung lexicon: A primer of terms & concepts.* Inner City Books.

Sieff, D. F. (2019). The death mother as nature's shadow: Infanticide, abandonment, and the collective unconscious. *Psychological Perspectives*, *62*(1), 15–34.

Sieff, D. F. (2022). *A brief introduction to the archetypal death mother.* Retrieved February 28, 2022, from https://danielasieff.com/the-archetypal-death-mother/

Stevens, A. (1982). *Archetype: A natural history of the self.* Routledge & K. Paul.

Tatar, M. (1987). *The hard facts of the Grimm fairy tales.* Princeton University Press.

Ulanov, A. B., & Ulanov, B. (1987). *The witch and the clown: Two archetypes of human sexuality.* Chiron.

Van Zyl Smit, B. (2002). Medea the feminist. *Acta Classica: Proceedings of the Classical Association of South Africa*, *45*(1), 101–122.

Woodman, M., & Sieff, D. (2015). Spiralling through the apocalypse: Facing the death mother to claim our lives. In D. Sieff (Ed.), *Understanding and healing emotional trauma* (pp. 64–88). Routledge.

Zimmerman, J. (2021). *Women and other monsters: Building a new mythology.* Beacon Press.

Chapter 3

The Infanticidal Mother

A Speaking Subject

The infanticidal mother has been consistently imagined in culture and in our psyches as monstrous or mad. If we go inward, deep inside the shadow to the archetypal core and to the body of her story, we may get closer to who she is beyond mad. In fact, it is possible that by hearing the infanticidal mother's inner experience—understanding her subjectivity—we can gain a resonance with both the Death Mother and the greater Divine Mother.

Just as the infanticidal mother is psychically set aside, she is physically locked up, institutionalized, or incarcerated; her story written for her. It is rare to hear her quoted in the aftermath of infanticide, and she is rarely seen again. If we want to gain any understanding of these events, it is essential for the infanticidal woman to be placed as the speaking subject of this book, not as the objectified Other—an Other upon whom we project our own denied rage, fear, and madness. In a deliberate effort to truly center her, to resist objectifying her through the appropriation of her subjectivity to serve my own authority, I use her story, her voice, her affect, and her image as much as I can. Removing the infanticidal mother from the object of discussion, where she is frequently misidentified and imprisoned, and putting her into the subject role reveals more of who she is, who she was, and who she is becoming. Moreover, by giving a maternal subject the space to be a speaking subject, a *sujet en procès*, to say "I am mortal, and I am speaking," allows her the potential for transformation (Kristeva, 1980, p. 74). This is a power that the patriarchal contract has taken from women (Kristeva, 1981). Our job, as writers and readers, is to listen analytically to the infanticidal mother, coming to know her as an ordinary woman while we seek to understand in and through her a psychological and cultural construct.

Astria's Story

Astria is a mother I worked with who, when born, was stuck in her mother's vaginal canal. When the doctor pulled her from the womb Astria incurred a brachial injury. She has a smaller left arm and no use of her curled-up, smaller left hand. Bullied and impoverished in a small town, she was often depressed. "I was sad and lost during that time . . . I didn't feel right being here. I didn't want to live anymore."

DOI: 10.4324/9781003412809-5

She was taken in by an older neighbor man who established trust and then sexually assaulted her. When she became pregnant, she reported him and decided to keep the baby. "I had to get over [my] fears. I was bringing another life into the world. I became happy. I knew someone else was going to love me. At the time, I felt like I wasn't being loved by anyone."

Astria had a second child with another man who was physically abusive. He shoved and punched her "almost daily" and mocked her for being overweight. He often hit her in the face and kicked her in the stomach several times while she was pregnant, resulting in her going into early labor and delivering stillborn twins on her couch. Astria told me that the violence "was too much for me to bear . . . . At times, I wanted to leave in the middle of the night, but I was scared of what he would do. He had threatened to kill me and my daughter." Pregnant again, Astria gave birth 2 months early and needed to stay in the hospital for 3 months. She attempted to visit daily, and when baby Jamie was released from the hospital, he came home with an apnea machine to monitor his breathing. Before Astria could bring him home, the NICU staff instructed her on how to use the machine and what signs to look for that would require her to bring him back to the hospital. They gave her vitamins for his formula, which she was required to feed him every 3-4 hours. The machine was connected to the baby with stickers over his lungs. She was to keep them on unless bathing him. Astria reported they had to explain it to her "more than 5 times for her to understand it."

Astria and Jamie returned to living with her abusive boyfriend, who was convinced the new baby was not his. He pushed Astria to conceive again to have a boy of his own. He did not participate in the parenting and would make it known that the baby was not his, saying, "Come get *your* son!" Astria described a debilitating depression during that time; she felt numb, did not enjoy anything, and was "just going through the motions."

The night before the incident, Jamie refused most of his bottle. He did this a few times, and Astria planned on taking him to the hospital the next day. They went to sleep that night, and Astria remembered waking up with the baby at least once. Astria said she thinks she reset the apnea machine when it went off at 5am. She remembers Jamie was breathing at 5am.

In the morning Astria was getting her children ready for school and ironing her boyfriend's shirt. After he left the house, she checked on the sleeping baby and noticed that he was not breathing. She gave him CPR until the ambulance arrived and took them to the hospital. They pronounced Jamie dead at the hospital. Astria refused to let go of her baby. She said, "I wanted to die right there with him." The police arrived and made her hand over her baby. They took her to the station, where they interrogated her for several hours. Astria was charged and eventually given 40 years in prison. About her boyfriend, Astria said, "Sometimes I'm happy I came to jail to get away from him."

The shockingly misrepresentative news story on Astria's case read, "A 2-month-old prematurely born boy starved to death while his mother was in another room, texting her boyfriend, a Peoria County prosecutor told a judge Monday" (Kravetz,

2012, para. 1). The article continued: "Assistant State's Attorney contends 20-year-old [Astria] was 'completely indifferent' to the condition of her son" (para. 2). The prosecutor also indicted her maternal history, arguing that Astria

> showed no remorse or empathy when she told the police detective that she delivered the children [her stillborn twins] and tried to hide their deaths because she didn't want her mother or grandmother to know. It was a 'complete lack of disregard,' [the prosecutor] said, and also showed her 'extreme self-centeredness' that carried through to how she dealt with [the infant].
>
> (Kravetz, 2012, para. 8)

The headlines and stories that reach the public hardly reveal the actuality of the story, instead highlighting grotesque details which are then spun into narratives for both our entertainment and to assure psychological distance. The truth of Astria's story is miles from the headline "Prosecutor: Baby Starved While Mother Was 'Completely Indifferent'" (Kravetz, 2012). It is a narrative that is largely misunderstood, layered with generations of trauma, physical disability, mental instability, and relational dysfunction. For an act that is meant to only be known in fairy tales or imagination, the truth of a child murder is an event that itself is unknowable, as it lives in the shadow carried by the mother and is outside the objectifying framework of the way in which we tell stories. A headline such as "Mother is Monster" or "Mother Committed Final Sin" could also read, "Mother with low physical and cognitive ability controlled and abused by man for years is co-parent to child who dies on malfunctioning heart monitor."

Subjectivity and Transformation

It is crucial that in the important goal of freeing females from being valued only as mothers and freeing individuals from being confined to gender roles, we not ignore the immutable reality that it is only in the specific and potent burden and power of reproduction that woman is differentiated, understood, and known. As such, motherhood carries the biological, psychological, and spiritual burden of what a woman is. To separate woman from womb—whether she is barren or fertile by choice or biology—further enables psychological matricide in the reduction and silencing of the experience of mothers by appropriating it as a "birthing person's event." In fact, in order to liberate women, it is essential to bring into focus the biological, sociocultural, autobiographical, and spiritual aspects of her procreative potential and burden that inform her subjectivity. Swedish feminist scholar Fanny Söderbäck argued that in returning motherhood as intrinsically belonging to women and "bringing the mother out of the shadows," Kristeva "provides women with a past (. . . a history hitherto repressed) and simultaneously with a future (in the sense of liberating them from pre-defined roles and positions—from motherhood as the only form of subjectivity available to them)" (2–3).

Söderbäck points out that the patriarchal account of a female fertility as "cyclical and repetitive" is plainly naive, when reproduction is all about "unpredictability, irreducibility, variation, singularity." The potency, energy, and rhythm of a woman's reproductive process is essentially subjective, making her subjectivity essential to the discourse of political philosophy. What the infanticidal mother needs is for the discourse to return to Mother, her political potential, her reproductive grammars, and her power of reproduction that shapes her history and future. This is crucial if, as Söderbäck argues in a podcast, we "want to save the baby" (2021).

Susan Ayres, a Texas A&M University law professor who has written prolifically on the law, gender, domestic violence, justice, and infanticide, is concerned with the construction of the infanticidal mother's subjective identity. Similar to Kristeva's concept of analytic listening, Ayres suggests we receive her story with "other love" or compassion for the Other (2004, p. 40). Ayres argues that our construction of motherhood must be re-examined and that the presumptions and foundations constructing motherhood must be challenged and subverted in order to allow the stories of infanticidal mothers to be heard with compassion, with "other love." Lawyers and judges can strive to develop this story more fully, both in the representation of mothers accused of infanticide and in the words and facts selected to craft judicial decisions. Indeed, rather than secularize, silence, and label mothers as "mad or bad," lawyers and judges should make every effort to give recognition to the "other" and should try both to represent and to judge mothers accused of infanticide with other love (110).

Drawer of Letters

I have a drawer where I keep all the letters I receive from women in prison. They ask direct questions and give honest answers. They are the words of women who have been muzzled. These beautiful lined pages tell stories of horrific childhood abuse, sex trafficking, murder, and then the difficult material: the first lawyer, the failed defense, the second lawyer who misrepresented her, the police who coerced a confession, the judge who made a speech at her expense, and the various psychologists and forensic psychiatrists who never got her story right. The letters that these women write to me and others like me are a way of writing themselves. They are an act of creation in which the transformation of self is possible. These incarcerated mothers have seen their own headlines, but their letters tell the actual story. Carefully, in their deliberate handwriting, page after page, their subjectivity takes form. These women contribute to what Cixous suggested is needed:

> Women must write her self; must write about women and bring women to writing from which they have been driven away as violently as from their bodies—for the same reasons, by the same law, with the same fatal goal. Woman must put herself into the text—*as* into the world and into history—*by* her own movement. The future must no longer be determined by the past.
>
> (1976, p. 875)

Ayres has analyzed trial strategies for women convicted of infanticide. She found that, if extensive videotaped documentation of the mother's mental state is provided to juries so that "the truth can come out," it is possible a defense team can "subvert conventional views of infanticidal mothers as mad or bad and give them a voice that can be heard with greater compassion and justice" (2006, p. 356). This is also my intent.

In my work with these women, I hear their stories not as evil or crazy, but as narratives in which the Subject, having lost all power, resorts to a terminal act. Rarely do we examine the tribulations and trials of an infanticidal mother's life. She is much easier kept as a catchall for what we need to think of as "unnatural" maternal drives. By perpetuating the infanticidal mother as Other, we keep our own dark drives hidden in the shadows. Approaching her as a speaking subject may shed light on and allow for a more whole experience of motherhood. I invite the reader to look beyond their own presuppositions of what an infanticidal mother is and allow the patriarchal narrative to be subverted by analytically listening, with other love, to an infanticidal mother's story.

The Media and Identity Formation

The identity of the infanticidal mother is multifaceted: she has a past, a present, and a future. She is caring for other children or facing her first, she is a competent employee or unemployed, she is a loyal family member or alone and isolated. Those who keep her present before us—media, literature, and film—accentuate her gory act and define her by it, leaving the many other aspects of her personhood behind. Hearing about maternal infanticide is a source of profound anxiety. It is unnerving to know of women—more so than men—who murder, transgressing gender constraints and moral tenets. Thus, stories of maternal infanticide are told in a way that makes female violence palatable by making her evil, mad, or scorned and locating her as outside civilized community. Because these women threaten the social order, controlling their narratives is a means of containing that threat. As a collective we dissociate her from our consciousness; so horrific is she that she cannot be discussed or even thought of as a familiar person.

There is a difference between telling the story of a woman and telling a woman's story. A recent headline read, "Monsters Walk Amongst Us" (WRGB Staff, 2021), referring to a young mother who was accused of assaulting her 10-month-old baby on Halloween. In the article Police Chief Joseph Centanni stated: "The defendant's actions are unequivocal proof that monsters walk among us" (as cited in Kalmbacher, 2021, para. 17). This *telling* of her story *makes* her a monster. Hearing her tell the story might sound different. It might sound like some of the other stories I've heard: I've been living in squalor, beaten daily by my boyfriend, just like how my father beat me. To ease the pain, I started taking painkillers; now I'll do anything for these pills, to keep the relief. It has changed my ability to control my impulses. So when he beat me, I was weak, and when the baby was demanding, I couldn't bear it and I beat the baby.

Often, the media plays a powerful role in dictating the defendant's blameworthiness and even in determining the resolution of these cases, parading guilt before a trial. The impact of media coverage is revealed in the headline, "A crowd chanted 'Death, Death' as a mother arrived at court to face charges of killing her 9-year-old daughter as she lay in a hospital bed" Bethany Dawson (April 9, 2022), Business Insider. The media had been reporting for weeks on this mother, and before her trial the public had already convicted her.

Criminology and psychology researchers Saavedra and Oliveira noted in their work on motherhood and media, "The media preserves the 'good' image of motherhood as an institution while treating all other forms of motherhood as 'othering' (e.g., Beauvoir, 1989), that is to say, as abnormal, whether due to being 'bad' or 'mad'" (2016, p. 9). Media comes from the vantage point that assumes women are naturally good mothers and only experience unconditional love and care for their child. Anything outside of this experience is either criminal or crazy. Media's compulsive imposition of a puritanical divide between what is good and bad leaves no space or tolerance for the full range of emotional maternal experiences. In this way, media representations of infanticidal mothers are pernicious to the institute of motherhood itself. Media uses psychological, relational, and social factors to constitute what is normative vs. transgressive motherhood. When violent crimes by women occur, they attract more media and public attention than crimes by men (including filicide), and the images used in the stories are bolder and more graphic, thus they tend to leave "a more long-lasting impression" (Poteyeva & Leigey, 2018, "Introduction", para. 2).

Social policy expert Anette Ballinger suggested that the "need to tell and re-tell" stories about murderous women is "a symptom of social anxiety about women's roles and the perceived abandonment of traditional femininity" (1996, p. 13). In the headlines of infanticide cases, the message sent to women is clear: A mother who has rageful urges toward her child is a shameful monster. I have a growing list of these internet headlines, each more degrading and gruesome than the last, as shown in this very small sampling:

Florida Times Union: "Jacksonville Mom Who Killed Baby While Playing FarmVille Gets 50 Years"

(Hunt, 2011)

Essence: "Woman Spitefully Texts Photo of Dead Toddler To Baby's Father During Fight"

(Rogo, 2020)

CafeMom: "Mom Who Killed 3-Year-Old for 'Interrupting Her Having Sex' Posts 'Apology' to Her Parents"

(Glassman, 2021)

People Magazine: "Florida Mom Charged with Death of 7-Month-Old Boy Left in Bathtub While She Had Her Nails Done"

(Balagtas, 2022)

And most recently,

> *KHOU*: "Mother accused of leaving young kids at home alone to go gamble, drink on Memorial Day"
>
> (McCord, 2023)

It is impossible to not feel some disgust at mothers who fail so miserably. Understandably, that feeling keeps us away from wanting to know more, but in fact learning what is behind the headlines, listening to a mother's account of events, would be a narrative subversion that could change consciousness and invite compassion toward motherhood.

Leora's Story

Leora is a young Lakota woman now serving 20 years in prison for killing a 5-year-old boy. She grew up on an American Indian reservation, and both her parents were addicts. Her father had bipolar disorder and regularly tortured and abused his wife and children. Once, in a jealous rage, he took his wife out to the woods and set her truck on fire and left her there. When punishing the kids, he put their hamster in the microwave and turned it on. From the ages of 4 to 12, he sexually molested Leora, telling her to put her underwear on her head as a "blindfold" and then putting a "snake between her legs while she stayed real still and quiet." When Leora's parents were arrested and separated for drug offenses, she was put in the child welfare system and lived with several foster families throughout her adolescence. She began experiencing rage, mania, and depression at a young age. Her chief complaint: "I keep trying to kill myself." She was regularly suicidal and got into fights with other kids, which landed her in hospitals and juvenile detention several times.

When she was 18, Leora met Steven and fell in love; they became engaged and had two daughters 12 months apart. After having her children, Leora experienced severe postpartum depression,[1] spending most of her days in bed with the babies nursing and sleeping while Steven worked a factory job. Steven was possessive and dominating and did not allow Leora to leave the house while he was gone. She often heard footsteps in the house and began to sense "the presence of the devil." Steven's 5-year-old son Tommy, who was from another relationship, came to live with them at this time, when the boy's mother was arrested for drug possession. Leora was now taking care of all three children.

Leora made healthy food for her children and dressed them in clean clothes, intent on giving them a better life than she'd had as a child. She treated Tommy the same way, teaching him to read early. Then, Tommy began playing sexual games with her daughters. He had been exposed to sexual trauma in his mother's house and was now acting it out with his new baby sisters. As Leora witnessed this behavior, she began experiencing flashbacks of her father's sexual abuse, for which she had never received treatment. Leora felt rage. At times she felt like a mother lion who was protective of her cubs, and she would yell at Tommy, "You cannot mate with my cubs!"

Leora cut her legs with a razor in the shower to relieve the emotional pressure. She was also making blood offerings to the devil, with the intention of making herself and the evil presence feel calm. The mania grew, as did the hallucinations. One day, when she caught Tommy making humping movements on her eldest daughter, she attacked him, kicking and stomping on him until he died. Leora immediately felt at ease knowing her daughters were no longer unsafe.

Today, from her prison cell, she tells me her story. "You're not supposed to get that mad," she says. "Do you know how much my girls mean to me? They're my girls . . . nobody's going to take better care of them." She asks me what "premeditated" means and then says: "No, I didn't plan for Tommy to do that to my daughter. I didn't plan to hurt him." She believes she has given her daughters a better life and now can relax because they are safe. She says, "If someone would have killed my dad that would have been awesome. I knew Tommy would grow up to be like my dad." She has also expressed her regret and feeling that others have a right to hate her.

Leora's words are poignant, and ones we would never read in the media. Now called the "baby killer" at the women's prison, she serves as the dark "other"— a Native girl in the White conservative law-and-order Republican state of South Dakota that historically has stereotyped and condemned the Native tribes as savage and violent. Leora has become a catchall for the shadow impulses disavowed by those around her; with barbaric impulses projected onto her, she is very convictable.

When the infanticidal mother is the subject, standing in the location of motherhood, speaking from the maternal body, we can hear her words—"I was scared he would kill me," "I couldn't live this way anymore," "I am so sorry, everything is heartbreak," "I love my children more than anything," "I only want to die," "I saw no way out for us," "I lost myself"—we gain a further understanding of her position, energy, and emotions.

The heartbreaking body-breaking accounts of a forced abortion, the detail of dressing one's baby in his finest Christmas outfit on the day of his death, the battered mother's body caring for a newborn who cannot breathe on his own: these are the potent maternal energies too long forbidden full acknowledgment. Western patriarchal institutions have had prohibitive authority over mothers' stories, "have had privilege over her gender and creative actions" (Jordan, 2016, p. 103), and maintain "the only words we have for women's sexuality are filthy, mutilating words" (Irigaray, 1987/1993, pp. 16–17). Yet these words, too, need to know the light of day, and fill in the outline of a mother's full experience.

Murderous Mothers and Film

There are many murderous mothers from movies that are worthy of examination, but the one I like for its haunting aspect is *The Others* (Amenábar, 2001). This film is an adaptation of Henry James's *Turn of the Screw*, a gothic horror novella focused on the eerie relationship of a governess and two children. The film presents shadowy short scenes of an English manor house, a rigidly mean and distracted mother, and two pale, curious children. After we come to believe the house is controlled by ghosts, a flashback to the past reveals that the mother had in fact gone mad while her husband was away at war. She smothered the children with a pillow and then put a rifle to her own head. The horror is now magnified as we see the impish children and evil mother become ghosts.

In their critique of films such as *The Others*, feminist film critics Alexopoulos and Power defined the genre as " 'maternal horror cinema,' films that centre on a maternal figure and perpetuate the 'unstable ideology of idealised motherhood.'" The authors concluded,

> While responsible for injury and death, the maternal figures are not all to blame. Rather than viewing the horror created via the mother as reinforcing normative gender roles and ideologies, the grotesque mother can also be read as a subversion of, resistance to, or a result of problematic gender dichotomies that assign domestic care and familial love exclusively to women. They are mothers alone and burdened by maternity in isolation. In each case conventional institutions that supposedly "protect" women, such as the family, fail.
>
> (2018, "Patriarchy and motherhood:" para. 1)

Although these films "question whether hegemonic ideologies of motherhood cause harm, ultimately, they reinforce normative conventions of gender by rendering women who transgress idealised motherhood as abject and grotesque sources of fear and horror" (2018, "Discussion", para. 1). The films ultimately declaim any uncertainty about the mother myth: the rewards go to the good mother, punishment to the bad.

The film title *The Others* is a nice play on the concept of Other—the *not me* that is kept in the shadows, namely the ghosts of the children and mother. The shadow is the dark unconscious material that we cannot see, the unknown dark side of the personality (Jung, 1951/1968). Jung suggested the shadow is instinctive and irrational. On the one hand, it is prone to psychological projection, in which a perceived personal inferiority is recognized as a perceived moral deficiency in someone else. On the other hand, shadow content has an "emotional nature, a kind of autonomy and accordingly an obsessive or, better, possessive quality" (1951/1968, para. 15). Through projection, the infanticidal mother carries the shadow of our society, and when the shadow side of motherhood is constellated in a state of dissociation, trauma, or psychosis through possession, she acts it out. What we see as a moral deficiency in our own motherhood—or what, as a culture, we deny as part of a mother's legitimate feelings, struggles, and behaviors, we project onto the infanticidal mother. It's not me, it's her.

Jung argued that withdrawing our projections and confronting the shadow is a moral struggle: We struggle not only to face what we do not want to accept in our own lives, but also, as a society, to accept and understand it when and where it appears. Kept split off from consciousness, the archetypal and instinctual energies associated with shadow content are raw, ego-autonomous, and possessive. Only through conscious attention and listening to the infanticidal or filicidal mother's story of trauma and distress held in shadow can both the conditions that constellate the Death Mother and her energies be humanized. As Cixous warned of women, "when the 'repressed' of their culture and their society returns, it's an explosive, utterly destructive, staggering return, with a force never yet unleashed and equal to the most forbidding of suppressions" (1976, p. 886).

The Story of Saint Omer

Alice Diop's French film *Saint Omer* is a rare film example of an infanticidal mother held in a steady light, as neither monster nor madwoman. The film, based on a true story, tells the story of Rama, a successful author living in Paris, who travels to the northern town of Saint Omer to attend the trial of a young Senegalese woman, Fabienne Kabou, who is accused of murdering her baby daughter. This film was exquisitely done. The uninterrupted close-up testimony and the portrayal of the mother's quiet yet burning emotion had the effect of evoking reverence for the mother and compassion for her experience in a way other films have not attempted.

The film begins with Rama giving a lecture on Marguerite Duras's work, *Hiroshima, Mon Amour*. Diop uses the lecture to prepare the audience for what Rama refers to as the power of narrative to sublimate a horrific reality. In *Hiroshima, Mon Amour*, Duras asks her audience to transform into a lyrical song the shock and feelings of revolt in seeing a line of women whose heads have been shaved being mocked and degraded for sleeping with the enemy—a commonplace punishment at the end of World War II. Rama says of Duras,

Listening to the text, the author's intention is crystal clear. This woman is humiliated, distraught, branded like a prisoner, albeit temporarily as hair does grow back, but branded forever on her memory and that of those around her. This woman, an object of shame, becomes, thanks to the author's words, not only a heroine but a human being in a state of grace.

From Diop's allusion to Duras's work, our psyches are cued to understand something that is brutal as something grace-filled.

As portrayed in *Saint Omer*, Fabienne Kabou portrays Laurence Coly, an isolated foreigner who has a secret pregnancy and a transactional relationship, followed by an agoraphobic postpartum mental illness, sorcery, and infanticide. Fabienne was sentenced to 20 years in prison in 2016. The tension of the film builds to a crescendo at the end, not with Fabienne's act of infanticide and the baby at the edge of sea, but with Fabienne's lawyer making an exquisitely compelling, convincing, and comprehensive statement to the court in which she explains Chimeric cells, the cells that migrate from a fetus to a mother, which are then lodged in her body, possibly forever. She says:

Like the Chimera, the mythical monster. A hybrid creature composed of different animal parts. A lion's head, a goat's body, a snake's tail. So, members of the jury,

I have come to believe that we women, we are all chimeras. We carry within us the traces of our mothers and of our daughters, who in turn will carry ours. It is a never-ending chain. In a way, us women, we are all monsters. But we are terribly human monsters.

Film and news media representations of infanticidal mothers are pernicious to the institution of motherhood itself. Knowing what is behind the headlines, listening to a mother's true story, is a narrative subversion that can change consciousness and compassion toward motherhood. If we go inward, from inside the shadow, the madness, and the body of her story, we come to see the infanticidal mother more compassionately, see the patriarchal conditions that confront mothers more clearly, and see motherhood more holistically and realistically. As Cixous asserts,

> Women must write through their bodies, they must invent the impregnable language that will wreck partitions, classes, and rhetorics, regulations and codes, they must submerge, cut through, get beyond the ultimate reserve-discourse, including the one that laughs at the very idea of pronouncing the word "silence," the one that, aiming for the impossible, stops short before the word "impossible" and writes it as "the end."
>
> (1976, p. 886)

The stories of mothers who kill their children speak not only to personal and cultural shadow and its relationship to the Death Mother; they speak to the systemic social and economic problems in which they are trapped.

Note

1 Historically, motherhood for American Indian women in the United States was controlled by colonizers through forced abortions, forced or coerced sterilization, and by limiting or restricting abortion and birth control access. This history influences motherhood for Indigenous women, contributing to their uncommonly high rates of postpartum depression. (Maxwell et al., 2022)

References

Alexopoulos, T., & Power, S. (2018, Autumn). "What did your mother do to you?" The others (2001), mama (2013), the conjuring (2013). *MAI: Feminism and Visual Culture*. https://maifeminism.com/what-did-your-mother-do-to-you-the-grotesque-abjection-and-motherhood/

Amenábar, A. (Director). (2001). *The others* [Motion Picture]. Turner Classic Movies.

Ayres, S. (2004). [N]ot a story to pass on: Constructing mothers who kill. *Hastings Women's Law Journal*, *15*, 39–110.

Ayres, S. (2006). Newfound religion: Mothers, God, and infanticide. *Fordham Urban Law Journal*, *33*, 335–356.

Balagtas, T. (2022, May 30). Florida mom charged with death of 7-month-old boy left in bathtub while she had her nails done. *People Magazine*.

Ballinger, A. (1996). The guilt of the innocent and the innocence of the guilty. In S. Wight & A. Myers (Eds.), *Women who commit violence* (pp. 1–28). HarperCollins.

Beauvoir, S. (1989). *The second sex*. Vintage Books.

Cixous, H. (1976). The laugh of the Medusa (K. Cohen & P. Cohen, Trans.). *Signs: Journal of Women, Culture, and Society*, *1*(4), 875–893.

Diop, A. (Director). (2023). *Saint Omer* [Motion Picture]. Dogo Digital.

Glassman, G. (2021, August 16). Mom who killed 3-year-old for "interrupting her having sex" posts "apology" to her parents. *CafeMom*.

Hunt, D. (2011, February 1). Jacksonville mom who killed baby while playing FarmVille gets 50 years. *Florida Times Union*.

Irigaray, L. (1993). *Sexes and genealogies* (G. Gill, Trans.). Columbia University Press. (Original work published 1987)

Jordan, N. (2016). Daughter of writing mother writ large with Hélène Cixous. *Journal of the Motherhood Initiative for Research and Community Involvement*, *7*.

Jung, C. G. (1968). The shadow (R. F. C. Hull, Trans.). In H. Read, M. Fordham, & G. Adler (Eds.), *The collected works of C. G. Jung: Vol. 9, pt. 2. Aion: Researches into the phenomenology of the self* (pp. 8–10). Princeton University Press. (Original work published 1951). https://doi.org/10.1515/9781400851058

Kalmbacher, C. (2021, October 17). "Monsters walk among us": Mom charged with trying to murder her 10-month-old baby by throwing him across a room, police say. *Law and Crime*. https://lawandcrime.com/crime/monsters-walk-among-us-mom-charged-with-trying-to-murder-her-10-month-old-baby-by-throwing-him-across-a-room-police-say/

Kravetz, A. (2012, September 25). Prosecutor: Baby starved while mother was "completely indifferent". *Journal Star*. www.pjstar.com/story/news/crime/2012/09/25/prosecutor-baby-starved-while-mother/42343126007/

Kristeva, J. (1980). Word, dialogue and novel. In L. S. Roudiez (Ed.), *Desire in language: A semiotic approach to literature and art* (pp. 64–91). Colombia University Press.

Kristeva, J. (1981). Women's time (A. Jardine & H. Blake, Trans.). *Signs: Journal of Women in Culture and Society*, *7*(1), 13–35.

Maxwell, D., Mauldin, R., Thomas, J., & Holland, V. (2022). American Indian motherhood and historical trauma: Keetoowah experiences of becoming mothers. *International Journal of Environmental Research and Public Health*, *19*(12), 7088.

McCord, C. (2023, May 30). *Mother accused of leaving young kids at home alone to go gamble, drink on memorial day*. KHOU.

Poteyeva, M., & Leigey, M. (2018). An examination of the mental health and negative life events of women who killed their children. *Social Science*, *7*(9), 168.

Rogo, P. (2020, October 26). Woman spitefully texts photo of dead toddler to baby's father during fight. *Essence*.

Saavedra, L., & de Oliveira, J. M. (2016). Transgressing motherhood: Media reports on infanticide' *Deviant Behavior*, *38*(3), 1–10.

Söderbäck, F. (2021). *New books in philosophy: "Revolutionary time: On time and difference in Kristeva and Irigaray"* [Podcast]. https://newbooksnetwork.com/revolutionary-time

WRGB Staff. (2021, October 27). "Monsters walk amongst us", mom accused of assaulting baby, says Watervliet police chief. *CBS News*. https://cbs6albany.com/news/local/monsters-walk-amongst-us-mom-accused-of-assaulting-baby-say-vliet-police-chief

Chapter 4

An Intersection of Systems

The infanticidal mother is not an event with a beginning and an end. She is a subject in process, a culmination of all the moments that came before the incident and gave force to what came next. Over her lifetime, she has been imprinted by an intersection of archetypal, social, political, historical, and economic forces, all of which have brought her to the newly constructed identity of an infanticidal mother. In my evaluations of infanticidal mothers, I see firsthand the intersecting forces that have affected them, which typically go unnoticed by the public eye. In the moment of her offense, her behavior is impacted by her psychological state, but rather than pointing to an inherent, aberrant psychological force within her, the more evident reality is that *normal women can kill their children when confronted by severe enough social and economic circumstances.*

Although infanticide occurs across race and socioeconomic status, the typical profile, or context, of an infanticidal mother includes women who have disadvantaged socioeconomic backgrounds, are socially isolated, are full-time caregivers, are women of color, are victims of domestic violence, and are under the age of 19 (Baek et al., 2019; Friedman & Resnick, 2007; Mailloux, 2014; Oberman & Meyer, 2008). Her context is essential to examine, as each component holds some responsibility for maternal aggression toward a child. Refusing to consider these factors perpetuates antiquated concepts, such as the belief that the infanticidal mother has an inherent madness or is simply bad. Whereas society is largely interested in placing the blame squarely on the mothers, the acknowledgment of these contextual factors points to much wider accountability. She is guilty, but who is to blame?

In my work I have become acutely aware of the way class, race, sexism, the police, the law, and the media contribute to the identity of an infanticidal mother, and how these intersecting factors are intractable from a discussion of who she is. I use the word *intersection* as it was coined by legal scholar Kimberlé Crenshaw (2018), who observed that in the experience of multiple discriminatory or subordinating structures, the force of their intersection is greater than their sum. This framework serves the following examination of the multidimensional experience of an infanticidal mother and her identity in the modern Western world.

DOI: 10.4324/9781003412809-6

Class

Like infanticide in animals, human infanticide is driven mainly by economic survival concerns, confirming the fact that infanticide is largely a poor woman's business. Current studies reflect the significant correlation between income levels and infant deaths at the hands of their mothers (Friedman & Resnick, 2007; Koenen & Thompson, 2008). Statistics range from upward of 80% of filicidal mothers having annual incomes below $20,000 (McKee & Shea, 1998) to 90% of fatal neglect occurring when the mothers were living below the poverty line (Meyer et al., 2001).

> The economic inequality of women leaves mothers with paychecks that are insufficient for home care, child care and health care . . . and they are powerless to change their situation. For the mothers who commit infanticide, the struggle overwhelms them, and they commit a terrible, heavily regretted act that costs them their child's life, their family, their freedom and their peace of mind for the rest of their lives.
>
> (Smithey, as cited in Young, 2020, "Social conditions", para. 7)

An economic stress hypothesis explains that poverty-stricken mothers who already have several children may commit infanticide when they believe that they cannot care for another child or when caring for another child would jeopardize the survival of the siblings. This means that acts of infanticide in cases of economic deprivation are evidence of a *committed* mother who may need to abandon a newborn to best care for her existing children (Hrdy, 1999, 2011).

Research also has shown that in the U.S., a nation known for high rates of child homicide, some areas are much more dangerous for children than others. Where mothers are in extreme poverty amid extreme wealth, there is a higher likelihood of stress-related violence against children. Relative deprivation, or the perception of income inequality, increased rates of infanticide (Baek et al., 2019; Gauthier et al., 2003).

In contemporary American society, the state supplements necessary resources for children in low-income families, yet despite these programs a mother who is unemployed or among the working poor still struggles with meeting basic needs, not only for food but other necessities. Financial stress can contribute to a mother having inadequate *emotional* resources—the ability to care, to be attuned to a child's needs, to show empathy, to create consistency, etc.—especially if compounded by issues such as isolation and postpartum depression.

> Scheper-Hughes' research led her to conclude that emotional scarcity can follow from material scarcity, and she warns against sentimentalizing "Mother." She writes that the image of all-nurturing, selfless mother is a modern artifact that has emerged only because we live in a sufficiently benevolent environment for mothers to trust that pretty much every child will survive.
>
> (Sieff, 2019, p. 24)

Hunger, famine, and food insecurity as a collective historical trauma may have left its trace in the cultural unconscious as a complex of affect-laden images (Scheper-Hughes, 1992). From the perspective of analytical psychology, the cultural unconscious shapes how a group of people define and experience archetypal aspects of human life; holds the effects across time of group trauma; and "operates both in the collective psychology of the group and in the individual members" (Singer & Kimbles, 2004, p. 2). The psychological effect on a group can take root in the cultural unconscious as an affect-laden cluster of images and beliefs and be passed across generations through attitudes, stories, and behaviors. When a mother living below the poverty line is struggling with multiple stressors and few resources, the deprivation may cue her psyche to access ancestral experiences of scarcity stored in the cultural unconscious, to which she may respond in an instinctual way that carries the archetypal fear of starvation and the energies of the Death Mother.

Low income has adversely affected most of my clients, creating an isolated world in which education on sexual health and resources for birth control are not available or adequate. Mothers living in poverty struggle "with substandard housing, hunger, homelessness, inadequate childcare, unsafe neighborhoods, and under-resourced schools" (American Psychological Association [APA], 2022, para. 7). Many of these mothers also face deficits from having grown up in poverty.

> Low-income children are at greater risk than higher-income children for a range of cognitive, emotional, and health-related problems, including detrimental effects on executive functioning, below average academic achievement, poor social emotional functioning, developmental delays, [and] behavioral problems.
> (para. 7)

Poverty sets a woman on a compromised path, one on which she is more likely to get pregnant at an age when she is neither capable nor prepared to care for a dependent, as evident in the fact that most neonaticides occur for girls under 19 who have had no prenatal care (Friedman & Resnick, 2007; Resnick, 1969).

The mother I met who grew up in an impoverished American Indian community persisted at a survival level for most of her life, rarely rising to a sense of thriving—most of her behavior was motivated by the need for food, shelter, and safety. She was unable to complete middle school, never educated about sexual health, and never offered birth control. This client spent much of her adolescence in juvenile detention and foster care, and as a young adult she was often homeless. The mechanism of poverty ushered her into motherhood in a way she was not prepared for, but having a baby meant more resources and more support for her. It upgraded her to a mother/baby shelter and access to medical services and helped her stay sober. Unfortunately, the trauma and stresses of her life left her vulnerable to postpartum psychosis, which ended in the death of her child and a life sentence in a women's prison, another unfortunate and unplanned way she has found regular housing.

This mother lived at the all-too-common intersection of sexism, classism, and racism: "In the United States, more women than men live in poverty . . . of the 38.1 million people living in poverty in 2018, 56 percent—or 21.4 million—were women" (Bleisweis et al., 2020, para. 1). The likelihood of being poor escalates if you are a woman of color:

> Poverty rates are disproportionately higher among most non-White populations. Compared to 8.2% of White Americans living in poverty, 26.8% of American Indian and Alaska Natives, 19.5% of Blacks, 17% of Hispanics and 8.1% of Asians are currently living in poverty.
>
> (APA, 2022, para. 4)

The Dark Other: Mothers of Color

Most of the women I see in my perinatal expert witness work are women of color. This has included Native American women, Mexican women, Guatemalan women, Pakistani American, and African American women, all of whom have their own cultural and religious beliefs about motherhood and childrearing and their own experiences of racism, which intrinsically affect their moment of infanticide. Infants of non-Hispanic White mothers accounted for 62.1% of homicides; however, rates among infants of non-Hispanic Black mothers (14.4), and non-Hispanic American Indian/Alaska Native mothers (14.9) were more than double the rate among infants of White mothers (5.9). Infants of Asian/Pacific Islander mothers had the lowest homicide rate (3.1) (Wilson et al., 2020). Without understanding the societal contributions of intersecting sexism, classism, and racism to these statistics, the status of an African American woman as criminal or subhuman is perpetuated. If you are a Black woman, the intersection of racism and sexism compounds your problems with healthcare:

> A new United Nations analysis of Black women's experiences during pregnancy and childbirth in the Americas has concluded that systemic racism and sexism in medical systems—not genetics or lifestyle choices—are the main reasons they are more likely to experience serious complications or even death. The United Nations Population Fund surveyed data from countries in the Americas, including the United States. It found that Black women were more likely than their white counterparts to report denial of medication or physical and verbal abuse in health care settings, leading to more severe complications, delayed treatment and worse.
>
> (Baumgaertner & Fassihi, 2023, paras. 1–2)

Race is a factor central to the constructions of motherhood, as the image of the idealized mother in the West is a fair White middle-class woman, an icon that immediately starts the mother of color at a disadvantage. Historically, American culture has cultivated very powerful images of Black mothers, from Mammy, the ideal Black mother figure who selflessly nurtures White children, to today's image of Black teenage girls who recklessly bear more children to collect welfare checks. With few exceptions, contemporary society views Black women mothering their own children as outside the category labeled *ideal mothers*.

Dorothy Roberts, a sociologist and law professor, noted that White Americans have long demanded that Black mothers leave their children at home in order to work at menial, low-wage jobs. "Americans expected Black mothers to look like Aunt Jemima, working in somebody else's kitchen . . . . American culture reveres no Black Madonna; it upholds no popular image of a Black mother nurturing her child" (1995, p. 146). Instead, "Black mothers' bonds with their children have been marked by brutal disruption, beginning with the slave auction where family members were sold to different masters and continuing in the disproportionate state removal of Black children to foster care" (146)

Black mothers face a complex web of obstacles: poverty, abuse, systemic racism, transgenerational trauma, shame, and violence—what humanities scholar Laura Dawkins in "From Madonna to Medea" called the "anguish of black maternity," in which "the Black mother's dead child functions as a trope for her mangled maternity, her 'unmothering' by a destructive society" (230).

It is crucial to consider the effect on the individual psyche of the historical trauma to Black mothers embedded in the cultural unconscious. Transgenerational trauma forms a "collective shadow process"—elements that were repressed as inconsistent with a racial or cultural group's collective ideals emerge from the unconscious laden with affect (Kimbles, 2003).

Transgenerational trauma has also been found to pass its effects on the expression of genes. The study of genetics has revealed that gene expression—how it develops and functions—is not only affected by one's lived experiences but is also inheritable from one's forebearers (Gibney & Nolan, 2010, p. 4). Black women in the U.S. have DNA familiarity with traumatic motherhood—accustomed to selling, losing, sacrificing, and taking in children as an effect of ancestral slavery and ongoing systemic racism as these patterns continue in today's communities. For Black children, there remains a disproportionate rate of placement into foster care. Stereotyping of Black children tracks them into the juvenile incarceration facilities rather than mental health services, and Black children constitute the largest population of infanticide victims (Ayres, 2004).

The history of trauma for Black women begins in slavery, with rape, forced pregnancy, and the loss of their children to the violent system of slavery. Their children were malnourished in the womb, born into enslavement, then forcibly separated from mothers and often sold to different masters. At times, mothers attempted to terminate their pregnancies or smother their female or weak infants to save them from slavery, rape, and abuse. In the mid-1800s, 94% of infant deaths in the U.S. were slave babies in slave counties (Johnson, 1981).

Toni Morrison's classic telling of the infanticide narrative in *Beloved* (1987) has been a significant container of this history for Black women. Morrison's novel, based on the true story of Margaret Gardner, beholds, embraces, and forgives the infanticidal mother Sethe, who killed her baby to save it from slavery, and of whom the character Stamp Paid says, "She ain't crazy. She love those children. She was trying to out hurt the hurter" (276). After Margaret Gardner was caught by deputy officers and later imprisoned, she confessed, saying "that her determination was to have killed all the children and then destroy herself rather than return to slavery" (Ayres, 2004, pp. 6–7).

Certainly, a mother's killing of her child is not consistent with the collective ideals of African Americans. History, literature, and research point to Black motherhood as culturally revered and exalted. Women's studies professor Andrea O'Reilly asserted that "the centrality and excellence of Black American mothers" has survived despite the "obstacle of the common white, educated, middle-class, feminist view of motherhood" (2004, p. 10). She added that "mothers and mothering are what make possible the physical and psychological well-being and empowerment of African-American people and the larger African-American culture" (11) This sentiment gets repeated by feminist scholars bell hooks in *Ain't I a Woman* and Patricia Collins in *Black Feminist Thought*, and points to the way infanticide is a particular wound for a Black mother when her identity as a mother is one of deepest importance.

Burdened by the historical and continuing intersection of sexism, classism, and racism, Black maternal infanticide stems from the *othering* of Black mothers, the projection onto them of the shadow of those in dominance. In this way, White dominators privilege themselves by pretending they contain only the nurturing positive maternal impulses of a "good" mother, exempting themselves from the need to attend to the lived struggle and authentic voices of mothers, especially Black mothers.

In many ways, Medea also played the role of the dark other in the Greek Corinthian society. In his introduction to Euripedes's *Medea*, Denys Page noted the importance of her foreignness to the construction of her character and infanticide:

> Because [Medea] was a foreigner she could kill her children; because she was a witch she could escape in a magic chariot. She embodies the qualities which the fifth-century Athenian believed to be characteristic of Orientals.
>
> (1938, p. xxi)

She has been presented as a Colchian, belonging to both a different ethnic group than the Greeks and to a black-skinned race (Leibu, 2019). Even if Euripides made no explicit mention of her race, Medea is clearly foreign, and the issues she faces are common to those who are not a part of the ethnic/racial majority and therefore subject to being treated as *other* and seen projectively as carrying the unwanted, unconscious content of the dominant group. This motif is not only present in the text but parallels the issues confronted by many oppressed groups, especially Black women in the U.S.

Ruth's Story

Ruth is an African American mother who grew up in a public housing project of predominantly Black residents, known for its dilapidation and excessive violence. While dodging violence in the darkened hallways of her apartment block, she raised her younger siblings in a small apartment with an alcoholic mother and a very violent father. Ruth was first pregnant at 13 years old, then lost that pregnancy at 6 months due to being kicked in the stomach. She became pregnant again at 18 and never considered having an abortion due to cultural beliefs. Forced out of her father's house, Ruth moved in with a boyfriend who was extremely physically abusive. After having her first child, she took in a toddler—a common occurrence in her community—who had prenatal drug and alcohol exposure and developmental delays, and whose mother was incarcerated. Ruth helped this child, who was partially blind, learn to walk and hold a bottle. Ruth eventually adopted the child. She then became pregnant again but was anxious about miscarriage due to the domestic violence she was experiencing.

Caring for both her bio child and disabled adopted child, at 8 months pregnant Ruth was exhausted, depressed, and literally beaten down by her boyfriend. One afternoon the adopted daughter put her hand to a hot burner. Ruth punished her with a whooping during which she snapped and lost control. At the end of the whooping the child was unconscious, and Ruth rushed her to a hospital that served mostly White patients. Ruth reported the whooping and what she thought was a seizure. The child was pronounced dead, and Ruth was arrested. In what suggests both sexist and racist profiling, Ruth, a Black mother who had gone over and above to care for her children, was presumed solely responsible, and the White male police never questioned the abusive partner for his possible role. Ruth was sentenced to prison shortly after she delivered her baby. Her oldest child and newborn went to be cared for by her sister, while Ruth was sent away for 55 years.

Intersection with the Law

The infanticidal mother uniquely violates many versions of the law: the law of God, the law of nature, moral law, Constitutional law, and criminal law. Her violation can be heard in Union County deputy sheriff Bobby Hicks remarks about Susan V. Smith, a South Carolina woman who killed her two children in 1994: "Momma is the loving person, the giving person, the sacrifice person—for them to do something like that is like denying God or something" (as cited in Kunkle, 2014, para. 5). Hicks was the first to interview Smith, who was severely mentally ill and let her car roll into a lake with the toddlers inside. Hicks's statement reflects the Law: A filicidal mother has not only committed a crime of moral turpitude but has rebelled against her God-given instinct and violated a law of nature.

Historically, women have been outside of the construction of the law. As outsiders to the U.S. Constitution written by the Founding Fathers in 1787, women are denied subjectivity but are included as a reflection of the male ego. This Law ignores the complexity of women's lives as mothers, and posits women as "the other, the object of the male gaze, the subject of the discussion, not the speaker" (Schutte, 1991, p. 71). The Founding Fathers' ignorance of a woman's lived experiences—her body, relationships, race, culture, sensations, etc.—has constructed and reinforced a version of woman that is rudimentary and totalizing. Although the Founding Fathers endorsed separation of church and state, their vision of the role of women in society clearly had at its roots Christian patriarchal beliefs that depotentiated feminine agency and self-possession in the iconography of the self-sacrificing, obedient Virgin Mary. Women were completely excluded from both the formulation and content of the country's Constitution, which guaranteed men's but not women's rights (Schwarzenbach & Smith, 2003). It wasn't until 200 years after Law was established in the U.S. for women to win the right to vote. U.S. law has long been founded on the oppression of women: a failure to recognize and value their agency and complexity of their lives, including their reproductive power and experience of motherhood; and the assumption that they belong hidden in the background of men's lives.

My work sits at the intersection of psychology and the legal system, both systems of a Western symbolic order. The law is in deference to a Constitutional code and an elected judge, whereas psychology relies on the DSM-5, the APA's authoritative guide to the diagnosis of mental disorders. In many ways, the two institutions speak separate languages. Whereas law tends toward the factual and binary—wrong/right, good/bad, legal/illegal—psychology tends toward the uncertain and variable and is more comfortable in the gray areas. Psychologists are trained to observe behavior on a continuum whereas the law presents as dichotomous in nature (Fulero & Wrightsman, 2009), making for difficult bedfellows. Psychology and law may love and hate each other, but they ultimately need each other. For example, psychology needs law when the mentally ill patient is a danger to self or others. Alternatively, law needs psychology to determine whether a defendant is competent to stand trial or that jury selection is fair and balanced.

A significant interaction between psychology and the law is found in the rule of sanity: Did the defendant know what she did was *wrong*? Did she *know* it was wrong and do it anyway? The standard definition of sanity is based on the M'Naghten rule, briefly introduced in the first chapter. The M'Naghten rule includes three criterion that a defendant must satisfy to qualify as legally insane: The defendant had a defect or disease of the mind at the time of the crime, did not understand the quality of their act, and did not know that the act was wrong (Manchester, 2002). The discernment of sanity is flawed and repeatedly fails as the word *insane* is a legal, not psychological, term. When psychologists evaluate clients, they refer to symptomatology found in the DSM-5. For example, an individual may have symptoms of psychosis (unable to distinguish fantasy from reality), an intellectual disability, or a neurocognitive disorder that impairs an understanding of facts, but they would never be evaluated as "insane."

In many of the cases I see, an attorney enters a plea of Not Guilty by Reasons of Insanity. They are not in court to prove the defendant innocent, but to prove that at the moment she killed her child she did not know what she was doing was wrong. If insanity is too difficult to prove, counsel will use a defense of *diminished capacity*, arguing that although she broke the law, she should not be held fully criminally liable for doing so as her mental functions were diminished or impaired. At this point, the court turns to a psychologist to conduct evaluations and provide subsequent testimonies to validate or negate the defendant's sanity or capacity.

In cases of infanticide, the court asks the infanticidal mother: Did you know killing your child was wrong and you did it anyway? (Meaning, are you a *bad* mother?). Or were you insane? (Meaning, are you a *mad* mother?). In this interaction, the law is obtuse on the subject of postpartum psychology and infanticide. The law does not want to know the function of a mother killing her child. There is very little interest in the context of her life, such as her poverty, transgenerational trauma, psychosis, or even self-defense. What the law cannot accept is that an infanticidal mother is neither mad nor bad nor criminal, but caught and overwhelmed in intersecting, oppressive systems.

Failure to Protect Laws

The legacy of mother-blame is pervasive in child welfare and criminal justice systems, most notably in Failure to Protect Laws, which state that caregivers have a duty to protect the child in their care from avoidable harm, deeming those who fail to fulfill this duty liable for the resulting harm or risk of harm (Azzopardi, 2022). These laws were developed to find a way to impose accountability for child harm on those who allowed it to happen. More women than men have been charged and convicted of this offense—biological mothers comprise 90% of those identified as primary caregivers in child maltreatment investigations, irrespective of sole-parent or multi-parent household demographics (Fallon et al., 2020; Michaels, 2022). For example, nonoffending mothers have been blamed for child sexual abuse as having been negligent or complicit (Azzopardi et al., 2018). Although family systems and psychoanalytic theory have debunked the idea that mothers consciously or unconsciously collude with abuse of their children, as social worker Corry Azzopardi observed, "the legacy of mother-blame lives on in gendered child welfare policies and practices through the contemporary doctrine of failure to protect" (para. 1). This leaves women, rather than the men causing harm, to be the recipients of scrutiny and punishment from hospital staff, police, and the courts. When a mother is seen as failing to meet the good-mother standard of protection, it deserves a stiffer penalty than the actual assault or rape of a child.

Feminist criminologist Sarah Singh studied the punishment of women for men's violence under the Failure to Protect clause. Her work highlights mother crimes as "doubly transgressive" in that they challenge both the criminal law and their gender role (2021, p. 184). When women are accused of failure to protect, they are tried as women and mothers, not as autonomous legal subjects, and "convicted according to their adherence to maternal ideology, rather than their actions and omissions" (184). When a woman is arrested, the stereotype of woman as good is already askew. Thus, when arrested because her child is dead, she is immediately subject to the harshest of prejudices—the disdain and condemnation reserved for bad mothers.

The July/August 2022 cover of *Mother Jones* magazine read "Lock Her Up: Forced to give birth. Prosecuted for miscarriages. Policed for raising kids." The issue featured an article in which the author, Samantha Michaels, analyzed court records from almost 2 million felonies and misdemeanors in Oklahoma, focusing on the ones affected by the Failure to Protect law. Michaels highlighted several cases in which a father inflicted abuse on a child,[1] yet the mother received a harsher sentence. For example, although Greg fatally abused Traci's 13-month-old when Traci wasn't home, Greg was sentenced to 10 years in prison, whereas Traci received 65 years in prison for not intervening. In another case, Kerry King was incarcerated for not protecting her daughter from her live-in boyfriend who, high on heroin, had been abusing both her and her daughter. The officers who arrested her after her boyfriend's near-fatal abuse of her daughter asked why she allowed the abuse and why she didn't call 911 when it was happening. King was sentenced to 30 years in prison, 12 more years than the boyfriend. Interviewed from prison, King requested that the public not look at the singular event, but the greater context of the experience: "They should look at every day and see all that I went through, and how I got to the point of that day" (as cited in Michaels, 2022, para. 116). Laws like Failure to Protect are much more successful at prosecuting women like King than they are at protecting kids, who regularly land in foster care or, worse, are left at home with an abusive male guardian while their mother is imprisoned. Michaels concluded,

> The criminal justice system makes these mothers ultra-culpable, blaming them for things that are largely outside their control, as if mothers have a magical power. They are blamed for the intersecting forces, for the sexism that leads to domestic abuse, for the poverty that makes it hard to escape, for the racist policing systems that don't protect them, for the circumstances that leave them with few options.
>
> (para. 28)

The law makes an example of these mothers, and prosecutors use them to teach morals to their audience by pointing to what a Bad Mother is. In King's case, the prosecutor went so far to suggest child murder victims were watching King's case from heaven and she was there to get justice for them (Michaels, 2022). I have been in courtrooms where, when a guilty verdict was announced, people stood up and cheered.[2]

Police

Police officers are often the first people to interact with a mother who has committed infanticide. They are called to a scene where they find a gruesome aftermath, or to a hospital where they find a baby having died and a nurse holding a mother unknowingly until the police arrive. Eventually, the police are queried by journalists and give statements on the case. Police are the most oft-quoted in articles and headlines on infanticide (Briggs, 2007); their opinions construct a discourse about infanticide that provides a very limited range of subjective positions—entirely omitting the mother's perspective.

The police force in the U.S. is largely comprised of White (60%) men (83%) (Zippia, 2023), who have a duty to model moral, legal, and ethical standards in the public eye, thus an infanticidal mother is an offender they may be motivated personally and politically to vilify and to see prosecuted. Mothers who kill do more than break a law or a moral code against murder; they offend a culturally sacrosanct order of behavior in which mothers are inherently nurturing and sacrificial toward their children. Police officers, as the dominant voice in a press release on an infanticide case, act as gatekeepers to public opinion and have the power to interpret and advance the narrative of the mother as a criminal, or more so, a monster.

For example, an article from *Fox News*, "Slain Dallas 3-year-old's mother 'recklessly killed' him, police documents say," reported that "Dallas police believe Lacravionne 'recklessly killed' her 3-year-old son, who died from a gunshot wound. Police say she attempted to get rid of the gun and faked a road rage incident" (Dial, 2022, para. 5). This is a common form of identity construction in which the foundation is laid for both conviction and seeing the accused woman as different from us in emphasizing the manipulative, brutal, selfish, and irreparable violence of an unnatural mother.

"A Baton Rouge mother was accused of murder after police say she punched her toddler in the torso for playing with her contact lenses, causing her to hit her head and die hours later, before the family reported her missing" was the headline of an article that reported:

> "Over the last several days, since we first received the call, it was our highest priority to bring Nevaeh [the toddler] home," Baton Rouge Police Chief Murphy Paul said Wednesday in announcing the arrests. "It saddens me to . . . discuss the fact that this beautiful, innocent angel is no longer with us."
>
> (Carmosina, 2021, para. 5)

The police chief's narrative paints a stark contrast between the infanticidal mother and law enforcement: a brutal heartless killer versus an emotional (sad, not angry), caring police officer who elevates the child from toddler to angel.

The *CBS News* article " 'Monsters walk amongst us', mom accused of assaulting baby, says Watervliet Police Chief" conjures up the exact image of what a mother is if she deviates from her allotted role. A chief of police calls a mother whose child is now dead a "monster," providing a headline to attract readers—for as much as we are shocked or repulsed by the eruption of shadow, so we are fascinated by it, relieved to be able to think it belongs to someone else. What the police are not sharing with the reporters are the actual findings of their investigation. Such a report might read: *Female co-parent with history of trauma suffering domestic abuse, psychotic delusion, and no paid maternity leave injures child.*

DNA Analysis

As DNA analysis and profiling has grown more accessible to law enforcement, police forces across the country have used this technology to take up cold cases of Baby Johns, that is, deceased babies who had been found but an arrest was never made. Of all the cold cases a police officer could choose to pursue, including serial killers and rapists, it is curious that so many of these Baby John cases have been making the news of late. In June of 2022, police used DNA technology to arrest a 58-year-old Lee Ann Daigle for the 1985 death of her baby, who had been discovered in a gravel pit. The police agency was quoted as saying, "This case was the culmination of decades' worth of investigative work from dozens of . . . detectives who never gave up finding answers and justice for Baby Jane Doe" (as cited in Stelloh, 2022, para.). Daigle had given birth alone in the gravel pit in sub-zero temperatures and panicked and fled instead of getting help (Stelloh, 2022).

The Connecticut police department arrested 62-year-old Janita Philips for the previously unsolved murder of her newborn in 1986. In 2020, the Connecticut police picked up the cold case, obtained a court order to exhume the body for testing, and traced the DNA to Ms. Phillips living in another state.

> [Phillips] confessed and said she hid her pregnancy from her husband. "I didn't want to crash his dreams and fall down the rabbit hole of having a bunch of kids and stuck with bills and not being able to care for them or get to achieve his dreams," she said.
>
> (ABC Eyewitness News, 2021, para. 9)

Police Deputy Chief Robert Berry announced on Facebook, "The investigation of his tragic death has taken many long years, but he has always been remembered and we hope this conclusion will bring him peace and recognition" (as cited in Keller, 2021, para. 19).

What motivation is there to pursue a mother who decades earlier killed or abandoned her child—as unthinkable as the act is—when the likelihood that the mother is a dangerous criminal is statistically low and two-thirds of rape cases are still unsolved (Merelli, 2019)? The extraordinary use of resources to convict a woman who is not a dangerous criminal reflects a fear-based persecution of mothers and denial of the pressures and deprivations they face. Police spend labor and resources, time and money on efforts that are not effectively preventing more crime but acting out a drive to publicly identify and hang a "bad mother."

Gina's Story

I worked with Gina, an African American woman from the south side of Chicago, after she had been in prison for 30 years. At 17 years old, Gina was convicted of the death of her 20-month-old daughter. Gina's entire life had been riddled with violence and poverty. All the relationships around her were physically abusive and transactional. It was a strain to identify a positive support in her past, although at the time I met her she had very close relationships with her children, especially her daughter, with whom she spoke every night on the phone, trying to help her daughter navigate the dating world.

Gina had been in a string of violent relationships. At the time when she lost her child, she was living with a man who was a violent gang member and habitually assaulted her. Gina had several children, and her youngest, a 20-month-old, often slept with her and her partner. The morning that the baby died, Gina was getting her other children ready for school when her partner came out of the bedroom holding the limp child. Gina rushed the child to the hospital but couldn't answer the doctor's questions as she did not know what had happened to the baby. Her partner had told Gina to tell the police that the baby had fallen down the stairs. Gina and her partner were taken to the police station and put into different rooms. Gina repeatedly told the police that the baby had fallen down the stairs. The police told her that the kind of injuries the baby had were not consistent with falling down the stairs.

The police then began to ask how she disciplined her children: Did she spank them? How often? With what? Where on their bodies? The police told her that the sooner she answered the questions, the sooner she could return to the hospital to see her baby. Gina's interpretation of this led her to believe the baby was still alive, which she later found out wasn't true. The police continued to focus on how Gina "whooped" her children. They asked about the last time she had disciplined them, and Gina reported a recent time when the baby had stuck her fingers in an outlet. Gina had slapped her hand away. The police told her she slapped her too hard, and she fell across the room and hit her head. Although untrue, Gina agreed to this confession. The police did not adequately investigate the child's father, who was the last adult with the toddler.

At the police station, Gina was in a state of shock having seen her child limp and unresponsive a few hours earlier. During the confession, Gina was in a position of weighing her options: telling the police that she didn't know what happened to the baby, which risked a violent retribution from her partner, or giving the police a confession, which kept her safe from violence and hastened the possibility of seeing her injured child.

Gina was convicted of murder and sentenced to 80 years in prison. During her trial, her lawyer provided inadequate representation, failing to investigate the father's role in the death or claims of police misconduct. The case got picked up by Northwestern University's Center on Wrongful Convictions. In their attempt to do post-conviction sentencing, they hired me to evaluate Gina. She had severe PTSD, with the subcategory of battered women syndrome, and postpartum depression at the time of the offense. With this mitigating evidence her appeal was successful and last year Gina was released after 30 years.

In cases of domestic violence and infanticide, I often see mothers who have made a coerced confession. The police promise her that if she gives them what they want—a confession—she can see her baby. Typically, the mother is a woman of color being questioned by White male cops. She has a submissive, pacifying fear response, both due to the chronic abuse from a male and the systemic racism from the police toward people of color. Thus, the mother is in a vulnerable situation in which it is almost impossible to experience her own agency or defend herself. So, although a male may have been the guilty party or the last one with the baby, the battered mother is trained to protect and deny any violence on his part. She fears further reprisal from him or the police; thus, she takes the blame. These are awful situations of child abuse and neglect, where a mother, although she may not be completely innocent, is often the only one to receive blame.

Failure to Protect legislation is most often utilized in cases of domestic violence, such that a mother's failure to protect often gets conflated with a failure to leave an abusive relationship. Legal authorities and the law demonstrate psychological ignorance in their failure to understand the consequences for a woman of leaving an abusive relationship, which range from being fatal to homelessness, lack of resources, or loss of children. In this way, the Failure to Protect statute criminalizes the actions of women who are victims of domestic abuse. In contemporary Western society, it is not only women's responsibility to care for children, but also to avoid and manage male violence. Case law consistently shows that women tend to select the least dangerous option, and most often that means staying in an abusive relationship (Stark, 1995). Singh argued that when mothers are accused of failure to protect,

> Juries are encouraged by prosecutors to interpret a mother's failure to meet this idealised standard of mothering as justifying the imposition of criminal responsibility on women who have experienced abuse (Panko, 1995; Herring, 2008). Archaic associations between femininity and suffering mean that the good mother is required to be self-sacrificing to the point where she will die for her child (Jacobs, 1998). It follows that . . . the threshold of what is reasonable is set too high in these cases.
>
> (2021, p. 194)

The expectation of maternal omnipresence plays a key role in the prosecution's contentions that the mother ought to have foreseen a risk of harm and been there to prevent it, whereas if a man was gone, it is aligned with our assumption that as the breadwinner he is of course out of the house. An example of this is found in the case of Lindsay Clancy, who heard a voice telling her to kill her children. She had a long and documented history of postpartum depression, of which her husband Patrick was aware. She had been previously hospitalized; she was taking various medications; she was posting on social media that she was struggling. Yet when harm came to his three children when he left them alone with her, he was not approached legally, nor by the court of public opinion, for failure to protect.

The most intimate way an infanticidal mother encounters the Law is when she meets her lawyer for the first time. It also tends to be the most decisive for her future. Recently, I received a phone call from a lawyer with his first infanticide case, and he was befuddled. He was a public defender in a small town in a conservative state, and he had never heard of postpartum psychosis. His client was a woman who heard a voice commanding her to kill her child with a sword. After we spoke for a while and I briefly educated him on postpartum psychosis, command voices, and infanticide, he admitted that he had only known to contact a perinatal expert witness because of a *Newsweek* magazine that had showed up on his desk with the article headline: "'I Wanted To Put A Knife Into My Baby': Moms On Their Postpartum Psychosis" (Collins, 2023). The lawyer recognized his client's story and pursued it as a defense. But for every one of these lawyers, there are more who remain ignorant.

Punishment

Contemporary justice is based upon the idea of "just laws," which means that the same punishment should be delivered to everybody who commits the same crime. Patriarchal justice is based on impartiality and the rule of law. As a result, infanticidal mothers in the United States, unless they can be found to be insane by the M'Naghten rule and a DSM-5 diagnosis (which does not include postpartum psychosis), are prosecuted and punished as murderers, generally without consideration of systemic or psychological factors. In the United States, infanticidal mothers receive the harshest sentences of all Western countries (Spinelli, 2019). In the United Kingdom and more than 20 other countries, a woman who causes the death of her child in the first year of life is assumed to be mentally ill. In lieu of prison or the death sentence, these women receive psychiatric treatment and rehabilitation (Friedman & Resnick, 2007). Canada has an Infanticide Law that is meant to draw attention to the social circumstances surrounding women who find themselves "with unwanted babies and no options" (Kramar, as cited in Gowriluk, 2022, para. 15). Kirsten Kramar, an expert on infanticide, noted that the faulty thinking is that harsher punishments will deter infanticide. Instead, she argued, "We need to be thinking about solutions other than prosecution and incarceration, particularly for [infanticidal mothers]" (as cited in Gowriluk, 2022, para. 7).

Although the British Infanticide Act became law in 1938 and has subsequently been adopted elsewhere around the world, nothing even approaching it became law in the United States until 2018, when the state of Illinois passed PA 100–0574, which recognizes postpartum illnesses as a mitigating factor in criminal cases. This reflects an improved ability of the legal system to listen to psychology: The infanticidal mother moves incrementally from the bad to the mad mother. Yet in 2021, a similar law was proposed in Massachusetts but failed to pass.

Most U.S. jurisdictions prosecute maternal filicide under the standard homicide laws. The result has been a tendency toward treating each maternal filicide case as exceptional, rather than recognizing the patterns that link these cases, which would illuminate the extent to which these crimes are linked to social expectations and conditions for mothers. The result is that U.S. maternal filicide case law is incoherent and often arbitrary. Women convicted of substantially equivalent crimes, such as neonaticide, receive sentences that vary from probation with counseling to life imprisonment, although most convicted mothers receive close to 30 years in prison (Spinelli, 2019). These mothers are at the bottom of the American legal system and rarely see effective appeals.

Mothers accused of killing their children face an issue in the criminal justice system linked to patriarchal beliefs that expect women to be compliant and passive while sanctioning male aggression. In the law's objectification of women and denial of their subjectivity, it denies their agency and reactivity—objects have neither. As such a woman may find herself punished not only for her crime, but also for threatening to destabilize women's subordinate and submissive place in the social order. As an example of this, a few years ago there was a man, with an extensive criminal history of drug and violence charges, who beat up a woman then drove his SUV into her. He was released on $1,000 bail. Around the same time, in the same county, a mother who was one week postpartum was led into gang gun violence by her abusive boyfriend, and she shot another woman, injuring her. She was jailed with no bail. Five days after the man was released on bail, he drove his SUV at top speed into a holiday parade in a small Midwestern town. He drove wildly, purposefully pegging off victims: the marching band, the "giving grannies," the children's choir (Wagner et al., 2021). Because the mother was held without bail, she couldn't nurse, bond with, or care for her one-week-old infant. Yet, the man was able to commit one of the most atrocious public attacks in that state's history.

This follows the general trend of punishment exacted on women in the U.S. It's notable that women who deviate from the maternal ideal receive some of the harshest punishments. For example, women are rarely sentenced to death in the United States and actual executions of women are even rarer, but of the women on death row, most have violated a Maternal Law—they have been a bad mother (Current Female Death Row Prisoners, 2022). Most recently, Melissa Lucio was sentenced to death for the murder of her 2-year-old daughter Mariah, who died two days after a tragic fall down a flight of stairs (Andone, 2022). In shock from the loss of her youngest child, Lucio was taken into police custody, blamed for her daughter's death, and ultimately badgered by a Texas Ranger into making a false confession. She was sentenced to death in 2008. Even with a high-profile defense team, petitions for sentence modification and clemency, and a national appeal, she was executed on April 27, 2022—killed without committing a homicide, but for being a bad mother. Another woman, Christie Scott, has been on death row since 2009 after a fire burned her house, killing her 6-year-old son. Christie had purchased a $100,000 life insurance policy on her son just 12 hours before his death. In all, she was accused of trying to collect $175,000 in insurance money. Yet, throughout trial proceedings, Christie maintained her innocence. Another mother, Patricia Blackmon, who has been on death row since June 2002, was 29 when she killed her 2-year-old adopted daughter. Tierra Capri Gobble has been on death row since December 2005 after being convicted of beating her 4-month-old son to death (CNN, 2014).

The sense of justice in the exacting of punishment is unquantifiable, inevitably both too much and too little. However, the mood in the courtroom around an infanticidal mother is akin to a funeral, but with a mix of dread, curiosity, and self-satisfaction. There is inevitably a focus on the mother's unnatural evilness. Bringing anything to attention aside from the tragic loss of a helpless child's life, such as a mother's past trauma, a severe mental illness, a break with reality, a decade of physical abuse, requires a careful and herculean strategy, yet is inevitably seen as barely touching the gravity of her violation of the Law. During the plea hearing for the American Indian mother, I first reported to the court that she was competent to stand trial. I then explained that at the time of the incident she had been experiencing untreated bipolar disorder with psychotic features, with no criminal intent. As the White jurors and the judge discussed the details and plea bargain in her case, the accused mother sat meekly with her long black braids hanging down her back, her jail scrubs like a bag around her. In the gallery was the extended family of the deceased boy, all wearing t-shirts that read "Justice for [the child's name]." When the procedure ended and I made my way out of the courtroom, I was slowed by the t-shirt-wearing crowd shouting to me, "She's evil, she deserves life in prison, she did it on purpose, she's lying to you!" "You came all the way from Chicago to help a lying baby killer!"

In Sum

What should happen to these women who have acted to end the lives of their children or who have failed to act to save them? What is the punishment, if any, that is deserved? The glaring punishment each infanticidal mother faces is the loss of her child. This is a life sentence. Every fiber of her being is forever aware of this brutal loss. For all the accusations of these mothers being cold or showing no remorse, I have not worked with a mother who did not grieve her act and the loss of her child.

Arriving at greater justice for mothers requires challenging the fundamental attitude in the American justice system and imagining a Law based on mothers' lived experience, considering the adversity of a misogynistic, racist, and classist system. It is possible that if the infanticidal mother's life is examined in all its context, she may have a different outcome within the legal system. It is also possible that her story brought to light would destabilize the social order and create change for mothers.

Revisioning the language of the law by exposing it to women's lives challenges the patriarchal constructions of motherhood. Just as her voice, her subjectivity, is worthy of attention, so are the historical and powerful systems that intersect in her identity. This deconstruction of the male gaze and the Law and illumination of the infanticidal mother gives us a better chance to respond to her needs, her desires, her cries for help, and ultimately her comments on the social order.

Notes

1 Just as maternal violence toward children in literature is often depicted in the stepmother character, paternal violence toward children may be carried by the archetypal energy of a wicked stepfather. Yet this archetype is notably absent in the literature because no matter how badly he treated his wife and children, he would simply be exercising his rights as a man to use his personal property in whatever way he wished (Brown, 2015).
2 For an exploration of changing the laws regarding neonaticide and infanticide, see Oberman (1996)

References

ABC Eyewitness News. (2021, November 19). Woman charged in 1986 murder of her infant son in Connecticut. *CONNECTICUT WABC*. https://abc7ny.com/janita-philips-cold-case-murder-arrestbaby-killed-infant/11253498//

American Psychiatric Association. (2013). *Diagnostic and statistical manual* (5th ed.). APA.

American Psychological Association. (2022, October). *Exploring the mental health effects of poverty, hunger, and homelessness on children and teens.* www.apa.org/topics/socio economic-status/poverty-hunger-homelessness-children

Andone, D. (2022, May 1). Melissa Lucio was sentenced to death. Courts will now look at these 4 claims to decide if she gets a new trial. *CNN.* www.cnn.com/2022/05/01/us/melissa-lucio-claims-new-trial/index.html

Ayres, S. (2004). "[N]ot a story to pass on": Constructing mothers who kill. *Hastings Women's Law Journal, 15.* https://ssrn.com/abstract=2493308

Azzopardi, C. (2022). Gendered attributions of blame and failure to protect in child welfare responses to sexual abuse: A Feminist critical discourse analysis. *Violence Against Women, 28*(6–7), 1631–1658.

Azzopardi, C., Alaggia, R., & Fallon, B. (2018). From Freud to feminism: Gendered constructions of blame across theories of child sexual abuse. *Journal of Child Sexual Abuse, 27*(3), 254–275.

Baek, S. U., Lim, S. S., Kim, J., & Yoon, J. H. (2019). How does economic inequality affect infanticide rates? An analysis of 15 years of death records and representative economic data. *International Journal of Environmental Research and Public Health, 16*(19), 3679.

Baumgaertner, E., & Fassihi, F. (2023, July 12). Racism and sexism underlie higher maternal death rates for black women. *The New York Times.*

Bleisweis, R., Boesch, D., & Gaines, A. (2020, August 3). The basic facts about women in poverty. *CAP.* www.americanprogress.org/article/basic-facts-women-poverty/

Briggs, C. L. (2007). Mediating infanticide: Theorizing relations between narrative and violence. *Cultural Anthropology, 22*(3), 315–356.

Brown, M. D. (2015, May 24). *Why you never hear stories about wicked stepfathers.* https://cc.bingj.com/cache.aspx?q=Literary+critic+Mary+Daniels+Brown%2c+Ph.D.+wicked+stepfather&d=4746574823840930&mkt=en-US&setlang=en-US&w=E43ROz255CRufl u37I-dZZEcQczkzp6F

Carmosina, E. (2021, September 29). Baton Rouge toddler died after mom punched her torso, causing her to hit head, police say. *The Advocate.*

CNN. (2014, September 18). *Women of death row.* https://edition.cnn.com/2014/03/25/us/gallery/byrom-female-death-row/index.html

Collins, A. (2023, February 4). "I wanted to put a knife into my baby": Moms on their postpartum psychosis. *Newsweek.* www.newsweek.com/postpartum-psychosis-lindsay-clancy-1778724

Collins, P. H. (2000). *Black feminist thought: Knowledge, consciousness and the politics of empowerment.* Routledge.

Crenshaw, K. (2018). Demarginalizing the intersection of race and sex: A Black feminist critique of antidiscrimination doctrine, feminist theory, and antiracist politics [1989]. In K. Bartlett & R. Kennedy (Eds.), *Feminist legal theory: Readings in law and gender* (pp. 57–80). Routledge.

Current Female Death Row Prisoners. (2022). https://deathpenaltyinfo.org/death-row/women

Dawkins, L. (2004). From Madonna to Medea: Maternal infanticide in African American women's literature of the Harlem Renaissance. *LIT: Literature Interpretation Theory*, *15*(3), 223–240.

Dial, S. (2022, April 18). Slain Dallas 3-year-old's mother "recklessly killed" him, police documents say. *Fox4*. www.fox4news.com/news/slain-dallas-3-year-olds-mother-now-charged-with-manslaughter

Fallon, B., Filippelli, J., Lefebvre, R., Joh-Carnella, N., Trocmé, N., Black, T., MacLaurin, B., Hélie, S., Morin, Y., Fluke, J., King, B., Esposito, T., Collin-Vézina, D., Allan, K., Houston, E., Harlick, M., Bonnie, N., Budau, K., Goodman, D., . . . Stoddart, J. (2020). *Ontario incidence study of reported child abuse and neglect—2018*. https://cwrp.ca/sites/default/files/publications/Ontario%20Incidence%20Study%20of%20Reported%20Child%20Abuse%20and%20Neglect%202018.pdf

Friedman, S., & Resnick, P. (2007). Child murders by mothers: Patterns and prevention. *World Psychiatry*, *6*(3), 137–141.

Fulero, S. M., & Wrightsman, L. S. (2009). *Forensic psychology*. Cengage Learning.

Gauthier, D. K., Chaudoir, N. K., & Forsyth, C. J. (2003). Sociological analysis of maternal infanticide in the United States, 1984–1996. *Deviant Behavior*, *24*(4), 393–404.

Gibney, E. R., & Nolan, C. M. (2010). Epigenetics and gene expression. *Heredity*, *105*, 4–13.

Gowriluk, C. (2022, June 12). Infanticide expert puzzled to see Winnipeg mother charged with manslaughter in newborn's death. *CBC News*. www.cbc.ca/news/canada/manitoba/jeanene-rosa-moar-infanticide-manslaughter-experts-1.6485231

Herring, J. (2008). Mum's not the word: An analysis of section 5, Domestic Violence, Crime and Victims Act (2004). In S. Cunningham & M. V. Clarkson Christopher (Eds.), *Criminal liability for non-aggressive death* (pp. 125–155). Ashgate.

hooks, b. (2014). *Ain't I a woman: Black women and feminism*. Routledge.

Hrdy, S. (1999). *Mother nature: Natural selection and the female of the species*. Chattos & Winduss.

Hrdy, S. (2011). *Mothers and others: The evolutionary origins of mutual understanding*. Harvard University Press.

Jacobs, M. (1998). Requiring battered women die: Murder liability for mothers under failure to protect statutes. *The Journal of Criminal Law and Criminology*, *88*(2), 579–660. https://doi.org/10.2307/1144291.

Johnson, M. P. (1981). Smothered slave infants: Were slave mothers at fault? *The Journal of Southern History*, *47*(4), 493–520.

Keller, A. (2021, November 9). Florida woman charged with murdering newborn boy in Connecticut more than 35 years ago. *Law and Crime*.

Kimbles, S. (2003). Cultural complexes and collective shadow processes. In J. Beebe (Ed.), *Terror, violence, and the impulse to destroy* (pp. 211–234). Daimon Verlag.

Koenen, M. A., & Thompson, J. W., Jr. (2008). Filicide: Historical review and prevention of child death by parent. *Infant Mental Health Journal*, *29*(1), 61–75.

Kunkle, F. (2014, September 27). What makes mothers kill their own children? *Washington Post*.

Leibu, D. (2019). *Myth, magic, and murderous mothers: An exploration of myth and Medea* [Honors thesis, Wellesley College]. https://repository.wellesley.edu/object/ir903

Mailloux, S. (2014). Fatal families: Why children are killed in familicide occurrences. *Journal of Family Violence*, *29*, 921–926.

Manchester, J. (2002). Beyond accommodation: Reconstructing the insanity defense to provide an adequate remedy for postpartum psychotic women. *Journal of Criminal Law & Criminology*, *93*, 713.

McKee, G. R., & Shea, S. J. (1998). Maternal filicide: A cross national comparison. *Journal of Clinical Psychology*, *54*(5), 679–687.

Merelli, A. (2019, March 5). At least two-thirds of rapists in the US get away with it. *Quartz: Economics*.

Meyer, C. L., Proano, T. C., Oberman, M., White, K., & Batra, P. (2001). *Mothers who kill their children: Understanding the acts of moms from Susan Smith to the "prom mom"*. New York University Press.

Michaels, S. (2022, August 9). She never hurt her kids. So why is a mother serving more time than the man who abused her daughter? *Mother Jones*.

Morrison, T. (1987). *Beloved*. Vintage.

Oberman, M. (1996). Mothers who kill: Coming to terms with modern American infanticide. *American Criminal Law Review*, *34*(1), 1–110.

Oberman, M., & Meyer, C. L. (2008). *When mothers kill: Interviews from prison*. New York University Press.

O'Reilly, A. (2004). *Toni Morrison and motherhood: A politics of the heart*. State University of New York Press.

Page, D. (1938). Introduction. In D. Page (Ed.), *The plays of Euripedes: Medea*. Clarendon Press.

Panko, L. (1995). Legal backlash: The expanding liability of women who fail to protect their children from their male counter parts abuse. *Hastings Women's Law Journal*, *6*(1), 67–92.

Resnick, P. J. (1969). Child murder by parents: A psychiatric review of filicide. *American Journal of Psychiatry*, *126*(3), 325–334.

Roberts, D. E. (1995). The unrealized power of mother. *All Faculty Scholarship*. 762. https://scholarship.law.upenn.edu/faculty_scholarship/762

Rose, J. (2018). *Mothers: An essay on love and cruelty*. Farrar, Straus and Giroux.

Scheper-Hughes, N. (1992). *Death without weeping: The violence of everyday life in Brazil*. University of California Press.

Schutte, O. (1991). Irigaray on the problem of subjectivity. *Hypatia*, *6*(2), 64–76.

Schwarzenbach, S. A., & Smith, P. (Eds.). (2003). *Women and the U.S. constitution: History, interpretation, and practice*. Columbia University Press. https://doi.org/10.7312/schw12892.

Sieff, D. F. (2019). The death mother as nature's shadow: Infanticide, abandonment, and the collective unconscious. *Psychological Perspectives*, *62*(1), 15–34.

Singer, T., & Kimbles, S. (2004). Introduction. In T. Singer & S. Kimbles (Eds.), *The cultural complex: Contemporary perspectives on psyche and society* (pp. 1–10). Routledge.

Singh, S. (2021). Punishing mothers for men's violence: Failure to protect legislation and the criminalisation of abused women. *Feminist Legal Studies*, *29*, 181–204.

Spinelli, M. (2019). Infanticide and American criminal justice (1980–2018). *Archives of Women's Mental Health*, *22*(1), 173–177.

Stark, E. (1995). Re-presenting woman battering: From battered woman syndrome to coercive control. *Journal Albany Law Review*, *58*(4), 973–1026.

Stelloh, T. (2022, June 14). Woman charged in murder of newborn who was found by a dog in Maine gravel pit in 1985. *NBC News*. www.nbcnews.com/news/us-news/woman-charged-murder-newborn-was-found-dog-maine-gravel-pit-1985-rcna33622

Wagner, M., Rocha, V., & Regan, H. (2021, November 22). Multiple fatalities after SUV plows through Wisconsin holiday parade. *CNN*.

Wilson, R. F., Klevens, J., Williams, D., & Xu, L. (2020). Infant homicides within the context of safe haven laws—United States, 2008–2017. *Morbidity and Mortality Weekly Report, 69*(39), 1385.

Young, G. (2020, August 3). Sociologist studies what leads mothers to kill their children. *Texas Tech Today*. https://today.ttu.edu/posts/2020/08/Stories/sociologist-studies-what-leads-mothers-kill-children

Zippia. (2023). *Police officer demographics and statistics in the US*. www.zippia.com/police-officer-jobs/demographics/

Chapter 5

Domestic Violence as Infanticide

The majority of infanticidal women I have interviewed have been subjected to domestic violence for most of their lives. Their relationships with their partners are volatile, unpredictable, and violent. More than once, in the midst of an evaluation, a woman has said to me, *Being in prison is the safest I have ever felt.* Contrary to what may be assumed, women who commit maternal infanticide are most often married or in long-term relationships. Moreover, they did not become mothers alone. This point, although obvious, is essential to keep firmly in mind to resist the media's sole focus on the mother or the police's folly in only interviewing her. The colliding institutional forces of mother-blaming and mother-exalting make it appear she conceived alone. The mechanism of being abused by a partner and then killing one's child is not straightforward; it is layered in misogyny, poverty, racism, and child neglect, but the chain of violence in a home almost always begins with a male abuser and ends at a child.

Studies on the topic concur that about 50% of infanticidal mothers were living in violent relationships (Meyer et al., 2001; Sidebotham & Retzer, 2018), or in another study, domestic violence toward the mother was found in up to 79% of cases of child death (Quigley, 2007). In a more recent study of infanticidal mothers, researchers found that *all* of the women in the sample were victims of violence by their partners (Kachaeva, 2015). The women who had committed infanticide displayed "pathological altruistic motivation," meaning they killed their child for reasons of saving them as they knew the world to be a violent one (751).

To bring the reader into what I call *domestic violence as infanticide*, the following is a graphic excerpt about Kerry King, her daughter Lilah, and violent partner Purdy from the article "She Never Hurt Her Kids. So Why Is a Mother Serving More Time Than the Man Who Abused Her Daughter?":

> King agreed to hold Lilah down like Purdy demanded, hoping that if she complied it would be over faster. But when she saw how hard his blows were, she threw her body over her daughter's, receiving Purdy's belt lashes on her own back. Purdy pulled King off Lilah, and King tried to run out of the house to get help from the neighbors or the police—but he blocked her at the door. You ain't going nowhere, she recalls him saying. "I was scared. I didn't know what to do,"

DOI: 10.4324/9781003412809-7

she later told me, adding that it felt like she "had been in chains." Purdy dragged King to the master bedroom by her hair and threatened to kill her if she didn't stay there. He reentered Lilah's room and locked the door, leaving King outside, listening to her daughter's cries.

(Michaels, 2022, para. 11)

This type of violence, in which a mother is recruited into abuse toward her own child, is a paradoxical horror difficult to comprehend. In these circumstances, a mother's instinct to keep harm from coming to her child still ends in the child suffering grave physical harm in which she participates. To be able to understand the mother's actions as rooted in a protective instinct to bring the least amount of harm to her child requires an expanded and contextual understanding of motherhood within violence.

Intimate Partner Violence

Violence from a man toward a woman in the home has been a tool of male domination since the beginning of humanity. The recognition of domestic violence (DV) has increased since it entered the English lexicon in the early 1970s, and it is now considered immoral and illegal by most institutions. Yet, DV has not subsided. In 2020 about 47,000 women and girls worldwide were killed by their intimate partners or other family members; on average, a female is killed by someone in her own family every 11 minutes. The statistics show that the magnitude of such gender-related killings remains largely unchanged, with only marginal increases and decreases over the past decade (United Nations Office on Drugs and Crime, 2020).

DV is defined as a pattern of abusive behavior in which a person uses coercion, deception, harassment, humiliation, manipulation, and/or force to establish power and control over his intimate partner. Perpetrators use economic, emotional, psychological, physical, sexual, and verbal tactics to sustain control over and achieve submission in their partners. The U.S. Centers for Disease Control and Prevention (CDC) replaced the term *domestic violence* with the more specific *intimate partner violence* (IPV), which acknowledges that violence can occur in a wide range of living arrangements.

In the U.S., one out of every three adult women experiences at least one physical assault by an intimate partner during adulthood (CDC, 2022). "Almost half of all women (49.4% or 61.7 million) reported any psychological aggression by an intimate partner in their lifetime, which includes expressive aggression (29.4% or 36.7 million) and coercive control and entrapment (46.2% or 57.6 million)" (Leemis et al., 2022, p. 6). Although domestic and sexual violence occur in all socioeconomic classes, being poor or in a minority group increases the risk of IPV. African Americans experience domestic violence at higher rates in comparison to all other populations in the U.S. For women of color, approximately four out of 10 women at some point in their lifetime have been a victim of IPV (Basile et al., 2022). The number of non-Hispanic black women was more than twice the number of non-Hispanic whites who reported "sexual violence, physical violence, and/or stalking by an intimate partner" (Leemis et al., 2022, p. 7).

The term *coercive control* is imperative to recognize when examining DV, and although coercive control has become a serious criminal offense in England, Scotland, Ireland, Wales, Canada, France, and elsewhere (Lambert, 2021), it currently has no legal standing in the U.S. Stark (2007) explained the how the concept of coercive control changes how IPV is measured and understood:

> In assessing harms, we shift from measuring the physical/psychological valence of specific violent acts to an emphasis on the concurrence, frequency, and duration of multiple forms of oppression. Extreme physical and psychological injury, or trauma, remains important in measuring the weight of these harms to individuals. But coercive control extends through social space to every type of relationship and relational setting where it affects our personal interface (harms to dignity, autonomy, personhood, etc.), our material interface (access to money, food, clothing, transport) and our political interface (speech, assembly, and so on) in all the ways that tie into the practice of citizenship.
>
> (2020, p. 270)

Coercion encompasses "psychological, physical, sexual, financial, and emotional abuse" in a pattern of controlling and threatening incidents (Stark, 2020, pp. 262–263). Coercion's end goal is to make a person subordinate and/or dependent "by isolating them from sources of support, exploiting their resources and capacities for personal gain, depriving them of the means needed for independence, resistance and escape and regulating their everyday lives" (263). Without the framework of coercive control, law and public attention center too exclusively on physical violence and ignores the perniciousness of psychological violence, which Stark stressed can lead to what he termed *child abuse as tangential spouse abuse*. This occurs

> when a partner's primary purpose in hurting a child is to subordinate his adult victim. Children in these cases are considered "secondary" victims because the coercive control of the adult partner usually antecedes the child abuse, the tactics used to harm the child(ren) are chosen for their effect on the adult victim primarily, risk to each is assessed by the cumulative danger to both, and ending the coercive control of the adult victim usually ends the risk to the child, often by pursuing criminal charges against the primary perpetrator.
>
> (263)

As described in the previous chapter, law enforcement in the U.S., failing to recognize the context of coercive control, has tended to focus solely on the mother for failure to protect the child. Stark found:

> Straightforward forensics is challenged in cases like this because adult victims are often a focus of criminal charges or other legal attention, often regardless

of whether they directly harmed the child or caused a death. The charges usually stem from the degree to which the adult victim is said to have "colluded"
in the child's abuse, "failed to protect" the child from harm, or actively abused
the child in ways that appear to be unrelated to whatever domestic violence
may have occurred. In no sense, is harm to the child secondary in importance,
of course.

(263)

I find Stark's framework and perception of the relationship between IPV and child
abuse useful as it resonates with the patterns of behavior I see in cases of infanticide. Once an abuser gains command over a woman's life, his strategy evolves
logically in response to challenges or dilemmas she poses to his singular interest
in dominance. He attempts to manage the threat of exposure—in school settings,
work settings, social settings—by escalating his coercive control of all parties,
including binding, isolation, starvation, and physical abuse. This "ongoing process
systematically diminishes and destroys the inner self of another" (Loring, as cited
in hooks, 2004, p. 57).

Understanding Male Violence

Patriarchal culture creates the expectation of power and status in men, especially
over women, as part of male identity (Gilligan & Snider, 2018). Men learn early
in their lives that part and parcel of being a successful man is dominating others;
they are "programmed from birth to believe that at some point they must be violent,
whether physically or psychologically" (hooks, 2004, p. 60). Power imbalance,
scorn, and embarrassment can provoke male violence toward women. These experiences threaten male identity, creating shame in a man. When men are unable to
tolerate the emotional distress, they act out violently toward women. This difficulty
tolerating emotional distress is a consequence of "the first act of violence that patriarchy demands of males . . . that they kill off the emotional parts of themselves,"
leaving access only to lust and anger (66). One study of male felons' accounts of
IPV found that all the study participants believed their partner disrespected them
"as a man," and they were therefore justified in using physical violence (Wood,
2004). In similar research, the men interviewed said they used violence because
they had to "maintain dominance" (Ptacek, 1988). Husbands who feel that they
have less power than their wives are more physically abusive toward them, as compulsive and physical compensation for and proof against their insignificance and/
or impotence.

Violence and Pregnancy

Pregnancy tends to be provocative for men's violence. In the World Health
Organization's multi-country study on domestic violence against women, most

women who reported physical abuse during pregnancy had also been beaten prior to getting pregnant, although around 50% of women in three sites stated that they were beaten for the first time during a pregnancy (García-Moreno et al., 2005). Approximately 20% of pregnant women experience physical abuse during their pregnancy; IPV is more common among pregnant women than pregnancy-related conditions such as gestational diabetes or preeclampsia (Kippert, 2019; National Coalition Against Domestic Violence, 2004). A 2021 study of maternal deaths in the U.S. found that women were more than twice as likely to die from homicide, often related to IPV, during pregnancy and the year following childbirth than from hypertensive disorders, hemorrhage, or infection (Wallace et al., 2021).

It is possible that women's increased physical vulnerability and perceived dependency in pregnancy creates a defenselessness that abusive men prey on. Also, abuse has been found to start or worsen during pregnancy due to partners doubting the baby was theirs (Campbell et al., 1998). Additionally, the impending birth may be interpreted by narcissistic abusers as a competitor for the woman's attention. Ultimately, the fetus is both an object of intense jealousy and competition, as well as an object with which to control the pregnant woman. A baby's birth often precipitates a crisis in relationships characterized by coercive control if for no other reason than the unpredictable demands of maternal caretaking, which wreak havoc on authoritarian regimes of time regulation and exclusive possessiveness (Stark, 2020). As a result of a woman's increasing intensity of focus and power as a mother, she is perceived as a provocative threat who must be controlled.

Jacqueline Rose added another possible trigger of male violence, suggesting motherhood is disconcerting due to its evocation of death. An impending birth can act as "an uncanny reminder that once upon a time you were not here, and one day you will be no more. Mothers alert us to the irreducible frailty of life" (2018, p. 25). Rose's observation can be threaded back to the drive for immortality as an instinctual aspect of the masculine archetypal principle pitted against the archetypal energies of the Death Mother. Death poses the ultimately unknowable and unconquerable reality, and fear of it lurks in the collective fear of the feminine and oppression of women who carry the cyclical nature of birth and death in their wombs. In this way, a woman's pregnancy can constellate a deeply unconscious and collective fear of the feminine and the Death Mother, a fear that destabilizes a man's sense of power and control over life such that he lashes out to reclaim his ascendency.

Battered Women Syndrome

Chronic IPV creates a complex traumatic syndrome referred to as *battered women syndrome* (BWS). The presentation is similar to posttraumatic stress disorder, but with symptoms including depression, anxiety, idealization of the perpetrator, and dissociation. It received its own name in 1979 from forensic psychologist Lenore Walker, who described the syndrome as

> the pattern of the signs and symptoms that have been found to occur after a woman has been physically, sexually, and/or psychologically abused in an intimate relationship, when the partner exerted power and control over the woman to coerce her into doing whatever he wanted, without regard for her rights or feelings.
>
> (49–50)

The diagnosis for BWS is not in the DSM-5 but can be found as a subcategory of PTSD. Like the lack of recognition for postpartum psychosis, in which the symptoms are specific and uniquely intense to a woman's experience, BWS has not been legitimated as a stand-alone diagnosis by the APA, leaving it and postpartum psychosis in the elusive space where jurors, lawyers, police officers, judges, partners, and women themselves wonder if their symptoms are real.

Trauma expert Judith Herman, in her seminal work on complex PTSD (1992a, 1992b), suggested that battered women suffer characterological changes in personality that leave them vulnerable to repeated harm. She emphasized that the reason for these changes is the perpetrator's actions rather than the woman's premorbid psychological functioning, although a history of abuse from childhood may make women more psychologically vulnerable. Herman argued that, typically, the perpetrator gains control over the woman's body through deprivation of sleep, food, or shelter. He then becomes the potential source of solace when he grants small indulgences. This dynamic greatly diminishes the woman's ability to initiate action; in fact, the traumatic reaction to the physical and psychological abuse is the mechanism through which many aspects of the battered woman's functioning may become impaired (Levendosky & Graham-Bermann, 2001). Often abusive relationships follow a cycle—stability, build up, explosion, honeymoon, repeat—that creates a perpetual trap of hope then shame for an abused mother.

BWS can lead to learned helplessness or psychological paralysis where the victim becomes so depressed, defeated, and passive that she believes she is incapable of leaving her abuser. Her belief system changes: She now believes her abusive partner is an incredibly powerful person and is all-knowing, and that she deserves the abuse he is delivering. She is further entrapped by a legitimate fear of being killed or being left alone with limited economic and social support. Although she is often assumed to be mentally ill, masochistic, or apathetic, she is in fact weighing life and death choices as a daily reality.

In my work with women who are currently in a chronic battered state, it is important as a clinician to not reenact the abuse toward them; to resist beating them over the head with some version of, "You should leave him. He's abusive. What's taking you so long?" Instead, I attempt to help them feel into the *hook* that keeps them ensnared, which is often "He needs me." And they are right. He is psychologically infantile.

The abusive man is like the toddler who hits his mother, an abuse the mother accepts as a natural violence from her son "who is allowed to assume the role of 'mini patriarch'" (hooks, 2004, p. 62). Although it is largely the responsibility of the father for raising a violent son, mothers may "standby and bear witness to their sons' brutalization at the hands of fathers, boyfriends, brothers, and so on" (61). By hitting and kicking when they do not get what they want, they learn that violence is an acceptable way to get their needs met. This coalesces with the indoctrination boys receive that teaches them to not be "pussies"—to split off from their emotional life and any relational need for others as effeminate. As a result, boys grow into men who remain childish; having not grown out of having violent tantrums, they use force to meet the needs they cannot express or admit to having.

A woman who finds herself in an abusive relationship with a man likely has a lot of 'good mother' energy to offer (i.e., caretaking, forgiving, softness, and empathy), so she naturally gets pulled into his pain and needs, which are great as he has little ability to recognize or cope with his repressed and unacceptable feelings of being hurt, weak, needy, or vulnerable. Unconsciously, in the role of mother, battered women let their man-child physically hurt them. With their children, this often starts with a bite of the nipple while breastfeeding. Many mothers tend to laugh over this or other forms of their boy child's violence, such as pushing and kicking. "Such a little boy!" she may say. "Taking it" from the child is what a good mother does.

Subsequently, of the abusive man in her life, she may say, *He is good on the inside; I know he is just frustrated*, and the dynamic of "taking it" is reenacted in an abusive relationship. If in the therapeutic relationship with a battered woman this insight is brought forth—that her partner is like an infant boy hurting his mother or having a tantrum—it tends to bring the patient into a potent experience of the dynamic, potentially to understand and resolve it. From there she has a greater sense of choice: is this the right dynamic for an adult relationship? But when a woman continues to be battered, the loss of her sense of self, dignity, agency, and choice—and the fear and repressed rage with which she lives—may lead her to a larger and disproportionate explosion of violence.

Intimate Partner Violence, Complex Trauma, and Infanticidal Mothers

In a 2022 article, gynecologist Leo Ankerstjerne et al. reported their systematic review of existing studies on the topic of IPV and postpartum depression (PPD). They found that women who experience domestic violence during pregnancy are three times more likely to report symptoms of depression in the postnatal period than women who did not experience domestic violence while pregnant (Ankerstjerne et al., 2022; Rabin, 1995). At the same time, the inverse has also been found to be true: experiencing PPD places women at greater risk for abuse by an intimate partner (Ankerstjerne et al., 2022). This may have something to do with the mother's increased vulnerability or their emotional distance/dissociation from the abuser.

Additionally, women who are abused during pregnancy are more likely to receive no prenatal care or to delay care until later than recommended, setting both mother and child up for poor health outcomes, including depression (Alhusen et al., 2015; Holmes & Kim, 2019). Similarly, women who experience IPV during pregnancy are about three times more likely than women who do not experience IPV to suffer the often-depressing event of miscarriages at all stages of pregnancy (Afiaz et al., 2020).

For mothers, coercive control and abuse from a partner increases their need to be vigilant in protecting themselves and their child, adding another layer of stress to their maternal responsibilities, keeping mothers chronically exhausted and unable to attend to their own needs. For a mother, caring for a newborn in the battlefield of IPV is depleting, forcing her nervous system into a state of survival. In an environment of coercion and abuse, she experiences a lack of choice and inability to affect change in her life, finding herself on course toward an inevitably dangerous outcome. In her inner world, she is struggling with chronic, complex trauma and the affective energies of the Death Mother.

The pathway from domestic violence to infanticide is paved with complex trauma from ongoing interpersonal abuse with no perceived ability to escape (Lucario, 2023). In childhood, physical or emotional abuse, neglect, caregiver substance abuse or mental illness, exposure to violence, racism, and/or family economic hardship can lead to a *toxic stress response*, a term coined by Surgeon General of California Nadine Burke (2018). This stress-response system can disrupt the development of brain architecture and increase the risk for stress-related disease and cognitive impairment well into the adult years. Children who witness or experience domestic violence will be more vulnerable to engaging in adult violent relationships, believing that violence, even sexual violence, is a regular part of a relationship. Burke described how pathology can move from the molecular level to the social level. A girl who grows up with domestic violence develops an overactive fight/flight/freeze response, which affects her brain development such that her stress-regulation system goes off track. This causes her to react to confrontation or coercive messages with a trauma reaction. Unable to (or having learned she cannot) fight or flee, she may freeze (become dissociated and numb) or react with a fawn response, developed as a result of childhood abuse from a parent or authority figure. This response involves "immediately moving to try to please a person to avoid any conflict" (Gaba, 2020, para. 4). Alternatively, she may not recognize risky situations because they feel normal, matching the chronic high level of stress that has become the baseline in her nervous system. Feeling comfortable only in her known reality of violence, she ends up and stays with a partner who is abusive. This creates a cycle of transgenerational trauma with generation after generation of women's nervous systems accustomed to violence. This cycle breeds maternal infanticide, where the Death Mother steps in from the collective unconscious in the mix of trauma, desperation, and toxic neurochemical stress—when a battered mother, as some might say, *goes off* or *snaps*.

Physician Gabor Maté explained that a history of trauma may mean we have difficulty interrupting impulses, such as the impulse to *snap* into violence (2018). Although this impulse may come as a total surprise, in most cases there has been a psychological buildup (Ash, 2012). Chronic abuse stored in the nervous system is akin to the accumulation of sticks of dynamite; with each episode of abuse a stick is added to the pile, one by one, until there is a trigger and the pile is lit, and there is a deadly and destructive explosion. The snap happens when the nervous system has reached its limit of what it can bear. This snapping may look like a fatal moment of self-defense or an uncontrolled beating of a child. Beyond it being a trauma response, it is also emblematic of a hierarchy of violence in the home, in which violence moves from the most powerful and aggressive abuser and ends at the most vulnerable in the home.

Ruth's Story

Ruth, who I discussed in the previous chapter, had grown up violently abused by her father, leaving her feeling like a "piece of crap"—worthless in the eyes of her father. When she miscarried at 6 months pregnant from her sister kicking her in the stomach, Ruth said, "The whole experience made me want to die." Consuming pills, Ruth attempted suicide. She described feeling intense shame and loss, describing herself as "an object with a voice."

At 16, Ruth left her home. In her early 20s, she became unexpectedly pregnant and had her first child, after which she went into depression. As described earlier, she then began fostering and doing all that she could for the special needs daughter Dina, whose mother was lost to addiction. Ruth and the two children began living with Jacob, a man who was horrifically abusive. Ruth was increasingly depressed. Expressing the symptoms of BWS, she felt "no will power, hopeless . . . reviewing my life and thinking nothing good came of it." Jacob was jealous and controlling and on a whim would physically and sexually assault Ruth. When Dina needed a permanent family, Ruth transitioned from fostering her to adopting her. Then Ruth became pregnant, and Jacob's coercive behavior increased toward her.

Between the ages of 13 and 29, Ruth was pregnant five times, tending to a newborn or a child for 16 consecutive years. The hormone changes that occur during pregnancy and postnatal significantly affect mood and anxiety. The levels of progesterone and allopregnanolone rise during pregnancy and plummet after childbirth, a drop thought to contribute to emotional dysregulation. This 16-year period put Ruth in a vulnerable state for postpartum depression. Her lack of resources (including food and shelter) increased that vulnerability. The trauma Ruth experienced as a child (i.e., abuse from her father, sexual assault by a neighbor, a violent and impoverished environment) resulted in complex trauma, compromised her cognitive and executive functioning limiting her capacity for thriving as an adult. Her trauma, never treated, was activated and increased with the cumulative abuse from Jacob and each perinatal experience.

Ruth attempted to create a family for her children, giving them a home and a father. Her choices in doing so, though misguided, depict Ruth's natural and corrective impulse toward health and betterment. Ruth never lacked love and care for her children; she lacked an ability to act confidently with and for them. But she lacked the emotional, cognitive, and physical safety and support to pull herself out of the cycle of complex trauma and toxic stress.

No one in Ruth's life addressed or acknowledged the abuse she received; neither had Ruth, as it was an accepted part of her family culture. The effects of that abuse were stored in her nervous system as sticks of dynamite with which she entered adulthood, when each additional episode of intimate partner abuse added a stick to her pile until there was a trigger at a vulnerable moment, her pile was lit, and the explosion was deadly.

When Ruth snapped, she was 8 months pregnant but in a deeply depressed state of pregnancy denial. At 8-months pregnant, the body is working to carry and feed a small baby, which exhausts a mother. Ruth was feeling hopeless, experiencing regular intrusive thoughts that she was worthless, and having extreme swings in mood and energy. Ruth knew she was not well; she was taking her kids to stay with other caretakers, she felt like she was "going crazy," and she was feeling suicidal. Ruth had very few resources to manage the moment when her dynamite was lit, when her rage was triggered, when she lost control.

In Ruth's case, she overreacted to the threat of a 4-year-old girl innocently, but dangerously, playing with a stove. The girl was not at fault nor was she a threat, but Ruth's traumatic memories and nervous system responded disproportionately. When her nervous system went into fight mode, her body released the hormones cortisol and adrenaline. She experienced rage and an inflated sense of strength, which she had little control over. Ruth described the moment as surreal and "cloudy"; she lost track of time and space when she chased and grabbed and beat and whipped Dina, only coming back to her senses when Dina was having a seizure.

Dina's death was not premeditated, intentional, or desired. Ruth stated, "I believe I snapped. I felt like I couldn't stop. I was angry. I was depressed. I didn't know who my baby daddy was. I didn't want to be abused by Jacob. I was trapped." The state of rage that overcame Ruth is indicative of a flashback, when one is dissociated from present and current events, in a state of sensory deprivation, possessed by the nervous system's dysregulated rage and fight reaction to cumulative past trauma and overwhelming fear.

Mothers who find themselves in the unthinkable circumstances of killing their own child are most often in the throes of postpartum depression or psychosis and intimate partner violence. They have not planned nor preconceived their crime; most often they have no criminal history and have never displayed signs of being a neglectful mother. A mother with very little support, under the control of a violent man, unable to care properly for her child, afraid for her own life along with her child's, with symptoms of fatigue, low self-worth, and suicidality, is in a perfect storm for an ultimate tragedy.

Legal Response to Domestic Violence and Infanticide

The legal world has struggled to effectively respond to DV as a mitigating factor in infanticidal cases. In circumstances of maternal infanticide where DV is brought forward as a factor, it is likely the information will be used against the mother, as she is now perceived as having failed to protect herself *and* her children, furthering the image of her as uncaring and irresponsible. The implicit message is that a *responsible* mother is not a vulnerable *victim*. For a woman to be a good mother, she must avoid men's violence, which the legal system and society at large have long conspired to both legitimate and keep secret. That protection of men's right to violence in the domination of women is systemic is evident in women receiving blame for being sexually harassed or raped (Bongiorno et al., 2019), in addition to being blamed for domestic violence (Kippert, 2017).

The courtroom fails to appreciate the numerous risks associated with leaving an abusive relationship. This includes risk to women and their children of bodily harm, destitution, homelessness, and loss of support networks. Leaving a violent relationship is equally hazardous for children as it can make the child more vulnerable to an abusive father's violence. Singh highlighted a court case she observed in England involving the death of a young child whose mother was being abused by the father. The judge emphasized that Critchley, the mother, could have easily left the abusive relationship, as her mother lived just streets away. Singh wrote,

> Due to class-based assumptions about space and resources, he failed to consider that several adults and children already lived in [Critchley's] mother's house. It would not have easily accommodated another adult and two children. Moreover, the fact that both houses were in such close proximity makes this more dangerous: she could never have fled to her mother's house without [the father] knowing where she and their children were residing. These cases underline judges' consistent failure to recognise that pregnancy and the postnatal period are especially difficult times to leave an abusive relationship, emotionally and financially.
>
> (2021, p. 196)

Singh concluded:

> [Critchley] was not only vulnerable on account of the interpersonal violence and abuse she had suffered, her vulnerability was further exacerbated by her role as caregiver (both in terms of responding to her children's dependency and the responsibility which is associated with the status "mother"), and broader socio-economic precarity . . . . Criminalising abused women for "allowing" their children to come to harm obscures the reality that intimate partner violence remains endemic, not a rare social problem experienced by a small minority of women.
>
> (199)

Gina's Story

A case I mentioned in Chapter 4 deserves a closer look in the context of DV as Gina suffered brutal abuse, which was what ultimately killed her toddler. Gina was raised by a father who was cruel to her. He physically abused her (hitting her, shoving her, and using his belt on her), ridiculed and threatened her with his words, picked on her, and criticized her. He accused her of ruining his marriage to her mother, insinuating she was destructive and bad. He told her she was not his daughter, and that he got a vasectomy after she was born because he would not want another child like her.

As Gina grew older, she saw more abusive relationships around her: Gina said her first memory of a relationship was of her cousin being hit on the head with a plank of wood by her boyfriend. Violent relationships like these were prevalent in her neighborhood. Gina said nobody ever said, "This is wrong." Nobody, including the police, stopped the abusers; moreover, nobody talked to women about the effects of abuse. There was, as couples therapist Terrence Real referred to it, "a conspiracy of silence" (2002, p. 85). Gina had never heard of a domestic violence shelter until she was in prison. Due to the regular domestic violence Gina witnessed, the lack of intervention in her community, and her low self-worth, as she began to date, Gina came to believe that violence, even sexual violence, was a regular part of a relationship.

Gina began a relationship with an abusive man with whom she had several children. Gina's partner was menacing and torturous, taking all sense of self, autonomy, and worth from her, rendering her powerless. He used degradation and dehumanization as tactics (i.e., withholding food and clothing, constantly monitoring her actions), along with omnipotent physical violence (punching, pushing, dragging, hair pulling, and kicking). He terrorized and punished Gina regardless of Gina's behavior (i.e., whether she gave him oral sex in front of his friends or refused to). He stalked her and held her children hostage; he brought other women in the house and had sex with them in front of her. He imprisoned Gina, isolating her from her family or any form of support. This violence confided in me by Gina was also witnessed and reported to me by her cousins.

Gina described her fear of leaving him. She wanted to leave but believed there was nowhere she could hide where he would not find her and kill her or her children. Gina lived in a gripping fear, and she believed he was all powerful and all-knowing. She believes she may have died at his hands if she had not been arrested and locked up.

As described in the previous chapter, the morning that the baby died, Gina's partner had handed her the limp infant. Knowing the violent abuse and threat under which Gina lived, it is easy to understand why she followed her partner's instructions and told the police that the baby had fallen down the stairs.

When I started working on Gina's case, she had already been found guilty and her appeal was limited to resentencing, so although it seemed clear she had not killed her child, that fact was unapproachable. Even in our confidential setting Gina did not defend herself. The social milieu in which women are blamed for men's violence and the strength of his violence toward her and her children lives on in Gina's absorption of the responsibility of the death of her child.

Thematically, Gina's case is not unique or new. An historical lens reveals how male dominance and control has affected women and children over time, playing an essential role in transgenerational trauma influencing how individuals and groups have adapted, resisted, survived, colluded, or succumbed to violence. In Western culture, violence against women throughout history is a remarkably commonplace event, originally codified by the Roman Empire as *pater* families: Fathers as heads of household were allowed to sell their family into slavery, abuse them, or kill them (PBS, 2006). A translation of a 2nd-century Roman magistrate's public address reveals the ancient antecedents of Western culture's double standard regarding morality, violence, and sexuality:

"If she has drunk wine she is punished; if she has done wrong with another man, she is condemned to death." It is also written, regarding the right to kill: "If you catch your wife in adultery, you can kill her with impunity; she, however, cannot dare to lay a finger on you if you commit adultery, nor is it the law."

(Diotíma, 2019, para. 2)

Eventually this double standard found its way into the Catholic Church's "Rules of Marriage" in 1452, which proclaimed the husband as judge over his wife, and recommended abusing her as an accepted form of discipline that would benefit her "soul" (Fortune & Enger, 2005, p. 2). In colonial America, the Puritans strictly adhered to their interpretation of Biblical commands about a wife's responsibility to obey and submit to her husband, which then laid the groundwork for the sociopolitical foundations upon which the country was built. Most importantly, the subjugation of women, both within and outside of faith traditions, persists as a reference point in the collective unconscious, which Jung described as the repository of "the whole spiritual heritage of mankind's evolution, born anew in the brain structure of every individual" (1931/1969, para. 342).

It was not until 1993 that the United Nations considered violence toward women an international human rights issue and adopted the Declaration on the Elimination of Violence Against Women. It was a year later, in 1994, that the U.S. finally passed the Violence Against Women Act, acknowledging domestic violence and sexual assault as crimes.

A nationwide grassroots feminist campaign was ignited in the mid-1970s by activist Susan Schechter (1982) to expose domestic violence against women, provide shelter and support, and demand radical change from law, medicine, and society. The first U.S. shelter for abused women was opened in Minnesota in 1974. The house was "always at capacity . . . . The demand for housing for battered women was such a big demand" (Beardslee, as cited in Kippert, 2015, para. 2). The general attitude at the time was that domestic violence was a private affair and few police departments were trained in DV intervention.

> The police told women that they could not do anything unless their husbands and boyfriends severely injured them. Women who left abusive partners were denied welfare because they were still legally married. Judges asked women, "What did you do to provoke him?" Clergy told women to try harder, pray harder. Clinical social workers considered the masochistic tendencies of women and recommended marriage counseling for relationship problems. Physicians and nurses looked the other way and did not ask women how they got their injuries. Friends and family members told women, "Work it out. Figure out what pleases him and stick with it. After all, children need their fathers."
>
> (Danis, 2006, p. 337)

This history is the tapestry of every instance of abuse toward a woman.

We perceive our worth according to how the world treats us. The message that is sent to women who are being abused in impoverished violent neighborhoods, where there is a lack of responsiveness by police and providers, is not very different from a wife abused by her husband in the Roman Empire. The women I interview describe horrific abuse: running out the door with the baby, being chased by her boyfriend, handing the baby to a cousin through a car window, being dragged back to the house by her hair. Years of this abuse continue in a woman's life with the occasional neighbor or aunt making a phone call to the police, and the police showing up but making very few arrests. Almost every woman I've interviewed had never heard of a domestic abuse shelter until they got to jail.

Recently I interviewed Shannon, a woman who told me about a police officer who took her and her children to the hospital after her mother-in-law called 911 during a particularly heinous incident of abuse. The abuser had dropped his wife on a concrete floor then stomped on her. While this woman and her two young children were evaluated in the ER, the officer waited. At discharge he drove them to a domestic violence shelter. This event happened 20 years prior to my interview with my client, yet in describing it to me she still sounded incredulous when she stated, "That white man tried to save my life."

Shannon stayed at the shelter for three months before she went back to her former life with her abusive husband at his mother's house. Less than a year later Shannon was arrested and sentenced for the death of her youngest child. When women such as Shannon grow up in violent neighborhoods, they are likely to see violence as a normal and inescapable part of their homelife as fused with the nature of love and care, making, in the face of having to create a life on her own with few advantages and a deeply scared sense of her value and possibilities, a return to her abusive relationship likely. Social structures such as class and race create zones within society where there is less access to education, birth control, and nutritional foods, and there tends to be a cultural desensitization to violence (Gartner, 1990).

References

Afiaz, A., Biswas, R., Shamma, R., & Ananna, N. (2020). Intimate partner violence (IPV) with miscarriages, stillbirths and abortions: Identifying vulnerable households for women in Bangladesh. *PLOS One*, *15*(7). www.ncbi.nlm.nih.gov/pmc/articles/PMC7386588/

Alhusen, J., Ray, E., Sharos, P., & Bullock, L. (2015). Intimate partner violence during pregnancy: Maternal and neonatal outcomes. *Journal of Women's Health*, *24*(1), 100–106.

Ankerstjerne, L., Laizer, S., Andreasen, K., Normann, A., Wu, C., Linde, D., & Rasch, V. (2022). Landscaping the evidence of intimate partner violence and postpartum depression: A systematic review. *British Medical Journal Open*, *12*(5). www.ncbi.nlm.nih.gov/pmc/articles/PMC9119188/

Ash, P. (2012). But he knew it was wrong: Evaluating adolescent culpability. *Journal of the American Academy of Psychiatry Law*, *40*(1), 21–32.

Basile, K., Smith, S., Kresnow, J., Khatiwada, S., & Leemis, R. (2022, June). *The national intimate partner and sexual violence survey: 2016/2017 report on sexual violence*. Centers for Disease Control & Prevention. www.cdc.gov/violenceprevention/pdf/nisvs/NIS-VSReportonIPV_2022.pdf

Bongiorno, R., Langbroek, C., Bain, P., Ting, M., & Ryan, M. (2019). Why women are blamed for being sexually harassed: The effects of empathy for female victims and male perpetrators. *Psychology of Women Quarterly*, *44*(1). https://journals.sagepub.com/doi/full/10.1177/0361684319868730

Burke, N. (2018). *The deepest well: Healing the long-term effects of childhood trauma and adversity*. Houghton Mifflin Harcourt.

Campbell, J., Oliver, C., & Bullock, L. (1998). The dynamics of battering during pregnancy: Women's explanations of why. In J. Campbell (Ed.), *Empowering survivors of abuse: Health care for battered women and their children* (pp. 81–89). Sage.

Centers for Disease Control and Prevention. (2022, October 11). *Fast facts: Preventing intimate partner violence*. www.cdc.gov/violenceprevention/intimatepartnerviolence/fastfact.html

Danis, F. S. (2006). A tribute to Susan Schechter: The visions and struggles of the battered women's movement. *Journal of Women and Social Work*, *21*(3), 336–341.

Diotíma. (2019). *Punishment for adultery*. https://diotima-doctafemina.org/translations/anthologies/womens-life-in-greece-and-rome-selections/v-legal-status-in-the-roman-world/111-punishment-for-adultery/

Fortune, M., & Enger, C. (2005). Violence against women and the role of religion. *Applied Research Forum*. https://vawnet.org/sites/default/files/materials/files/2016-09/AR_VAW Religion_0.pdf

Gaba, S. (2020, August 22). Understanding fight, flight, freeze and the fawn response: Another possible response to trauma. *Psychology Today*.

García-Moreno, C., Jansen, H. A., Ellsberg, M., Heise, L., & Watts, C. (2005, February 24). *WHO multi-country study on women's health and domestic violence against women: Initial results on prevalence, health outcomes and women's responses*. www.who.int/publications/i/item/924159358X

Gartner, R. (1990). The victims of homicide: A temporal and cross-national comparison. *American Sociological Review*, *55*(1), 92–106.

Gilligan, C., & Snider, N. (2018). *Why does patriarchy persist?* Polity.

Herman, J. L. (1992a). Complex PTSD: A syndrome in survivors of prolonged and repeated trauma. *Journal of Traumatic Stress*, *5*(3), 377–391.

Herman, J. L. (1992b). *Trauma and recovery*. Basic Books.

Holmes, M., & Kim, J.-K. (2019, April). *Prenatal exposure to domestic violence: Summary of findings*. https://case.edu/socialwork/traumacenter/sites/case.edu.traumacenter/files/2019-04/PrenatalDV.pdf

hooks, b. (2004). *The will to change*. Washington Square Press.

Jung, C. G. (1969). The structure of the psyche (R. F. C. Hull, Trans.). In H. Read, M. Fordham, & G. Adler (Eds.), *The collected works of C. G. Jung: Vol. 8. Structure and dynamics of the psyche* (2nd ed., pp. 139–158). Princeton University Press. (Original work published 1931). https://doi.org/10.1515/9781400850952.139

Kachaeva, M. (2015). Infanticide in women who are victims of domestic violence. *European Psychiatry, 30*(Suppl 1), 751.

Kippert, A. (2015, December 9). *I helped open one of the first women's shelters: What's gotten better, worse since the movement to end domestic violence began in the 70s.* www.domesticshelters.org/articles/heroes/i-helped-open-one-of-the-first-battered-women-s-shelters

Kippert, A. (2017, August 23). *Why we blame victims for domestic violence.* www.domesticshelters.org/articles/identifying-abuse/why-so-many-are-quick-to-blame-victims-of-domestic-violence

Kippert, A. (2019, June 10). *Postpartum depression linked to domestic violence.* www.domesticshelters.org/articles/identifying-abuse/postpartum-depression-linked-to-domestic-violence

Lambert, C. (2021). Coercive control becoming criminalized. *Psychology Today.*

Leemis, R., Friar, N., Khatiwada, S., Chen, M., Kresnow, M., Smith, S., Caslin, S., & Basile, K. (2022, October). *The national intimate partner and sexual violence survey: 2016/2017 report on intimate partner violence.* Centers for Disease Control & Prevention. www.cdc.gov/violenceprevention/pdf/nisvs/NISVSReportonIPV_2022.pdf

Levendosky, A. A., & Graham-Bermann, S. A. (2001). Parenting in battered women: The effects of domestic violence on women and their children. *Journal of Family Violence, 16*(2), 171–192.

Lucario, L. (2023, July 24). *12 life-impacting symptoms PTSD survivors endure.* https://themighty.com/topic/post-traumatic-stress-disorder-ptsd/life-impacting-symptoms-of-complex-post-traumatic-stress-disorder-ptsd/

Maté, G. (2018). *In the realm of hungry ghosts.* North Atlantic Books.

Meyer, C. L., Proano, T. C., Oberman, M., White, K., & Batra, P. (2001). *Mothers who kill their children: Understanding the acts of moms from Susan Smith to the "prom mom".* New York University Press.

Michaels, S. (2022, August 9). She never hurt her kids. So why is a mother serving more time than the man who abused her daughter? *Mother Jones.*

National Coalition Against Domestic Violence. (2004). *Domestic violence and pregnancy fact sheet.* https://vawnet.org/sites/default/files/assets/files/2016-09/DVPregnancy.pdf

PBS. (2006). *The Roman empire in the first century.* www.pbs.org/empires/romans/empire/family.html

Ptacek, J. (1988). Why do men batter their wives? In K. Yllö & M. Bograd (Eds.), *Feminist perspectives on wife abuse* (pp. 133–157). Sage.

Quigley, L. (2007). The intersection between domestic violence and the child welfare system: The role courts can play in the protection of battered mothers and their children. *William & Mary Journal of Women and the Law, 13*(3). https://scholarship.law.wm.edu/cgi/viewcontent.cgi?article=1077&context=wmjowl

Rabin, B. (1995). Violence against mothers equals violence against children: Understanding the connections. *Albany Law Review, 58*(4), 1109–1117.

Real, T. (2002). *How can I get through to you? Closing the intimacy gap between men and women.* Simon & Schuster.

Rose, J. (2018). *Mothers: An essay on love and cruelty.* Farrar, Straus and Giroux.

Schechter, S. (1982). *Women and male violence: The visions and struggles of the battered women's movement.* South End Press.

Sidebotham, P., & Retzer, A. (2018). Maternal filicide in a cohort of English serious case reviews. *Archives of Women's Mental Health, 22*(1), 139–149. https://doi.org/10.1007/s00737-018-0820-7

Singh, S. (2021). Punishing mothers for men's violence: Failure to protect legislation and the criminalisation of abused women. *Feminist Legal Studies*, *29*, 181–204.

Stark, E. (2007). *Coercive control: How men entrap women in personal life*. Oxford University Press.

Stark, E. (2020). The coercive control of Daniel and Magdalena Lucek: A case of child abuse as tangential spouse abuse. *International Journal of Applied Psychoanalytic Studies*, *17*, 262–276.

United Nations Office on Drugs and Crime. (2020, November). *Killings of women and girls by their intimate partners or family members: Global estimates 2020*. https://static1.squarespace.com/static/5b7ea2794cde7a79e7c00582/t/64813af3e7775c60a32430a2/1686190837677/killings-of.pdf

Walker, L. (2017). *The battered women syndrome* (4th ed.). Springer.

Wallace, M., Gillispie-Bell, V., Cruz, K., Davis, K., & Vilda, D. (2021). Homicide during pregnancy and the postpartum period in the United States, 2018–2019. *Obstetrics & Gynecology*, *138*(5), 762–769.

Wood, J. T. (2004). Monsters and victims: Male felons' accounts of intimate partner violence. *Journal of Social and Personal Relationships*, *21*, 555–576.

Chapter 6

Motherhood
From Genesis to Modernity

The first conceptions of Mother, as identified by archaeologists and anthropolo-
gists, point to divinities extending back into the Bronze Age and earlier, a time
when woman was in position of religious authority. Marija Gimbutas, an archae-
ologist known for her cross-discipline work in Indo-European archaeological artifacts, posited that "it was the sovereign mystery and creative power of the female
as source of life that developed into the earliest religious experiences" (1992,
p. 222). From major excavations of Neolithic sites in southeastern Europe, Gimbutas uncovered artifacts that revealed a peaceful and matrilineal (nonhierarchical/not
matriarchal) culture in Old Europe that largely worshiped nature/earth and mother
goddesses such as Gaia. These societies were replaced in a series of incursions that
established a patriarchal warrior society that worshiped the father god/sun/King.
Anthropologist Riane Eisler found that the ancient objects recovered in the Indo-
European areas depicted a round figure giving birth, with a baby, or with a bulg-
ing vagina, evidence of mother goddess worship. Similarly, Gimbutas suggested
that these Paleolithic images and artifacts held a symbolic language of worship in
which the Mother Goddess was recognized in both her birth-giving and nourishing and life-taking and rebirthing functions. In other words, for these Paleolithic
peoples, there was as yet no sharp distinction between the goddess who creates new
life and the goddess who brings death to all things.

> The Great Mother who gives birth to all creation out of the holy darkness of her
> womb, became a metaphor for Nature herself, the cosmic giver and taker of life,
> ever able to renew Herself within the eternal cycle of life, death, and rebirth.
> (1992, p. 222)[1]

Mythologist Richard Stromer, in "The Good and the Terrible: Exploring the Two
Faces of the Great Mother," discussed the ancient Egyptian Mother goddess Hathor
and warrior goddess Sekhmet, the pre-Homeric Greek goddess Gaia, and the Hindu
goddess Kali as reflecting both the nourishing and destructive aspects of the Goddess. Gaia, as likely worshiped by the Paleolithic societies, is an Earth Goddess,
described as "the deep-breasted earth," the first being to emanate from Chaos,
which was "vast and dark" (Guirand, 1968/1987, p. 87). In her true Great Mother

DOI: 10.4324/9781003412809-8

archetypal nature, she has equal potential for both destruction and creativity. Gaia was suppressed with the establishment of patriarchal culture and laws, when nature (and women) began to be treated as a force to control. In *The Chalice and the Blade*, Eisler outlined the transition from partnership (matrilineal and egalitarian) to dominator (patriarchal and hierarchical) societies, which she said led to women's dependence, loss of their sexual agency, rape, prostitution, and the acceptance of chronic war. Neumann discussed the effect this had on humanity's relationship to the Great Mother: "The overpowering dynamism of the archetype is now held in check; it no longer releases paroxysms of dread, madness, ecstasy, delirium, and death" (1954/1973, p. 324).

Neumann added that in this shift in human consciousness from devotion to the Great Mother to the worship of an all-powerful Father, the "the Good Mother is split off, recognized by consciousness, and established in the conscious world as a value," whereas "the Terrible Mother, is in our culture repressed and largely excluded from the conscious world" (324). He concluded that in the continued development of patriarchal control "the Great Mother becomes simply the Good Mother, consort of Father-Gods" and "her dark animal side, her power as the uroboric Great Mother" gets forgotten (324). Gaia, as an all-powerful female, was a threat to the increasingly patriarchal nature of early state-based societies; she was relegated to "lesser" duties concerning births, marriages, and sometimes prophecy, and ultimately, along with other Goddesses, suppressed entirely. And, although as von Franz pointed out, in order for industrial development to succeed, it was necessary to put emphasis on the masculine principle—linear, competitive, and goal-directed—in the wake of Christianity we lost a feminine godhead and were left with the Virgin Mary. Jungian analyst and theologian Ann Belford Ulanov points out how in this way the Christian Trinity was left incomplete: "The feminine, the mater and the dark substance of the flesh and the devil should be added" (1971, p. 135).[2]

Eve and Lilith

The Old Testament of the Western Christian narrative depicts Eve as the first mother. Her myth begins in Genesis, thought to have been written in the 5th and 6th centuries BCE (Van Seters, 1998). According to Genesis 3:20, Adam and Eve lived piously in the Garden of Eden until Eve sought wisdom and the serpent led her into temptation. "Then the eyes of both of them were opened, and they knew that they were naked" (Genesis 3:7). Adam hides from God because of his nakedness, a verse that suggests the awakening of shame both for the body and for disobedience to the Father. Discovering that they had eaten the fruit of the tree of knowledge, for their disobedience (or Eve's self-agency and what is now called "original sin"), God turned them out of Paradise. It is the unconscious psychic load projected onto "bad mothers" and battered women and with which all mothers struggle. The image of the all-good mother is an unattainable standard, but to be a bad mother is to be neglectful, sexual, shameful, and demonic.

Adam, after being cast from the Garden, named his wife *havāh*, Eve, which means *life* in Hebrew, because she was the "Mother of all living" (Genesis 3:20), the progenitrix of all human beings. Without a role model or mentor, while carrying the blame for the sorrows of mortal life and mortality itself, she became the mother of all succeeding generations. Evicted from the Garden, she fulfilled her role in God's plan to prevent humans from being able to "take also of the tree of life, and eat, and live forever" (Genesis 3:22), and thus the capacity for birth and inevitability of death became forever fused in the sinful body of the woman/mother. Moreover, God deprived Eve of agency, declaring, your "husband . . . shall rule over thee" (Genesis 3:16). In this way, human patriarchy—the unquestioned rule in the "Name-of-the-Father" (Lacan, 1956/1968, p. 127)—is rooted and justified by Christian mythology.

Eve is a symbol, an archetypal image, that carries the feminine energy responsible for the "fall of man" and justifies the rule of men. She is a complicated archetype who represents desire, shame, and original sin. Medieval art works often depict Eve as a snake with a human female head, conflating the subtle serpent of Genesis with Eve and demonizing her. One of the most painted women in Western art, almost all depictions of Eve portray her as naked, except with a leaf, hand, or her long hair covering her genitals, with a snake nearby. With more telling and retelling, depictions and projections, Eve began to be a symbolic container of the chaotic impulse of life, intuitive and nonrational, and feminine knowledge, which threatens a culture that elevates the rational and social order. In this way, Eve became both mother and evil. As Marie-Louise von Franz pointed out, "with Eve's prominent role in the Fall of Man, the tendency to associate woman with evil has constantly manifested" (1994/1999, p. 14). Woman and snake are cursed, along with all women who descend from Eve, meaning all women.

In pre-Christian, Judaic mythology the first woman and Adam's first wife is Lilith, who has been shunted into the mythological and cultural shadow of Eve. Ancient Jewish scholars described Lilith as the "first Eve" (Ben-Amos, 2016). Genesis states that in his act of creation God made them "male and female" (1:27), but in a separate act of creation (Genesis 2:21–22), God creates a woman from Adam's rib. To resolve these two accounts, a midrash or ancient Hebrew scriptural commentary identified Adam's first wife as Lilith.

A story recorded in "The Alphabet of Ben Sira" midrash tells that Lilith refused to lay beneath Adam during sex. She believed they were created equal, both from the dust of the earth, thus she should not have to lay beneath him. After Adam disagreed, Lilith fled the Garden of Eden to gain her independence. Adam told God that Lilith had left, and God sent three angels to retrieve her. The angels found Lilith in a cave bearing children, but Lilith refused to come back to the garden. The angels told her they would kill 100 of her children every day for her disobedience. In revenge, Lilith is said to rob children of life and is responsible for the deaths of stillborn infants and crib deaths (Lesses, 1999, para. 1). Thus, the dark baby-killing mother is born in ancient Christianity. Mythologically she is associated with female independence and agency, demonized, and split off from human nature.

Figure 6.1 Adam; Eve. Oil painting depicting the biblical story of the temptation of Eve. By Giuliano di Piero di Simone Bugiardini (ca. 1495–1554). Bequest of Edward Fowles, 1971.

After Lilith departs, God makes Adam a wife from Adam's rib, and Adam declares his ownership: "Flesh of my flesh: She shall be called woman because she was taken out of Man" (Genesis 3:23). Identifying the first woman as Lilith gives a legendary, demonic origin to female agency, associating evil with a woman's refusal to submit to male authority. When female agency creeps back in through Eve's disobedience, it wreaks havoc and she is to be controlled, shamed, and punished: "In sorrow thou shalt bring forth children . . . [and] thy husband . . . shall rule over thee" (Genesis 3:16).

The Virgin Mary

Mary arises in the New Testament to redeem the sexual temptress Lilith and the sinful Eve. Mary is the all-loving, pure virgin and martyr who achieved the fantastical deed of bearing God's son. The Biblical evidence for seeing Mary as the new Eve is found in Luke 1:45. When both Eve and Mary were approached by an angel, doubt crept into Eve's heart, whereas Mary's faith was steadfast. Moreover, 2nd-century Christian writers proclaimed, "Death through Eve, life through Mary" (as cited in Thurmond, 2007, p. 33), and "the knot of Eve's disobedience was untied by Mary's faith" (Swafford, 2017, para. 1).

Mary was Immaculate, without sin, so that her son Jesus was conceived and born without the stain of original sin. Her entire life was a martyrdom. Father Donald Calloway, of the Marions of the Immaculate Conception, wrote that she is called the " 'Queen of Martyrs' because by uniting herself closest to Jesus, who has endured more suffering than anyone, she took on more pain than any other created person" (2019, para. 7). She is both naturally loving and *supernaturally* loving—loving Jesus as her son *and* as her God, placing the male child in authority above the mother. Catholic doctrine expounds upon Mary's glory as a mother

Figure 6.2 Madonna and Child. Devotional painting by Titian (Tiziano Vecellio) (1508). The Jules Bache Collection, 1949.

more loving than all others, always serene, sorrowful, pristine, and nonsexual. The archetypal image of the perfectly suffering Virgin Mary remains an incomparable and unachievable model of motherhood across the globe.

As psychoanalytic theory suggests, where there is all-good purity without stain, there is an equally alive but repressed stain waiting for its moment to emerge. In the inverse of martyrdom and self-sacrifice, repressed selfish and distinctly self-acting behaviors are alive, haunting the unconscious and waiting to act. In this way, the Virgin Mary only represents one side of Mother. As Jesus is believed to have taken on the sins of humankind and models the divine ideal to which all should strive, so is Mary seen as taking on the suffering of all and modeling the divine ideal to which all mothers should strive. However, as Julia Kristeva, who was raised Catholic, cautioned, the Virgin Mary as a maternal construct is problematic for the feminine psyche. As she noted in her essay, "Stabat Mater," or Sorrowful Mother, the idealization of Mary's self-sacrificial purity and love brings with it the abjection of actual women in their lived experience.

The Idealization and Institutionalization of Motherhood

In graduate school, as young burgeoning psychologists, we were told the quickest way to uncover the dynamics of a patient is to ask: Tell me about your mother. It

took me many years of work, mothering, and study to fully understand that statement and its implication: The mother is responsible for everything. Although this
is a question a therapist of almost any training will arrive at, it is thanks to Freudian
psychoanalysis that we have made the mother ultimately accountable. His work
established the mother's relationship with the child as the greatest major event of a
human's first years of life and the main source of mental illness. In this way, Freudian psychoanalysis greatly contributed to creating the myth of the ideal mother.

> If Freud had been less preoccupied with Oedipus and more observant of Medea
> when he remarked that "aggression forms the basis of every relation of affection
> and love among people," Loraux writes in *Mothers in Mourning*, "he would
> certainly not have added: 'with the single exception, perhaps, of the mother's
> relation to her male child.'"
>
> (Rose, 2014, para. 33)

Freud perhaps longed for the omnipotent mother, and he is not alone. An archetypal longing for a human mother to fulfill the image of the all-good Mother—the
forever-warm womb—contributes to the projection onto the mother in which she is
seen as *only* womb. Freud's theories remained ignorant of the other half of Mother,
her natural possibility for destruction; so deep was his boyish need for mother that
his office was said to be cluttered with statues of the Virgin Mary and Madonna.

The myth of motherhood is based on the maternal ideal: the unity of mother
and child in pure love; the woman and child in mutuality. Western culture repro-
duces this sentimental idealization of motherhood in baby food, clothing, and child
accessory commercials. A quick internet search for "pregnancy photo shoot" will
reveal women wearing all white, with gentle smiles, projecting perfect attunement,
undiluted love, and unending devotion, some even donning angel wings. She is the
all-giving safe haven/heaven. These images of the mother as young, pristine, and
calmly exuding oneness with a child perpetuate the myth of women's *only* natural
attitude as mothers as loving and giving, and as finding ultimate fulfillment in the
blissful state of motherhood.

One of the most subtle but insistent mandates of Western society is that women
are expected to *want* to be mothers. What might be called *The Mother's Mandate*
continues from there. She is to relinquish personal ambitions to care for her family;
deplete herself to support her family and raise children; be the primary caretaker
of the household; constantly serve other's needs (especially her husband's) while
not attending to her own; handle everything with ease; have well behaved children;
perform a high standard of beauty; maintain a sex drive; cultivate a successful
career; and present a solid marriage.

Nancy Chodorow, in *The Reproduction of Mothering*, answered the question,
"Why do women mother?" by psychoanalytically examining the states and creations of motherhood, concluding that women mother because they were mothered;
in effect, the mother is first a daughter. It is in the cyclical transmission from mother
to daughter that motherhood is reproduced, and that a mother has innate knowledge

of the needs and subjective states of her infant because she was mothered. In this genesis of mother, the woman has a "sense of self-in-relation" that spans herself as daughter and now as mother (107). This tends to be unique to mothers and daughters because typically a son does not identify with the mother—his opposite-sex parent—the way a daughter does. It's possible that women's mothering is purposed toward recreating and transmitting this primary intimate, mother–child relationship. Thus, an instinct of mothering is received but also limited by one's own mother.

Matrescence[3] and Maternal Subjectivity

The experience of motherhood begins with pregnancy. When a woman first realizes that she is carrying new life within her womb, all the feelings, both positive and negative, that she begins to experience are the beginning of her motherhood. "To become a mother is to enter a chaotic time, in which one is no longer recognized as a unified agent by others and can no longer easily regard oneself as a unified agent either" (Stone, 2014, p. 325.) When childbirth arrives for a mother, Jungian analyst and author Esther Harding describes this essential perennial experience:

> Then when her hour comes she must give herself up to be merely the medium for this new life, her body merely the prison whose doors must yield to the violent assault of the being who would live free. In that hour the woman must experience a gradual descent into the depths; the distinguishing marks of her personality, of her social grade, of her race, are stripped off, until she, like her remote ancestress of old, is revealed only as woman—as female creature engaged in her most fundamental task . . . . In spite of the pain, childbearing is most deeply desired by many women because of the contact with the deepest meaning of life which has come to them by this road and by it alone.
>
> (1935, p. 172)

When a new mother emerges from the chaos of birth, there is a process of transformation and an internal rearrangement of psychical relationships, cultivating a new subjective experience, a maternal subjectivity. Her perceptions and sensations are recruited into this new identity: she may hear sounds differently, such as large vehicles that could now bring harm to her child; she may smell things differently, such as toxins and smoke; she may experience space differently, large crowds suddenly no longer appealing. Lisa Barrister suggests there is a *maternal time*. "Neither linear nor cyclical: instead it is characterized by moments of dissolution and syncope" (Rodgers, 2014, p. 384). A mother interacts with the world and herself differently, changes which may be unique to each woman, but that represent similar transformations in all mothers. Feminist theorist Suzanne Juhasz detailed the maternal subject as a process weaving between multiple relational positions: those of mother and child, the mother and her own mother, mother and woman, and ideal and real mother (Stone, 2014, p. 334). Although generating meaning from her new maternal subjectivity, a mother has not lost her former female or independent subjectivity in its nuances, desires, and history.

In contemporary Western culture, although a baby shower may announce a woman's pregnancy, bringing the baby home is notably bereft of ritual or celebration. Once she has truly entered motherhood, there is a scattering of visits, intended to view the new baby rather than support the new mother. Robbie Davis-Floyd, in *Birth as an American Rite of Passage*, pointed out that although there are some rituals that recognize and welcome the infant, such as the traditional Jewish Bris celebrating the birth of a son and the ritual of christening in some Christian faiths, the mother has no welcoming party of her own.

Motherhood Is Powerful

Giving birth and taking life are the two most powerful acts a human can engage in; women can do both, men can do only one. Adrienne Rich observed, "All human life on the planet is born of woman. There is much to suggest that the male mind has always been haunted by the force of the idea of dependence on a woman for life itself" (1976, pp. 10–11). In this way, Mothers' unique power is a threat to men, who at the same time long to regain their prenatal state of wholeness and primal narcissism with Mother. Complicating this further is the idea of merging or entering the mother-world, in which men fear annihilation of their individuality. Mother who as womb is oceanic and symbolically evokes fluidity, water, the unconscious depths, is a threatening concept that not only incites violence from male partners during pregnancy but also incites the patriarchal system to transfigure and enslave her. Mary is an archetypal example of enslaved motherhood. She is silenced, put into the passive position; any means of autonomy are taken from her; she becomes the vessel for Joseph, Jesus, God, and the sorrows of the world.

When the respect for the power of motherhood turns into an idealization and an unconscious collective association with archetypal forces, it is dangerous for women. Although on the surface it may appear that idealization boosts mothers' place in society, the impossible standards perpetuate women's guilt and disempowerment. Everyday challenges, mistakes, and setbacks become sources of deep shame. We have the expectation that mothers should never be angry or jealous. Asking for help or feeling overwhelmed are seen as symptoms of failure. Mothering is expected to be instinctual—a natural built-in ability to play the role of the socially acceptable mother, happily accepting that she has no power beyond the position that the patriarchal society gives her. The institution of motherhood contains women within the home and devalues her potency anywhere else, except in child-based activities. In these designated spaces mothers are expected to unfailingly perform a series of never-ending visible and non-visible tasks. A mother is expected to give herself over to the child entirely if the child is to succeed. Chodorow observed that especially in industrialist-capitalist societies, the longing for mothering may put more expectations and pressure on the mother, as extended families are rarely nearby to help provide nurturance and companionship.

In *Mother, Madonna, Whore: The Idealization and Denigration of Motherhood*, British forensic psychotherapist Estela Welldon argued that the idealization of motherhood is also dangerous for children. If we assume perfection and love from mothers, it conceals a mother's capacity for child abuse. Munchausen by proxy, in which a mother fabricates or causes symptoms of illness in her child, is a perfect example of this. While the mother's family, friends, and medical providers assume the best of her as a caring and dedicated mother, especially the mother of a handicapped or ill child, they miss the signs of her poisoning or harming a child to keep it ill.

The conventionalized norms of motherhood in patriarchy and Christianity demand of women a performance of humility rather than intelligence, selflessness rather than self-realization, relation to others rather than the creation of self. Feminist theorist Sara Ruddick highlighted this internalized rhetoric of maternal selflessness by pointing to a Jewish folk poem in which a son rips out his mother's heart; when he stumbles and falls, still holding her heart in his hands, the mother asks him whether he hurt himself (1980, pp. 342–343).

If she acts in her own self-interest and rejects the traditional expectations of motherhood, she is a Bad Mother, a social deviant who does not want to only care for children, she does not always like children, she wants to work outside of the home. She is not nurturing, soft, or kind, she is selfish, she is single, she is introverted, she has a messy house, she never cooks meals, and she likes having sex.[4] Adrienne Rich argued that "female possibility has literally been massacred on the site of motherhood" and that motherhood has incarcerated women in their bodies (1976, p. 13).

> Essentially, the ideal of motherhood is a culture-specific, socially constructed concept in which the images of the socially acceptable and the socially deviant mother are established. The socially acceptable mother will be selfless and will act the role given to her that benefits society rather than creating a version of herself that she wants to be, a version of herself that is best for her.
>
> (42)

I write in a small cottage 90 minutes from my house when my children are with their father. This morning I got an email from him wondering, "How sustainable is this, you being away while the children are with me, how can you still be available?" Per our custody agreement the children are not in my care for half the week; they are at their father's house; he takes them to school; he makes them dinner; he covers their care. Yet I must be available. There is an invisible perimeter beyond which my body cannot cross. The mother is a locus of power and an expectancy, her maternity is required but her agency is ignored. The expectation of maternal omnipresence is more than being physically present, it is an essence of care to be available on command.

Rose's book *Mothers: An Essay on Love and Cruelty* is at its best when she observes that mothers are expected to create both a good child *and* a good world for that child. A natural mother is invested in the whole world, a world that must be flawless for her baby. The figure of the mother is "held accountable for the ills of the world, the breakdown in the social fabric, the threat to welfare" (6). We expect them to "repair the world and make it safe" (177).

> Mothers of the western world are punished (by economy) for being mothers and instructed to love without reservation. The hate is proportionate to the love—the intensity of demands matches the deluded expectation, the veneration is a cover for reproach.
>
> (37)

The exaltation of Mother sets up grand impossibilities: Heal the world, create good citizens, and end war.

> Motherhood is, in western discourse, the place in our culture where we lodge, or rather bury, the reality of our own conflicts, of what it means to be fully human. It is the ultimate scapegoat for our personal and political failings, for everything that is wrong with the world, which it becomes the task—unrealisable, of course—of mothers to repair
>
> (1)

Mother holds the evils of the world, mitigating them for her children. Akin to the ancestral practice of pre-mastication, we make the world palatable for our children, while like "Queen of the Martyrs" we contain the weight of its horrors. With each horror the world presents, I have felt the fracturing of my promise to my children of a safe and beautiful world, the one a mother is meant to supply. Because the world is built of tragedy, the mother is forever racked with guilt.

> With the suffering of the whole world etched on her face, the mother carries and assuages the burden of human misery.
>
> (Rose, 2018, p. 12)

Recently, a friend of mine was asked by her ex-husband to meet for coffee to "discuss the children." She arrived at this meeting with a box of homemade scones and her eyes filled with tears, feeling intense worry for her children's health, anticipating condemnation from their father, experiencing guilt at her failings, and having sudden regret that she divorced their father—a man who one time on a bike ride in an urban area lost track of them. At their meeting he told her the older child needed more help with college applications and the younger one had a painful tooth he was scared to face. With this non-urgent news, she was able to take reprieve from her maternal guilt and left the meeting relieved. Later, he texted her, "You worry too much. But thanks, I ate all the scones."

Rozsika Parker, in *Torn in Two*, embraced the profound ambivalence and intolerable levels of guilt that are pervasive for mothers.

> A mother's psychic guilt in relation to the confluence of love and hate she feels towards her children is exacerbated by the social conviction that mothers are

truly culpable. Mothers mobilize what defenses they can against intolerable levels of guilt.

(1995, p. 259)

Humanity is projecting and expecting divine omnipresence from human mothers because of a yearning for the archetypal Good Mother. As Jung warned, "In all fairness [we cannot] load the enormous burden of meaning, responsibility, duty, heaven and hell onto the shoulders of one frail and fallible human being" (1954/1969, para. 172). In a way, the infanticidal mother illuminates this projection. Her arrival screams, "Mother is not all good and pious. She does not have bottomless energy or an endless capacity to love and serve, she may in fact be murderous. Accept these parts of her; end this myth in which you have attempted to cage her." Perhaps in the moment of infanticide, the child, who is appropriately demanding and needy, is a stand-in for the infantile and narcissistic demands of the culture that press upon the human mother and need to be terminated.

Maternal Solicitude and Finitude

Jung described the qualities associated with the mother as: "maternal solicitude and sympathy; the magic authority of the female; the wisdom and spiritual exaltation that transcend reason; any helpful instinct or impulse; all that is benign, all that cherishes and sustains, that fosters growth and fertility" (1954/1969, para. 158). He added,

This is the mother-love which is one of the most moving and unforgettable memories of our lives, the mysterious root of all growth and change; the love that means homecoming, shelter, and the long silence from which everything begins and in which everything ends. Intimately known and yet strange like Nature, lovingly tender and yet cruel like fate, joyous and untiring giver of life-mater dolorosa and mute implacable portal that closes upon the dead.

(para. 172)

Jung suggested, as I am, that this exaltation of Mother and conflation of human mothers with the Virgin Mary—who is "great enough to include in herself both the Queen of Heaven and Maria Aegyptiaca" and is "glorified in all ages and all tongues" (para. 190)—lends itself to the overdevelopment of the maternal instinct.

In my practice treating mothers I repeatedly see an over-investment in their parenting behaviors, concerns, and expectations. This maternal solicitude is an earnest, anxious, protective, and caring attention to their child, and entire therapy sessions, for years, may be consumed in discussing their children's behaviors, achievements, dietary habits, sleep schedules, etc. Women sometimes enter therapy with a singular focus on discussing a child who is causing them anxiety because they will not behave or sleep well or because they are afraid of their child's vomit.[5] Mothers often drive their children to several therapy appointments per week and almost daily organized activities. Although I encourage fathers to join therapy and activities for the children, they rarely attend.

The expectations of motherhood have intensified. Since the 18th century, there has been a rise of moral conscience regarding infants and children, heightening empathy and sensitivity to the birth of and care for children; as a result mothers began to form strong attachments to their children (DeMause, 1974). In the mid-20th century, a greater emphasis was placed on child-centered parenting and respecting children's integrity. Family members, teachers, and religious organizations invested more to enhance young children's learning and growth, as their future held great promise (Fass, 2016). An even sharper rise in attention toward child-rearing has taken place in the last 50 years, resulting in accelerated expectations of walking, talking, potty training, and reading, among other cognitive and physical achievements that are pushed up on the timeline, perfected and manipulated. Scores of parenting books have their own sections at bookstores. Books on parenting tactics, parenting to produce the best child, parenting to create the best attachment, advice on behavioral, medical, academic, psychological issues, with the largest consumers of these books being mothers. The most oft-cited, well-respected, best-selling books about the caretaking of babies have been and are mostly still written by men (Winnicott, Spock, Sears, Weissbluth), although that has shifted in the last several years. Advice that historically would have come from elder women in a community, the grandmothers and the aunts, is now largely left to Google searches.[6] The websites and mommy blogs intended to help mothers induce more anxiety by perpetuating the sense that there is an answer *out there*, moving mothers further away from not only a maternal community, but from their maternal instincts.[7]

In treating parenting as if it were a PhD program, we have produced the pursuit of the gifted child, like a divine child, to be tenderly tended to, nourished, and accommodated. Tutors enter children's lives earlier than ever before, and competitive sports teams are now mainstream for middle schoolers. The child, having become an extension of the adult's tendency toward competition, serves to fulfill a mother's hope that she will be rewarded for all the hard work she has put into this child.

In my practice I see college students who work on setting boundaries with a mom who continues to press for the same contact they had when the child lived at home, including daily text messages and calls. Both child and mother, accustomed to an enmeshed relationship, now struggle with separation. I will often encourage both parties to harness their individual energy and put it toward their own interests and agency outside of the relationship. Inevitably there is a spike in anxiety with this suggestion, but if it is followed the child especially gains a sense of autonomy and confidence.

Sarah Singh, who has followed the course of women criminalized in the justice system, pointed out how the intensified focus of mother on child has been damaging to mothers:

More contemporaneously, the impact of neoliberal privatization of care has led to expectations of intensive mothering, which re-emphasizes the demand for maternal omnipresence and selflessness. The naturalization, then later normalization, of these conventional constructs of mothers have ultimately led to a contemporary culture of mother blaming which means that when tragedy befalls children, mothers are presumed blameworthy.

(2021, p. 184)

Maternal solicitude mistakes being consumed with one's child for caring for the child. Mothers who become overly invested in and focused on their child can become overactivated and transformed into obsessional mothers. To be clear, their impulse to be invested and focused is often born of a loving maternal instinct but perverted by an over-demanding social norm. Burdened with a pathological need to protect their children, they engage in pathological self-sacrifice. Their helicopering, hovering, devouring, and smothering can all too easily become a literal danger to the child's life. Writing in 1902, John Baker, renowned British medical superintendent, observed that many of his maternal filicide patients were not vicious by nature but driven by their own maternal instinct. "It may seem paradoxical, but it is not vice that leads to the death of the infant, rather it is morbid and mistaken maternal solicitude" (Gregory et al., 2018, p. 16).

Mary was like this. She was hyper-interested in her baby. Meticulous in her planning and thoughtful in her care for him. Mary researched the best forms of clothing, the best foods, sleep styles, bedding, stimulation, education, discipline, and play. She paid close attention to his needs, shopped only at certain stores for him, and allowed only a few close people to hold him. She vetted daycares and quit them when they did not meet her standards. Mary wrote down every detail of her baby's small existence. Her carefully tended journals detailed when he ate, when he pooped, when he smiled, etc.

Mary is like many mothers who kill their children. These are women about whom others would later say, "She would never do something like that. She was the best mother I ever knew; all she cared about was her child." Carol Coronado, who in 2014 killed her three daughters with a knife and marked a cross on their heads afterward with their blood, would often be seen happily walking her kids down the sidewalk. Her neighbor later said, "It's not Carol, Carol would never do that" (as cited in Harrington & Watkin, 2019). The collective praise for and expectation of an overdeveloped maternalism colludes with our inability to see and respond to a good mother's experience of difficulties—which in Carol's case was postpartum psychosis: "No one could see it, so no one could stop it" (Not Carol, n.d., para. 1).

The phenomenon of an overinvested mother is ubiquitous in middle- or upper-class white families. Her social media may be full of mommy-baby content, her house is never clean enough, the relationship with her mother likely is strained, a hidden eating disorder is usually lurking, she tends to have underlying contempt for a subtly narcissistic husband, and she is smiling for the camera. She is happy with baby; baby is her world.

A recent *Atlantic* article, "The Gravitational Pull of Supervising Kids All the Time," suggests the vigilant style of American parenting is pervasive, and although it may have to do with a history of safeguarding children, it is driven by the competition to raise successful children and the proliferation of showcasing one's children/parenting on social media. Once a parent is ushered into this social norm of helicopter parenting it is almost impossible to back out of, for fear of social shame. In this way, the hyper-attentive parenting style is emboldened. The article author, Stephanie Murray, noted,

> Compared with children of generations past, modern American kids tend to live under a high degree of surveillance. That's not to say they have no autonomy. If anything, children today have more say over what they eat and wear than kids have had through much of history—just very few opportunities for "some degree of risk and personal responsibility away from adults," as a trio of researchers recently put it.
>
> (2023, para. 3)[8]

Mary Harrington has similarly noted the intensified parenting styles, and the emotional deadly energy behind it, in her article, "Devour me, Mummy":

> According to a new survey from the American Cato Institute, three in ten Americans under 30 support the installation of cameras in the home to monitor for wrongdoing. We can probably also map this emerging support for intrusive digital surveillance onto the growing body of studies indicating that faith in and support for democratic norms is falling with every generation, even as the same group turns against open debate and academic freedom. In other words: there has been a pronounced turn away from the foundational liberal norms, and toward a baseline of authoritarian control and surveillance in the name of safety, care, and the avoidance of harm: an outlook I think of as Actually Existing Post-Liberalism, in the sense that all these values depart noticeably from core liberal assumptions on autonomy, the positive value of constructive disagreement, and a central assumption of a relatively robust sense of self.[9]
>
> (2023a, para. 1)

In her book *Feminism Against Progress*, Harrington called this dynamic *the devouring mother*, acknowledging its reference to the Jungian archetype of the ouroboric Mother who nourishes herself by consuming her own children.

The devouring mother is a version of the Death Mother, or as Clarissa Pinkola Estés referred to her, the "Life/Death/Life Goddess" (1992, p. 95). The Death Mother symbolizes the archetypal nature of death as the devouring of lives to sustain life—the need to eat to live and die for others to live. When this overarching, instinctual commitment to life is out of balance and becomes all-consuming, she becomes the Terrible Mother, also referred to as the "Too Good Mother" (181). She prioritizes safety over freedom, restraining and stunting her child's developmental growth, which provenly requires unattended play and the level of risk inherent in exploring self and world. But what choice does a mother have when she feels society threatening, as a hovering, punitive and shaming parent, expecting her to be a perfect (Too Good) mother, so that if she has allowed her child distance, she suffers the worst fate: that of a bad mother?

When the pendulum swings too far toward the Good Mother and the fear of death and imperfection, we find this Too Good Mother. The Too Good Mother is a variation on maternal solicitude; she has bypassed Winnicott's advocacy for an imperfect but "good enough mother," fleeing the possibility of failure into the manic CEO of motherhood. A too good mother feels great sympathy for every fragile creature; she consistently roots for the underdog; she is pulled to save the victims and the most vulnerable populations. Commercials of the 1990s for starving children in Africa were meant for her, along with the Society for Prevention of Cruelty to Animals (SPCA) advertisements featuring the desperate eyes of abused animals in need of homes (mothers). The maternal tendency has been hijacked from the needs, desires, and expectations of a good mother and channeled into an overabundance, almost a militarism, of care. Psychically overloaded with her emotional availability—mothering all the foundlings, even emotionally, is exhausting—a mother inhabited by this Too Good Mother often explains and protects herself with pious designations such as that of an empath (I feel too much) or introvert (I need silence and alone time). This is also a way to gain care and create boundaries.[10]

Mothers are not endless saviors, martyrs, nurturers, or containing wombs, but singular humans who have human capacity; that is, limited and flawed. Maternal finitude subverts the traditional belief that a mother could satisfy our desires if she really wanted to (Griffin, 2001, p. 37; Silverman, 2009, p. 94). Critical theorist Kaja Silverman referred to finitude as the point where one ends and another begins:

> Since finitude marks the point where we end and others begin, spatially and temporally, it is also what makes room for them—and acknowledging these limits allows us to experience expansiveness for which we yearn, because it gives us a powerful sense of our emplacement within a larger Whole.
>
> (2009, p. 4)

Although motherhood implies a space shared with the child, theorists such as Silverman, Kristeva, Cixous, and Rich renounce the concept of the unity or oneness of mother and child and the maternal ideal as a sacrifice of self. They claim that such definitions reinforce the Christian ideal of Mary's martyrdom, forcing women into an impossibility. Second-wave feminist theory worked hard to subvert the myth of the selfless mother for the rest of us. Kristeva pointed out the crucifixion of mother, forced to self-sacrifice and become anonymous, is in service to stabilizing a patriarchal society. Yet even these mothers who have been recruited as wives of the patriarchy do not have an infinite capacity to give and nurture; in fact, there is a finitude of maternal love and selflessness. She has limits.

In her memoir *The Mother Knot*, feminist author Jane Lazarre gives an honest account of how maternal self-sacrifice is almost always tied not only to a mother's psyche but also to her body. The realities of maternal finitude are often dictated by the limits of the mother's body, such as her "weak back and a nagging pain from carrying the baby carriage down the stairs every day" (1997, p. 62). Like millions of other mothers, Lazarre mourned rather than celebrated the physical sacrifices she made for her son.

Physically, a mother's exhaustion, sweat, shaking, tears, and blood lead to maternal finitude. Psychologically, fear, love, worry, dread, shame, guilt, confusion, and crisis create natural limits for a mother. Yet, these realities of maternal finitude are often silenced by society; it is too dangerous to know that a mother's love is not limitless. Once a woman disappears into motherhood, her voice and boundaries are lost. Feminist literary scholar Michelle Walker Boulous suggested, "Women are silenced most effectively by their association with maternity. The maternal body operates as the site of women's radical silence" (1998, p. 1).

The Modern Mother

Contemporary American society's lack of care for a mother's body is reflected in maternal death rates. This is worse at the intersection of sexism and racism: The maternal mortality rate for Black mothers is 2.6 times that of white mothers, which is still higher than in any other developed country. *New York Times* columnist Nicholas Kristof asked in 2017, "If Americans Love Moms, Why Do We Let Them Die?" He wrote,

> We love mothers, or at least we say we do, and we claim that motherhood is as American as apple pie. We're lying. In fact, we've structured health care so that motherhood is far more deadly in the United States than in other advanced countries. An American woman is about five times as likely to die in pregnancy or childbirth as a British woman—partly because Britain makes a determined effort to save mothers' lives, and we don't.
>
> (2017, para. 1–2)

This continued disregard for the physical limits and challenges of mothers is compounded by the modern expectation that motherhood includes a successful full-time job *and* full-time attendance to children. Although women now make up close to half the U.S. workforce and over half of them are mothers (U.S. Department of Labor, 2022), men have not entered half the domestic force. Many women I see as therapy patients complain about this division of labor: I work but I'm still the only one in the house that knows the dosage of the children's Tylenol and how to balance our budget. This work that mothers do, that women do, is essential and imperative. "There is no constitution, development or renewal of the social body without women's work: their cathartic function as loved mistress or wife, their function as reproducing mother, their functions as carer and housewife assuring life and survival" (Irigaray, 1986, p. 15).

I often suggest mothers identify their role and give themselves a title as House Manager, honoring their in-home work and insisting upon its respect. Although this may support their self-respect, it does not address the systemic problem with which she is afflicted. My mother, in the 1990s, created a system in which she tallied up her domestic hours—cleaning, cooking, organizing, planning, driving—and collected payment from my stepfather. Although this may have felt empowering for a while, it didn't last. Inevitably, it is still "women's work," now receiving an allowance as if a child doing chores.

The pressure to be a full-time working mother is a guilt trap and a double bind that is now regularly identified in mommy blogs: Mothers have two full-time jobs and feel they are not good enough at either.[11] When the mother is working, she is failing at every school event or pick-up and every scraped knee; taking days off work for choir concerts and doctor appointments means she is failing at work, using up paid time off and missing meetings her male colleagues do not miss. There is an expectation for mothers to embrace and fulfill both these roles, having "the best of both worlds," but the workload is unsustainable. Jacqueline Rose pointed out the capitalist structures at work in these fantastical expectations of the working mother:

> To lean in, to use the ghastly imperative in the style of Sheryl Sandberg's bestseller—as if being the props of neo-liberalism were the most that mothers can aspire to, the highest form of social belonging and agency they can expect . . . what Angela McRobbie described as the "neo-liberal intensification of mothering"— perfectly turned-out middle class mainly white mothers with their perfect jobs, perfect husbands and marriages whose permanent glow of self-satisfaction is intended to make all women who do not conform to that image feel like total failures.
>
> (2018, p. 17)

With 70% of mothers in the workforce, women are expected to fill the role of mother, wife, family caregiver, and employee without the guarantee of paid family leave. Some of the most important work women do—raise children—is still going uncared for and unrecognized in the United States. On average, maternity leave in the top 40 wealthy countries lasts 18 weeks. Women who have paid maternity leave do not face the terror of financial loss versus separation from their baby. The U.S. is the only country of the top 40 wealthy countries that offers zero paid maternity leave (Organisation for Economic Co-operation and Development, 2022). In the U.S., the income of single pregnant mothers drops an average of 42% at the time of birth because of reduced work hours related to her pregnancy (Ingraham, 2018). This is compounded by the fact that women's wages average only 85% of what men are paid.

American women have been working later into their pregnancies and going back to work sooner after birth. This is bad for working mothers, who need time to recover from the physical and mental trauma of childbirth. It's bad for kids, who need extra attention and care in the crucial months after birth. And it's bad for the economy: Research has shown that paid maternity leave is associated with better job performance and retention among mothers, increased family incomes, and increased economic growth.

(paras. 14–15)

Women, mothers, make a human from their body. The work that women do, the mothering, remains unrecognized and unpaid. Irigaray, long a proponent of the financial assessment of mothering, commented,

Procreation has been the value underlying our societies for thousands of years. The question isn't expressed in these terms—the "work" is unpaid, the job is enveloped in an intangible aura of sacredness, in masks commensurate with the repressions and ignorance which is presupposed and continues to demand.

(1986, p. 14)

Our society assumes the mother should raise the child without pay as it is her "natural" place and sacred duty. The mother must "nurture both man and society— *a totem before any designated, identified or represented totem*" (Irigaray, 1986, p. 13). As Irigaray pointed out, when money is not given where it is due and work is not credited adequately, the entire system is deregulated. By positioning mothers as undervalued nurturers, where labor is obfuscated by ideology, a dysfunction in capitalism emerges, a specific dysfunction pertinent to mothers that traps them in being uncompensated, overburdened yet invisible.[12]

The lack of compensation and care for the modern mother reflects our assumption, expectation, and insistence that she can do it all without help. Because of our perpetual belief in the omnicompetence of Mother, we do not make changes in society that benefit mothers. Mothers are assumed to be sufficiently proficient and that the need to care for them via paid maternity leave, funded childcare, and flexible work times is moot. Moreover, idealizing motherhood enables and perpetuates oppressive social institutions, such as unequal division of family and household responsibilities, paternal negligence, and attribution of blame and criminal responsibility to women.[13]

In this context, in which negative mother energy and maternal limitations are unacknowledged and unacceptable, Lilith is pushed out for Eve, who is then redeemed by the Immaculate Mary, Queen of Martyrs. Mothers assume and attempt the maternal ideal, which forces them to suppress their negative feelings about motherhood and parenting. She sacrifices these parts of herself in a Sisyphean attempt to be the Good Mother—a cruel practice in which one's own sense of one's goodness has been subverted by impossible patriarchal expectations. The secularized ideal mother embodies an unrealistic and oppressive standard, which inevitably exposes all mothers to themselves as imperfect and failures. A festering loathing for herself and baby gains the potential to boil over into toil and trouble. More so for women whose bodies and psyches are burdened with poverty, racism, complex trauma, domestic violence, and/or postpartum depression or psychosis.

Notes

1 Gimbutas was originally dismissed for her Kurgan hypothesis, but it is now a widely accepted theory to explain the spread of Indo-European language and culture (Mallory, 1989; Gimbutas & Dexter, 1999).
2 The concept of a male God has been used by men to disavow their debt to femininity and maternity. Men regard themselves as formed by and in the image of a male divine omnipotent being and thus partake in His divine creativity. They effectively contain women in a sphere outside of the divine with women's relations to God mediated by men while continuing to rely on women's resources (Grosz, 1989, p. 152).
3 *Matrescence*, a term coined by anthropologist Dana Raphael in "Matrescence, Becoming a Mother," is a developmental passage where a woman transitions through preconception, pregnancy and birth to the postnatal period and beyond.
4 While a good mother must conceal from the world her voracious sexual desire, MILF ('Mothers I'd like to F*ck') is one of the most visited categories on pornography websites. A "mother" is allowed sexuality if she is fetishized and in service of men, especially to fulfill an unconscious desire for the exclusive love of a man's mother (Vannier et al., 2014). Consuming mother in pornography is a form of disavowal of man's maternal debt: "In order to become men, they continue to consume . . . [the mother], draw on her resources and, at the same time, they deny her or disclaim her in their identification with and their belonging to the masculine world. They owe their existence, their body, life and they forget or misrecognise this debt" (Irigaray in Grosz, 1989, p. 121).
5 Emetophobia (fear of vomit) in mothers deserves more analysis as it seems to singularly affect white mothers and is likely connected to a shame-avoidance response.
6 From an evolutionary perspective, the point of life is to procreate and pass on genes. That's why most animals keep reproducing until their deathbeds. Yet in humans, females tend to live for decades after they're no longer fertile, while few other primates ever live long enough to make it through menopause. The phenomenon of the grandmother, or crone, who cares for her grandchildren *and* her daughter-as-mother has been theorized as a component of evolution. The *grandmother hypothesis* states that women live well past menopause so that they can help raise successive generations of children. Yet there is balking at this concept as it again relegates women, even in their hard-won golden years, to being caretakers. The desire for pure self-oriented agency in grandmotherhood is salient as many women did not experience agency in their motherhood years, and now see their daughters as having more than they did. The effects are sometimes seen in the *glamma* (short for Glamorous Grandma), an identity for grandma that has developed in the last decade, but largely removes *grandmother* as an active identity. There is a successful line of products for this new variation of the archetype with mugs and tee-shirts that declare: I'm not grandma, I'm glamma.
7 The question of maternal instincts is addressed in Chapter 7.
8 As Murray didn't acknowledge projections onto motherhood, examine differing gender roles in parenting, or interview any fathers, there seems to be a subtle, perhaps unconscious, endorsement of mothers as the omnipotent parent.
9 Harrington noted the effect of hovering parents on generations of children as already apparent in Generations Y and Z: "The further the Devouring Mother cohort of intensely post-liberal young people moves into adulthood and meaningful power, the more we can expect this form of Actually Existing Post-Liberalism to consolidate as a political force" in which safety is valued over freedom (2023a, para. 12).

10 Estés argued that "the ever-watchful, protective, psychic mother is not adequate as a central guide for one's future instinctual life" (1992, p. 81). When a mother can refrain from indulging the too-good-mother, she is "developing [her] own consciousness about danger, intrigue, politics. Becoming alert by [herself for herself] . . . . As the too-good mother dies, the new woman is born" (81).

11 The *Huffington Post* has run a blog on the double standards for a working mother for the last 10 years.

12 In the increasing eradication of motherhood, not only is she hidden behind a stroller or a kitchen counter, but there also is a growing anti-natal movement, a withholding of procreation due to concerns about bringing a child into precariousness of the contemporary world with climate change, overpopulation, and the threat of nuclear disaster (Tuhus-Dubrow, 2019). Additionally, the denoting of mothers in scientific papers, medical information, HR policies, and legal statutes as *breeders, birthing parents, hired gestators*, *exowombs*, and *full-body gestational donators* erases women from maternity (Harrington, 2023b).

13 In this regard, one might ask: When the police force is exhuming dead babies and testing their DNA to make a match to a mother 30 years after the newborn was abandoned, why are they neglecting to search for the father's DNA?

References

The Alphabet of Ben Sira. (1990). *Rabbinic fantasies* (D. Stern & M. J. Mirsky, Eds., pp. 167–202). Yale University Press.

Ben-Amos, (2016, May–June). From Eden to *Ednah*-Lilith in the garden. *Biblical Archaeology Review*, *42*(3).

Calloway, D. (2019, October). The blessed Virgin Mary, apostle and martyr. *Litany of Loreto*. https://marian.org/articles/blessed-virgin-mary-apostle-and-martyr#:~:text=We%20call%20Mary%20%22Queen%20of,title%20%22Queen%20of%20Martyrs.%22

Chodorow, N. (1999). *The reproduction of mothering*. University of California Press.

Davis-Floyd, R. (2004). *Birth as an American rite of passage*. University of California Press.

DeMause, L. (1974). The evolution of childhood. In L. DeMause (Ed.), *The history of childhood: The untold story of child abuse* (pp. 1–73). Peter Bedrick Books.

Estés, C. P. (1992). *Women who run with the wolves*. Ballantine Books.

Fass, P. (2016). *The end of American childhood: A history of parenting from life on the frontier to the managed child*. Princeton University Press.

Franz, M.-L. V. (1999). *Archetypal dimensions of the psyche* (W. H. Kennedy, Trans.). Shambhala. (Original work published 1994)

Gimbutas, G. (1992). *Civilization of the goddess*. HarperCollins.

Gimbutas, Marija. (1997). Dexter, Miriam Robbins; Jones-Bley, Karlene (eds.), The Kurgan Culture and the Indo-Europeanization of Europe: Selected Articles from 1952 to 1993, *Journal of Indo-European Studies Monograph Series*, vol. 18, Washington, DC: Institute for the Study of Man, ISBN 978-0-941694-56-8.

Grosz, E. (1989). *Sexual subversions: Three French feminists*. Allen & Unwin.

Gregory, J., Grey, D. J., & Bautz, A. (Eds.). (2018). *Judgment in the Victorian age*. Routledge.

Griffin, S. (2001). Feminism and motherhood. In M. Davey (Ed.), *Mother reader: Essential writings on motherhood* (pp. 33–46) Seven Stories.

Guirand, F. (1987). *New Larousse encyclopedia of mythology* (R. Aldington, Trans.). Crescent Books. (Original work published 1968)

Harding, E. (1935). *Woman's mysteries; ancient and modern*. Longmans, Green.

Harrington, E., & Watkin, J. (Directors). (2019). *Not Carol* [Documentary Film]. Artemis Rising.

Harrington, M. (2023a, June 7). Devour me, mummy. *Reactionary Feminist.* https://reac tionaryfeminist.substack.com/p/devour-me-mummy

Harrington, M. (2023b). *Feminism against progress.* Regnery.

Ingraham, C. (2018, February 5). The world's richest countries guarantee mothers more than a year of paid maternity leave. The U.S. guarantees them nothing. *Washington Post.* www. washingtonpost.com/news/wonk/wp/2018/02/05/the-worlds-richest-countries-guarantee-mothers-more-than-a-year-of-paid-maternity-leave-the-u-s-guarantees-them-nothing/

Irigaray, L. (1986). Women, the sacred and money. *Paragraph, 8*(1), 6–18.

Jung, C. G. (1969). Psychological aspects of the mother archetype (R. F. C. Hull, Trans.). In H. Read, M. Fordham, & G. Adler (Eds.), *The collected works of C. G. Jung: Vol. 9, pt. 1. Archetypes and the collective unconscious* (2nd ed., pp. 75–110). Princeton University Press. (Original work published 1954). https://doi.org/10.1515/9781400850969.75

Jung, C. G. (1971). *The collected works of C. G. Jung: Vol. 6. Psychological types* (H. Read, M. Fordham, & G. Adler, Eds., R. F. C. Hull, Trans.). Princeton University Press. (Original work published 1921). https://doi.org/10.1515/9781400850860

Kristof, N. (2017, July 29). If Americans love moms, why do we let them die? *New York Times.* www.nytimes.com/2017/07/29/opinion/sunday/texas-childbirth-maternal-mortal ity.html

Lacan, J. (1968). *The language of the self: The function of language in psychoanalysis* (A. Wilden, Trans.). John Hopkins University Press. (Original work published 1956)

Lazarre, J. (1997). *The mother knot.* Duke University Press.

Lesses, R. (1999). Lilith. In *The Shalvi/Hyman encyclopedia of Jewish women.* https://jwa. org/encyclopedia/article/lilith

Mallory, J. P. (1989). In Search of the Indo-Europeans: Language, Archaeology, and Myth, London: Thames & Hudson, ISBN 0-500-27616-1.

Murray, S. (2023, July 13). The gravitational pull of supervising kids all the time. *Atlantic.* www.msn.com/en-us/news/us/the-gravitational-pull-of-supervising-kids-all-the-time/ ar-AA1dsy4C

Neumann, E. (1973). *The origins and history of consciousness* (R. F. C. Hull, Trans.). Princeton University Press. (Original work published 1954)

Not Carol. (n.d.). *Artemis rising foundation.* www.notcarol.com/

Organisation for Economic Co-operation and Development. (2022). *Parental leave systems.* www.oecd.org/els/soc/PF2_1_Parental_leave_systems.pdf

Raphael, D. (1975). Matrescence, becoming a mother, a "new/old" rite de passage. In D. Raphael (Ed.), *Being female: Reproduction, power, and change* (pp. 65–72). De Gruyter Mouton.

Rich, A. (1976). *Of woman born: Motherhood as experience and institution.* W. W. Norton.

Rodgers, J. (2014). Exploring the possibility of a positive maternal subjectivity: An intro-duction to Lisa Baraister's maternal encounters. In P. Bueskens (Ed.), *Mothering and psychoanalysis* (pp. 373–390). Demeter Press.

Rose, J. (2014). Mother. *London Review of Books, 36*(12). www.lrb.co.uk/the-paper/v36/ n12/jacqueline-rose/mothers

Rose, J. (2018). *Mothers: An essay on love and cruelty.* Farrar, Straus and Giroux.

Ruddick, S. (1980). Maternal thinking. *Feminist Studies, 6*(2), 342–367.

Silverman, K. (2009). *Flesh of my flesh.* Stanford University Press.

Singh, S. (2021). Punishing mothers for men's violence: Failure to protect legislation and the criminalisation of abused women. *Feminist Legal Studies, 29*(2), 181–204.

Stone, A. (2014). Psychoanalysis and maternal subjectivity. In P. Bueskens (Ed.), *Mothering and psychoanalysis* (pp. 325–342). Demeter Press.

Stromer, R. (n.d.). *The good and the terrible: Exploring the two faces of the great mother.* www.soulmyths.com/goodterrible.pdf

Swafford, A. (2017, May 3). *Mary: The new eve and our spiritual mother.* https://media. ascensionpress.com/2017/05/03/mary-new-eve-spiritual-mother/

Thurmond, G. J. (2007). Ecology and Mary: An ecological theology of Mary as the new Eve in response to the church's challenge for a faith-based education in ecological responsibility. *Catholic Education: A Journal of Inquiry and Practice, 11*(1), 27–51.

Tuhus-Dubrow, R. (2019, November). I wish I'd never been born: The rise of the anti-natalists. *The Guardian.* www.theguardian.com/world/2019/nov/14/anti-natalists-childfree-population-climate-change

U.S. Department of Labor. (2022). *Women's labor force participation rates by age of youngest child since 1975.* www.dol.gov/agencies/wb/data/mothers-families/Laborforce participationrates-women-ageyoungestchild

Vannier, S., Currie, A., & O'Sullivan, L. (2014). Schoolgirls and soccer moms: A content analysis of free "teen" and "MILF" online pornography. *Journal of Sex Research, 51*(3), 253–264.

Van Seters, J. (1998). The pentateuch. In S. L. McKenzie & M. P. Graham (Eds.), *The Hebrew bible today: An introduction to critical issues.* Westminster John Knox Press. ISBN 978-0-664-25652-4.

Walker, M. B. (1998). *Philosophy and the maternal body.* Routledge.

Welldon, E. (1988). *Mother, Madonna, whore: The idealization and denigration of motherhood.* Routledge.

Part II

Why She Does It

Chapter 7

Your Mother Wanted to Kill You

There was the time I told your cradle I was done
Locked you in the van then shopped at Walgreens
I didn't feed you vegetables
I let the car slide into the lake, watched you drown and blamed Medea
I held each of you one by one under the porcelain water.
Dozed as a man who wasn't your father broke your arm
I slapped your faces when your grades failed
When you were arrested I denied you were mine
I confess to being the mother of all bombs
Sometimes I disdained you
I confess I am not good
Sometimes the sound of the hawk
Chasing after the crow was the only thing I cared about
But I learned the word fontanel
Buried my face in the soft spot and oh the smell
The world of your skin the first morning after the night of your birth
Even the landscape of the heel of your day-old foot
The day gone to sleep and breast—your mouth opening
Then closing as if to tell me the story of what you saw—light
Glinting off a window and into your face—my
Large face like the ocean you would later swim in
Even as I love you and hold all of you
My children I'm the good mother the bad mother
The one who makes you
Then bombs your world to bits

"American Mother," by Pamela Hart, copyright © 2017 Sarabande Books.
Used by permission of Sarabande Books

(Hart, 2018, p. 54)

At times the Death Mother archetype is taken up by mothers who aren't infanticidal but are psychologically deadly for their children. Earlier I identified Medea, Kali, and La Llorona as carrying the energy of the Death Mother, but there are

DOI: 10.4324/9781003412809-10

endless variations on these dynamics. They come alive in films such as *Ordinary People* or *Mommy Dearest*; modern-day versions of the Death Mother archetype, aside from the infanticidal one, are often examples of the acting out of an unconscious complex. Enough conflict or stress can constellate a woman's personal mother complex such that unconscious affect (often fear and rage) and beliefs take over and interfere with her perceptions. She can become possessed by the Death Mother's archetypal energies arising from the core of the complex, which overwhelm her conscious will and cause her to act out in her relationships with her children, akin to the neurobiology in which a nervous system reacts to the triggering of complex trauma. The reaction bypasses the executive (decision-making) functions of her brain and interferes with her perceptions and conscious intentions, causing her to behave in ways that communicate the presence of the instinctual energies of the Death Mother. This chapter explores some of the ways the Death Mother expresses in mothers whose complex behavior has a psychologically deadly or defeating impact on their children: the Vampire (stage/helicopter/narcissist) mother, the dead (depressed/addicted) mother, the *puella aeterna* (little girl) mother, the Aphrodite (overly sexual) mother, the Munchausen by proxy mother, and the ambivalent mother.

Your Mother's Shadow

The experiences of motherhood are on a continuum; mothers can move through variations and experiences of motherhood, sometimes cycling through, sometimes staying fixed. If we look again at Neumann's schema of the Great Mother (see Figure 2.1), we see the lower shaded area as her shadow, and in this shadowy area we have many variations of destructive mothering: madness, dissolution, deprivation, dismemberment, devouring, fixating, and death. This shadow side of motherhood is the archetypal energy a mother may experience when feeling negatively or ambivalently toward her child. Jung identified the Whore of Babylon as an example of the Terrible Mother archetype (1952/1967, para. 315). The Bible's Book of Revelations depicts the Whore of Babylon as an image of spiritual ignorance, inhibiting a path of self-realization. Her full title, as was written on her forehead, is "Mystery, Babylon the Great, the Mother of Harlots and Abominations of the Earth" (Rev. 17:5). She is the "mother of all abominations" (Jung, 1952/1967, para. 313), the queen of corruption, the progenitor of end-time (apocalyptic) power that wars against God's people. She is Mother as creator and destroyer:

> For all the nations have drunk the maddening wine of her adulteries. The kings of the earth committed adultery with her, and the merchants of the earth grew rich from her excessive luxuries. Then I heard another voice from heaven say: "Come out of her, my people, so that you will not share in her sins, so that you will not receive any of her plagues."
>
> (Rev 18:2–4)

Figure 7.1 The Whore of Babylon. Watercolor by William Blake (1809). © The Trustees of the British Museum.

From the genesis of Lilith and Eve, sin and suffering are associated with the feminine, but when we arrive at Revelations, we have truly reached the drudges of mother's shadow in Babylon. As immaculate as the Virgin Mary is, the Whore of Babylon, the shadow mother, is in equal measure stained; she is a container for all of humankind's evil. The idea that, like Lilith, she is to be disavowed, left behind, and excommunicated to the unconscious was reinforced in the New Testament.

The experience of motherhood is an initiation, and as a woman enters motherhood she has unique access to layered experiences of mothering through time, including those relegated to the shadow, where we find the primordial and ancient autonomous energy of the infanticidal drive and other iterations of the Death Mother archetype. Her threatening power, along with infanticide, is embodied in the whore of Babylon and in the sorceress or medicine woman, all of whom are seen in Medea. As seen in Figure 7.2, Medea carries the energy of Blake's *Whore of Babylon*, a type of archetypal image mimicry found in art throughout the centuries.

Figure 7.2 Medea. Oil on wood by Frederick Sandys (1866–1868). Presented by the Trustees of the Public Picture Gallery Fund, 1925.

Not all women will be conscious of this drive; most will repress it. Unfortunately, left unconscious it possesses unmediated and affect-charged energy that will resurface in destructive ways. Women who experience destructive maternal sentiments in dreams, fantasies, or urges may be able to work with the images and feelings in mediums such as therapy, art, or journaling that allow their nondestructive expression. Some mothers have been able to vividly capture these emotions through writing, including poet Sylvia Plath, who experienced postpartum depression after the birth of her children. Death Mother feelings come alive in a lesser-known verse play for radio, broadcast on the BBC in 1962 and written from the perspective of three different women on a maternity ward. The first woman's voice:

There is no miracle more cruel than this . . . .
I am the centre of an atrocity.
What pains, what sorrows must I be mothering?
Can such innocence kill and kill? It milks my life.

(From "Three Women," from Winter Trees by Sylvia Plath. Copyright (c) 1962 by Ted Hughes. Used by permission of HarperCollins Publishers.)

Yet even for those who cannot access the feelings, every mother has a voice like this within her; it is as true as it is difficult to accept. Because mother-as-loving-martyr has been a consistent historical representation in the culture, to experience something different as a mother can be quite jarring, and yet it is inevitable that every mother, even the reader's mother, even this author, had urges to kill her infant. If we insist motherhood is natural and fulfilling, that a mother is meant to nurture, to self-sacrifice, that motherhood is the pinnacle of femininity—the ultimate goal and final purpose of womanhood—why is it that when women become mothers, they have a negative reaction? A debilitating depression? A murderous rage?

A woman who arrives at motherhood and finds she is not connected—finds that she does not like her baby, her husband, or herself—may dissolve in a desperate and silent sense of failing, a falling into an abyss, confused, frightened, ashamed. We want to believe becoming a mother will be an absolute joy when we as women get to play the role we were meant to play, as suggested by literature and film, media and capitalism, our parents, and even other mothers (talking about the pain of birth, their exhaustion, and their lack of support as the sacrifices that halo motherhood). Yet, having a child is a profound, frightening, and exhilarating experience at the boundary of life, from which one comes back a transformed person. Kristeva described motherhood as "the most intense form of contact with the strangeness of the one close to us and of ourselves" (2005/2010, p. 115).

Most women bear this monumental transition to motherhood with hardship. Experiences range from tearfulness, exasperation, and nervousness to more extreme feelings of obsessiveness, helplessness, and homicidal mania. After the birth of my daughter, I described my state of mind to my psychiatrist, who reflected to me what he heard as he took notes: "not suicidal, but homicidal." My friends and I were able to laugh every time I repeated his summation, bringing us all great relief to have a dramatic and bold enough word to contain our unspoken feelings toward having our bodies and lives completely taken over and rendered out of our control. Most mothers experience negative feelings and thoughts toward their children. A pediatric study of mothers in the general population found that 70% of mothers with colicky infants experienced explicit aggressive thoughts toward their infants, and over a quarter (26%) of them had infanticidal thoughts during colic episodes (Jennings et al., 1999).

[Mothers] are caught up in a conspiracy in which we are both the conspirators and the victims of the plot. In the face of all this "M is for the million things she [mother] gave me" mythology it becomes difficult to admit that occasionally you lock yourself in the bathroom just to be alone . . . when someone is depressed after having a baby, when everyone is telling her that it's the happiest damn time of her life, there's no space to admit what she's really feeling. So that when someone does something as horrifying . . . there is no room for even a little bit of understanding . . . the world says. How could anyone do that to her children?

(Quindlen, 2001, paras. 6–7)

You Better Run from Your Mother

Most women can at least imagine having the feeling of wanting to murder their children, if only momentarily. It is one of the ways a woman expands once initiated into motherhood: she has access to her own capacity for murder. Certainly, women who are not mothers have also experienced a murderous impulse or a fantasy of destruction, but there is a certain sweaty potency in a new mother's murder plot. I witnessed this for the first time at a psychology conference where for the duration of the lectures I sat, pregnant for the first time, next to a lovely mother who, although young, seemed more seasoned than me. We discussed birth and motherhood, and eventually she shared with me her experience following the birth of her first child.

This woman and her husband were living with her in-laws when she became pregnant. They all worked in the medical field and her in-laws were excited for the birth of their first grandchild. The mother-in-law tended toward being nosy and bossy. After the baby came home, disagreements began around the topic of the baby's care. Unfortunately, the new mother's husband almost always sided with his mother. As the tension in the house grew, this new mother began spending more time separate from the others. Sleep-deprived from waking in the middle of the night with the newborn, the intrusive nature of the house started to fray her nerves. She began spending days on end in her room, moving between the bed and the rocking chair with the baby. She also began writing in her journal to express some of her distress. Eventually, while feverishly rocking for days, she wrote out a detailed murder plan in her diary. Because the family worked in health care, she had access to medications that she fantasized could kill them in the right doses. She planned to murder her in-laws in the evening while her husband worked the night shift. When he returned, she would do the same to him.

In her reporting on the Andrea Yates infanticide case in 2001, journalist Anna Quindlen wrote, "Every mother I've asked about the Yates case has the same reaction. She's appalled; she's aghast. And then she gets this look. And the look says that at some forbidden level she understands" (2001, para. 2). Everyday experiences of mothers are layered in an exquisite design of mental, physical, and spiritual conquests. Mothers carry in their minds and bodies hidden yet pervasive guilt, shameful dread, pain, and exhaustion, most of which create a dark and heavy sensation. When repressed these feelings can manifest into any variation of the negative mother. Years ago, I read an essay by Lily Gurton-Wachter that helped me relax, knowing there are other mothers and writers capturing the existential crisis of motherhood. Gurton-Wachter wondered aloud,

How will having a baby disrupt my sense of who I am, of my body, my understanding of life and death, my relation to the world and to my sense of independence, my experience of fear and hope and time, and the structure of my experience altogether?

(2016, para. 7)

The entry into motherhood tends to literally be a life-or-death situation. Women are at more risk of experiencing new-onset severe mental illness in the early post-partum period than at any other time in their lives, and women with mental illness have an increased risk of obstetric complications and a higher mortality rate during the perinatal period (Howard & Khalifeh, 2020). One study found that almost a quarter of women who died between 6 weeks and one year postnatally died from psychiatric disorders (Knight et al., 2016). The number of mothers who died dur-ing or shortly after pregnancy rose to 1,205 in 2021 for a maternal mortality rate of 32.9 deaths per 100,000 live births, according to the National Center for Health Statistics (Hoyert, 2023). This marked a 40% increase from 861 maternal deaths in 2020 and 754 in 2019. The CDC lists the leading causes of pregnancy-related death as hemorrhaging, cardiovascular conditions, and infection or sepsis. When related directly to psychiatric implications, the deaths are due to suicide.

Maternal deaths among Black patients remain especially high compared to other groups, with a rate of 69.9 deaths per 100,000 live births, or 2.6 times that of non-Hispanic white patients. Maternal deaths overall are also much higher in the United States than in any other high-income country. For example, as reported by the Organisation for Economic Co-operation and Development, Australia, Austria, Israel, Japan, and Spain all hovered around 2 to 3 deaths per 100,000 births in 2020.

If a mother survives childbirth, she has gone through an initiation. As author and analyst Lisa Marchiano pointed out in *Motherhood: Facing and Finding Your-self*, one is separated from one's former reality, undergoes an ordeal, then returns to one's life with a new status: Mother. But in this initiation, the sorrow of every mother is the loss of self, or what French novelist Marguerite Duras called the "colossal swallowing up," a "mad love," and a "bursting of the ego" (As cited in Husserl-Kapit, 1975, p. 433)

This swallowing up echoes what a new mother, vacillating between dissocia-tion and depression, described to me as her inability to see herself in the family picture. This mom had twin baby girls with whom she was not bonding. She felt like a machine going through the mechanical motions of caretaking; she fantasized about her babies getting taken away; she fantasized about walking to a bus stop and not returning. After her first sessions in treatment with me, where she unburdened herself of the sadness and shame that she carried for not experiencing motherhood the "right way," she was able to start to locate herself. Her experience points to the invisibility some women feel as mothers. The baby is here, and the mother is gone.

He is the baby unchaotic
he is born and I am undone—feel as if I will
never be, was never born.
                        (Notley, 1998, p. 39)

Charlotte Perkins Gilman declared, "Such a dear baby! . . . And yet I *cannot* be with him, it makes me so nervous" (2016, p. 14). In her harrowing classic, Gilman was ostensibly writing of her own postpartum experience, as we read in her journal entries such as, "Every morning the same hopeless waking. Every day the same weary drag. To die mere cowardice. Retreat impossible, escape impossible. . . . he [her husband] cannot see how irrevocably bound I am, for life, for life." (1998, p. 91). Gilman wrote over 100 years ago about feeling imprisoned and isolated with a burgeoning sense of madness, an experience distinctly like what I hear in my therapy office today. Escape from this madness is impossible as the maternal monster is *within* the mother, going where she goes.

In "Stabat Mater," Kristeva accounted for the pain of a woman condemned as a mother to an eternal separation, an alienation without recovery, as when the Virgin Mary weeps at the feet of her crucified son: a part of flesh that once belonged to her within her womb is now dead. A part of the woman dies when she becomes a mother. It is a life reduced to nurturing and mourning—milk and tears. Kristeva referred to the dark underbelly of maternal bodily and psychical experience, that which is woven with tremendous suffering and is now a split experience of subjectivity:

> My body is no longer mine, it doubles up, suffers, bleeds, catches cold, puts its teeth in, slobbers, coughs, is covered with pimples, and it laughs. And yet, when its own joy, my child's, returns, its smile washes only my eyes. But the pain, its pain—it comes from inside, never remains apart, other, it inflames me at one, without a second's respite. As if that was what I had given birth to and, not willing to part from me, insisted on coming back, dwelled in me permanently. One does not give birth in pain, one gives birth to pain: the child represents it and henceforth it settles in, it is continuous. Obviously you may close your eyes, cover up your ears, teach courses, run errands, tidy up the house, think about objects, subjects. But a mother is always branded by pain, she yields to it. "And a sword will pierce your own soul too."
>
> (1983/1985, p. 241)

The overall effect of Kristeva's text is the unrelenting realization that the experience of motherhood is inextricable from pain and the grief of separation. Mothers "live on that border, crossroad beings, crucified beings . . . A mother is a continuous separation, a division of the very flesh. And consequently a division of language—and it has always been so" (254).

According to Western societal expectations, a mother's life is to be fulfilled once she surrenders herself to absolute selflessness, just like Mary did for Christ; in other words, she is expected to die for her offspring, either literally or figuratively, by giving up her own self. But, as humans do not live in such idealisms or absolutes, we must expect that the mother has another side to her: the inverse of masochism—sadism. Every nurturing mother also wants to deprive. Every mother who fully sacrifices themselves wants to absolutely destroy.

Mother Complexes

Complexes are organized around archetypes—that which is universal or instinctive in human nature and experience, but the emotions and beliefs they contain are based on our personal experiences of wounding. Jungian analyst Murray Stein explained how one's familial and cultural milieu can coalesce with archetypal elements to influence one's instinctual (automatic and unconscious) behavior:

> Complexes act like instincts in that they produce spontaneous reactions to particular situations or persons, but they are not purely innate in the same way that instincts are. Mostly they are products of experience—trauma, family interactions and patterns, cultural conditioning. These are combined with some innate elements, which Jung called archetypal images, to make up the total package of the complex. Complexes are what remain in the psyche after it has digested experience and reconstructed it into inner objects. In human beings, complexes function as the equivalent of instincts in other mammals . . . complexes are, in a manner of speaking, constructed-human instincts.
>
> (1998, p. 48)

The etiology of a complex tends to be a trauma or traumatized aspect of self that has been split off into the unconscious as too overwhelming to hold in consciousness. Jung described complexes as the "little people" who live within us, have varying degrees of autonomy, and are often resistant to assimilation. Laden with split-off energy, a complex can take over and interfere with perception and behavior; compensating for or defending against the complex and repeated trauma may become an intractable part of the persona, the socially acceptable self that one shows others. The persona hides aspects of oneself, including abilities, desires, and dreams that have been split-off into unconscious complexes as unacceptable, leading to a sense of an unlived life. This can be inherited from our parents and grandparents, who pass on to us their wounds related to their unlived lives and unsolved problems: A mother with a negative mother complex will tend to be a negative mother for her daughter, passing on the mother wound.

To be unconsciously enmeshed with a wounded and wounding negative mother "is to be outside of relationship with the polarities of mother and soul," unable to be in relationship "with matter's three attributes: nourishing goodness, orgiastic emotionality, and dark depths. We tend to find ourselves either taken over by them or we run madly away from them" (Rand, 2016, p. 34). When overtaken by a complex, one can experience a sense of power, although it may be a destructive power. For example, the "crushed hope of an unlived life" can express unconsciously in the impactful power of negative mothering on one's children (Woodman, as cited in Sieff, 2009, p. 191).

The essence of the negative mother complex is the Death Mother. In her patriarchal dismemberment from her place in the Life–Death–Life Mother, she can be seen as having become an archetypal embodiment of crushed hope and an unlived life. Turned out from the life she was meant to live, she turns against life and becomes destructive toward her children.

The Death Mother manifests in a wounded mother; a mother who, unable to face her own traumas and story and reintegrate disowned aspects of herself, has not been able to live an authentic life. Trapped in her crushed hope for her life, to survive without confronting her wound, she attempts to control the lives and souls of her own children with unconsciously wielded power and judgment, unknowingly forfeiting their livelihood for her own survival. Her message is, "If you love me, you will do as I say. Be who I want you to be. I know you better than you know yourself; I know what is best for you" (Woodman, 2005, p. 32). A mother can be possessed by the Death Mother archetype lying in wait at the core of her negative mother complex, and like all possessions, she is completely unconscious of it; her motivations (to parent obedient, successful children) are cannily disguised from everyone, even from herself. Jungian analyst Marion Woodman offered a close look at the harm to women out of which the Death Mother takes hold:

> Death Mother is born out of despair. It is incubated by the crushed hope of an unlived life . . . . When you look into the eyes of Death Mother you see that they are glazed over with hopelessness . . . . You see an unconscious, frozen, and profoundly wounded body-psyche devoid of authentic feeling. You see somebody with a desperate need to be in control. You see somebody who is driven by will-power. A person who acts out the Death Mother archetype will have had to split off much that was vibrant, creative, and unique in herself. In fact, the adults who carry the most ferocious manifestation of Death Mother may have been the most creative of children. Tragically, their intense imaginations collided with the rational, rigid world of their parents and teachers who demanded they "be good", where "being good" meant, "Swallow your anger, initiative, and creativity and reflect me, rather than expose all that I have had to push into the shadow."
>
> (As cited in Sieff, 2009, p. 191)

Negative Mother complexes were first introduced to me by Jungian analyst Patricia Vesey-McGrew in her talk "Passion, Obsession, Depression: Exploring Dynamic Images of the Dark Mother." Her insights expanded my understanding of maternal possibilities and mother complexes to include the disappearing mother and the vampire mother. I have expanded upon these as I continue to witness, observe, and research them in practice.

The *disappearing mother* is constellated when something happens to the actual mother, and she fades away physically or psychologically. She may have an illness, possibly depression or migraines; she leaves for her room, but she is also gone emotionally. The more extreme experience of this complex is the *dead mother*: she is chronically depressed, unavailable, numb. A dead mother was once alive, attentive, attuned then suddenly something manifests; her libido is withdrawn from the baby; she becomes a distant inanimate figure. A dead mother may also be an addict; she is generally negligent and unable to meet a child's needs. Lack of maternal presence and care leaves the child thrown back on her own resources to care for herself and her mother (and often other family members) (Green, 2005). Thus, the mother inadvertently steals her child's childhood and the self-discovery it might have held. She passes on to her child her wound of an unlived life.

The *vampire mother* is a mother who survives by feeding off her child. In her talk, Vesey-McGrew described this mother as attuned to something she has projected onto the child rather than the real child. The vampire mother continues to go after the child, insisting on a response that reflects her projection and in turn overstimulating the child. A vampire mother is not nurturing but draining. Vampire mothers include stage moms (pressuring and competitively showcasing the children), helicopter moms (hovering over and depriving their children of independence), and tiger moms (aggressively protecting and promoting their child). In their intrusiveness, they ask their child to compensate for their unlived life, thus crushing the child's hope for their own life.

The *devouring mother*, a complex described well by Woodman, is an abusive mother. She may be a narcissist such that she treats her children as objects that reflect on her, substantiating her sense of self, or she may have borderline personality disorder with a pattern of unstable relationships and difficulty managing her behavior and emotions. She may prefer one of her children over the others, a preference that can change. She may use excessive punishment. She can be both obsessive with her children and perceive her child as a threat to her independence, her marriage, or her success. The devouring mother's narcissistic rage is continually present in the background, about to erupt with the slightest provocation, including any sign of rejection. She is also attuned to her husband's abandonment/rejection of her and at times may try to possess or destroy him. She splits the husband from the children and the children from each other, locating herself as a deadly black widow at the center of the family web. Faye Dunaway's portrayal of Joan Crawford in the 1981 movie *Mommie Dearest* is an image that captures the devouring mother. She exhibits many of the characteristics of borderline personality disorder. A larger-than-life self-projection compensates for her deep insecurity; she sees her daughter as a threat and an object to control. She regularly tears into her daughter with a fierceness meant to devour her. Lacking the ability to feel safely secure in her world and perceiving her children's selves and lives as a threat to her own, the devouring mother consumes her children's self-confidence and ability to live their own life.

The *martyr mother* compulsively sacrifices herself for the child. Not attending to her own needs, she is hollow but caretaking; she is also codependent and potentially enables an addict father. Revering Mother Mary, the original sacrificial mother, the martyr mother gains a great sense of piousness and power through an identity of selflessness. She victimizes herself—"no, you take that last bowl of soup, I'll go hungry"—and burdens her children with guilt and a confused sense of entitlement.

The *vain mother*, or a mother with an *Aphrodite complex*, prioritizes her beauty over the needs of the child. This mother may have an eating disorder or body image disorder. She attempts to control her size, appearance, and existence in compliance with the male gaze, all of which thwarts her maternal instincts. She may be overly sexual, she may have affairs, she may have trouble with female friendships. She may also press the same values on her daughter, monitoring her diet and criticizing her appearance and behavior. Alternatively, her obsession with attracting love and attention can turn her vicious toward a daughter who she may perceive as a threat (i.e., "Snow White and the Evil Queen"). Sometimes a daughter will work to appear grotesque in order not to compete with her mother; will attempt to individuate a vain mother by becoming neglectful of her own appearance; or will become obsessed with and ashamed of her appearance to please or be like her mother. Such a mother's preoccupation with external beauty standards and male attention will intrude on her daughter's ability to develop a healthy sense of self in relation to her own body.

A *Munchausen mother* physically sacrifices her child for her own needs, whether they be caretaking, attention, sympathy, financial gain, and/or notoriety. These mothers use their child to create a sense of self as both savior and victim. Dee Blanchard, mother of Gypsy Rose, was a celebrity-status mother who appeared to be caught in this complex, exhibiting an enmeshed relationship with her child who she persistently identified as ill and requiring extensive unnecessary medical attention (Ketter, 2021). In 2015, Gypsy rebelled and got her boyfriend to kill her mother. A hallmark feature of this complex is that the need to medically sacrifice the child does not end after one illness is "cured." The child will continue to perform illnesses (consciously or unconsciously), or the mother will fabricate or initiate a new one. The medical abuse of one's child has been shown to arise in mothers who were not adequately cared for as children (Faedda et al., 2018), having a history of neglect or abuse or the loss of a parent during childhood. In fabricating their child's illness to gain, they compensate for their own loss through the theft of their child's health and ability to live their own life.

Mama Bear is the overly protective, anxious, hypervigilant, controlling mother who likely has unresolved trauma and PTSD, with her unconscious fear of being retraumatized projected onto her child as constantly in danger. She is a mother who never let anyone else hold her baby, she never hired a babysitter, her child has a few closely vetted friends and a curfew. This mother's fear of the dangers in the world borders on paranoia, and her child is the vulnerable object to be protected. Mama bear, like the Munchausen mother, never wants to relinquish her children, instead keeping them infantile forever.

The *puella aeterna mother* never grew up; she dresses in young clothing and does not initiate her child into adult life. She attempts to maintain a childlike world, she enjoys Disney movies, she bakes or knits, or has collections of objects, such as dolls. A young girl-like mother is often dependent on the child and will ultimately turn to the child for guidance. This mother may also align as a friend or best friend with her daughter, usually remaining at an adolescent stage even as the daughter becomes an adult.

Finally, the *ambivalent mother* experiences exaggerated mixed feelings about a child, vacillating between active love and active hate, resulting in inconsistent responses toward a child's needs. A "good mother" may suddenly think, "what do my . . . children expect of me? . . . Go away. There's nothing left" (118). In her feeling of being trapped, of being torn asunder from herself and her own life, her negative mother complex constellated, she may find herself possessed by the Death Mother, unconsciously trying to preserve, rescue, or sustain herself. "Spoken or unspoken," a mother's grief and rage about her own trauma, unlived life, and sacrifices "weigh heavily on the child," forming in the child's psyche a negative mother complex at the core of which lurks the Death Mother (Woodman, 1985, p. 118).

Ambivalence, the Too Good Mother, and the Bad Child

Ambivalence may be where most mothers are located, in the place of equal parts loving and hating their child(ren). As Jacqueline Rose put it, "Giving it with one hand and taking it back with the other" (2014, para. 25). Ambivalence is such a powerful maternal experience that it has been given its own attachment style. In the 1950s, John Bowlby, a British psychologist, in became interested in children's behavior as it relates to the bonds with their parents. He found that the style and consistency of care with which a mother responded to her young child created either a secure or insecure attachment for the child. Bowlby further identified insecure attachment as either ambivalent or anxious and as disturbing to children's development (1968). Whereas Bowlby was focused on children's behavior, his colleague Mary Ainsworth became more interested in the dyad of the child and the mother. In her "Strange Situation" experiment, Ainsworth observed mothers (no fathers) responding to their children after a brief separation in which a stranger is introduced to the child to assess how securely attached the child is to the mother and thus able to be comforted and return to play (Ainsworth & Bell, 1970). Ainsworth found that 20% of the mother–child dyads exhibited *insecure ambivalent* attachment, in which the children cling to their mothers in a new situation, are extremely distressed when left alone by their mother, and fear strangers. When the mother returns and the child goes to her for comfort, the child cannot be comforted and may show signs of anger toward the mother. Most attachment theorists like Bowlby and Ainsworth tend to focus on the effects these styles have on children (Ainsworth et al., 1978), but who are these ambivalent mothers and what are they up to?

Lowinsky argued that ambivalence is at the very center of motherhood because mothers have what she calls an *ambivalent soul* (2009, p. 68). This ambivalence arises from the child existing as part of the mother. The child begins within her, inseparable from her; requiring "the sacrifice of physical and emotional boundaries . . . she suffers the loss of her body's integrity and her personal identity" (68). Even after delivery mother and child share genetics, cells, fluids, and psychic space; the mother's being split between herself and feeling in her soul the imperative of the child's behavior, personality, and relationships. "Throughout life the boundaries between mother and child are not clearly defined" and ambivalence sets in as from "the moment of conception a mother faces this two-edged threat: that she will be destroyed by having a child; that she will destroy her child" (68).

Psychiatrist and psychoanalyst Barbara Almond related her experience in pediatrics and doctoral research on first-time mothers, stating that "maternal ambivalence," loving and not loving one's child, "is a normal phenomenon. It is ubiquitous. It is not a crime or a failing" (2010, p. 1). In her treatment of mothers, Almond recognized their difficulty in expressing their maternal ambivalence. Almond explained that although it is within the realm of normal to hate one's neighbor, friend, sibling, or even parents, to hate one's child is seen as immoral, evil, and monstrous, thus making it imperative that woman repress or deny this information about herself. Almond's astute theory is that the denied ambivalence sometimes manifests as a compensatory Too-Good Mother.

Part of the unconscious self-expectation of the too-good mother is that she has no ambivalence. Since this is impossible, her ambivalence takes very subtle forms, often masquerading as a deep concern to do the best she can for her child, to do motherhood in the absolutely right way. In a culture such as ours that has such limited tolerance for the negative side of maternal ambivalence, there are bound to be many women struggling to be perfect. The harm they can do to themselves and to their children is hidden and pervasive (Almond, 2010, p. 38).

Almond gave a plethora of clinical examples with evidence of variations on ambivalence, finding that most often women internalize a feeling that they are pathological. The more extreme forms of ambivalence are characterized by the mother's projection of "badness" onto the child or the child's taking on a monstrous or negative identity. I have seen mothers such as these pathologizing their children, evident in the mother's constant flippant comments of how awful the brat is or her picking on a child's appearance or personality. Her child may express the projected badness in behaviors such as obsessive hand-washing or the obsessive cleaning of her vagina after urinating. Almond identified infanticide as the most extreme form of maternal ambivalence, in which mothers chose to

> return their children to a womb, albeit a cold and deadly one. In their deranged and deadened states of mind, they could not care for the children but did not want to let them go, so they symbolically reclaimed them.
>
> (2010, p. 186)

Welldon would refer to this as a *maternal perversion*: "A desire to engulf, to dehumanize, to invade, take control of and merge with children" (1988, p. 37). There perhaps is a need to take back the projected badness, to resolve the ambivalence of a split self and the two-edged danger of loss of self or child.

Hate, one angle of ambivalence, was articulated by psychoanalyst Donald Winnicott in 1949. Having worked with children, then mothers and children, for decades, Winnicott was adamant that the mother "hates her infant from the word go" and must be allowed to feel that hate, especially when she is hurt by the child or even because she "mustn't eat him or trade in sex with him" (1994, p. 355). Winnicott famously listed 18 reasons a mother may hate her child. The mother, like the analyst, must know she is feeling the hate and stay with it if the infant (or patient, in the case of the analyst) is to have any chance whatsoever of experiencing true affect or feeling in himself. Jacqueline Rose made a sound interpretation of Winnicott ideas about hate:

> He is talking about a form of hatred which, against all her better "instincts", as one might say, the mother needs to know she is feeling, and to stay with, if the

infant is to have any chance of experiencing, other than by means of a violent ejection, true affect in her or himself. The alternative is masochism. Winnicott is therefore making a political point: "If, for fear of what she may do, she cannot hate appropriately when hurt by her child she must fall back on masochism, and I think it is this that gives rise to the false theory of a natural masochism in women." The baby, he writes, "needs hate to hate". Sentimentality, he concludes, "is useless for parents."

(2014, para. 26)

Adrienne Rich bravely described her own ambivalence, her own maternal vacillations, quoting her journal from when her children were young:

My children cause me the most exquisite suffering of which I have any experience. It is the suffering of ambivalence: the murderous alternation between bitter resentment and raw-edged nerves, and blissful gratification and tenderness. Sometimes I seem to myself, in my feelings toward these tiny guiltless beings, a monster of selfishness and intolerance. Their voices wear away at my nerves, their constant needs, above all their need for simplicity and patience, fill me with despair at my own failures, despair too at my fate, which is to serve a function for which I was not fitted. . . . And yet at other times I am melted with the sense of their helpless, charming and quite irresistible beauty—their ability to go on loving and trusting—their staunchness and decency and unselfconsciousness. I love them. But it's in the enormity and inevitability of this love that the sufferings lie.

(1976, p. 1)

Of course, hate is a part of love; that is the tension and paradox that Winnicott, Rose, and Rich are suggesting needs containment. Ideally, the mother finds a way of sublimating her hate, singing the infanticidal song "Rockabye Baby." She gently rocks her child to sleep while allowing fantasies, conscious or unconscious, of the wind blowing, the bough breaking, to hold the perverse maternal aggression she has stored in her mind and body.[1]

Psychoanalyst Rozsika Parker described the ambivalence mothers face as having to navigate between "the Scylla of intrusiveness and the Charybdis of neglect," referring to Homer's hazardous sea monsters, between which sailors safely passed by avoiding the greater of two evils (2005, p. 140). Parker likened this to the task of mothers who must walk the fine line between intrusiveness and neglect, or extreme solicitude and finitude. Parker considered the impact of maternal ambivalence on the mother's capacity to mother, as the ambivalence can provoke increased consciousness. In this way, maternal ambivalence may contribute to the growth of a mother, bringing awareness to what is going on between her and baby. "It is the unruly, unacceptable nature of hatred that breeds thought and concern; the aggressive fantasies, the violent impulses bring women face to face with themselves—and with their children. Some can bear it. Some find it unbearable" (169). Parker encouraged mothers to accept their own ambivalence in order to build resilience. Some mothers may find relief in identifying their hate as toward the role of mother rather than toward the child. Even though we may dread the relentless dinners, the laundry, the whining, and the persistent demands, our actual raw love for the child is intact.

In a society that does not tolerate a mother's ambivalence toward motherhood, shame is used to condemn her. Moreover, when a mother's ambivalence toward a child is not acknowledged, it can turn to shame.

> Maternal shame leaves women isolated in an emotional wasteland. Terrified to expose their supposedly inhuman inadequacy to both themselves and others, mothers strive to deny and dissociate their feelings, thus becoming alienated from themselves (and, of course, from their children). In this place, there can be no transformation or healing.
>
> (Sieff, 2019, p. 29)

A mother's internalized shame at her ambivalence becomes self-hatred or self-disavowal and may get acted out against the child. It is as if the self that has been buried in the shame erupts from the unconscious in a rage to be rid of the source of shame—the child. Her inner dialogue, conscious or unconscious, is *I'm getting it all wrong, I am bad, I am useless. See how bad I am?* And she hurls her child down the stairs.

Maternal Instinct

Could we explain these negative maternal behaviors and complexes by a lack of maternal instinct? Does a lack of maternal instinct explain a "bad mother"? An instinct is a "stereotyped, apparently unlearned, genetically determined behaviour pattern" (Beer, n.d., para. 1). The concept of a maternal instinct entails automatic protectiveness, cherishment, and devotion, and a specific type of love that only a mother can have for her child. There is much study in the field of sociology and psychology that demystifies the existence of an innate maternal instinct. Its existence has been investigated by neuroscience and some feminists have been working to dismiss it since its introduction. Studying an instinct is complicated, as instincts per se are inherently unconscious and unquantifiable, and thus suffer the risk of being reduced to a single variable when a maternal instinct, if there is such a thing, is likely a vast primordial force.

The book *Mother Brain*, by journalist Chelsea Conaboy, has been lauded by feminists and psychologists for its ability to separate women from motherhood, to make room for negative maternal experiences, and to offer maternal instincts to non-biological mothers. Conaboy included research on the parental brain that contests "the notion that care is distinctly female. It is not" (2022, p. 251). And she made a good point:

> The notion that the selflessness and tenderness babies require is uniquely ingrained in the *biology* of women, and only women, is a relatively modern

[and pernicious] one. It was constructed over decades by men selling an image of what a mother should be, diverting our attention from what she actually is and calling it science.

(26)

Denying an innate maternal instinct explains women not wanting to have children, freeing them from the accusation of just being bad unloving women. The lack of a maternal instinct specific to women also supports the argument for equalizing parenting between the sexes. If women do not have a maternal instinct, or maternal instincts are found across genders, there is no reason that a mother is better at parenting or should be expected to do more of the parenting work.

Conaboy was not the first to come to this conclusion. "Maternal love is not a given but a gift," contended French feminist Elisabeth Badinter:

it is a human feeling, and like any feeling, it is uncertain, fragile and imperfect. Contrary to many assumptions, it is not a deeply rooted given in women's natures. When we observe the historical changes in maternal behavior, we notice that interest in and devotion to the child are sometimes in evidence, sometimes not.

(1981, p. 26)

Badinter critiqued a culture that is overly focused on the child and fought for the recognition that mothers have desires outside of motherhood. Badinter rightly problematized the word *natural* when it comes to mothers—natural breastfeeding, natural sleep styles, natural attachment, natural birth—all of which are setups for mother to fail at not being natural, aka *good*. Badinter critiqued Sarah Hrdy and John Bowlby for driving an ideological conviction that females across species possess an innate maternal instinct and that the mother's attachment style is of primary importance to their children.

The claim that the lack of an inherent maternal instinct explains maternal violence is inaccurate at best, cruel at worst. Of the mothers I have interviewed, charged with abuse, neglect, and/or violent crimes toward their children, there were none that were without a maternal instinct—an automatic, seemingly unlearned, impulse to care for their child. In fact, it was often the activation of their maternal instinct that ignited the violence.

In my evaluations I have traced the defendant's violent act to an overreaction of her maternal instinct as it confronts unconscious ambivalence and shame, oppression, postpartum depression/psychosis, or the Death Mother at the core of a negative mother complex. If instinct is a pattern of behavior in animals in response to certain stimuli, maternal instinct consists of innate behaviors from a mother toward a child. These impulses may not all qualify as what an outsider or our sociocultural norms would judge as good. To correlate maternal abuse with a lack of maternal instinct reinforces the binary in which the maternal instinct equals good mother, and bad mother equals no maternal instinct. To say there is no maternal instinct cruelly strips a woman of her innate ability to mother—whether she chooses to do so or not, or whether she is a good enough mother (who may at times be infanticidal), or a mother who was good until she snapped and killed her children. Both positions obfuscate the instinct of the full range of motherhood (the Great Mother), denying the role of the Death Mother in a woman's maternal life as she navigates the ambivalent terrain between self and child.

From a Jungian perspective, archetypes are psychological images of instincts and contain constructive and destructive poles as seen in the polarity of birth and death held within the activity of the Great Mother across time and cultures until her dismemberment in Western patriarchy. These images, emerging in myth and iconography from the depths of the human psyche, suggest that a woman's maternal instinct has both a positive life-giving and negative death-dealing pole.

Importantly, placing the burden of mothering on a maternal instinct without reference to the Death Mother as an instinctual reaction to intolerable circumstances internalizes the problem to mothers, excusing society of culpability. If the problem is solely a lack of maternal instinct, there is no need to hear mothers' voices or to address the systemic forces and cultural attitudes that drop sticks of dynamite into a mother's lap, prepping the deadly side of her maternal instinct to blow. From my experience with hundreds of mothers, I have been unable to refute an innate maternal instinct, available and alive for all women.

Western medicine has long been complicit in denying or overriding women's maternal instincts. There are many examples of this, but a foundational one is during labor and delivery. In a shift to medicated deliveries, modern medicine has assumed a magical or godlike mastery, usurping a mother's instinct and voice. The medical model has replaced women's traditional medicine, from a dim red tent with hushed female supportive voices and a birthing stool to a sterile overstimulating hospital environment, directives and tools, then separation of mother and baby. It is not the mother who delivers the baby, but the doctor. A colleague of mine who studies the anthropology of birth suggests the hospital acts as a Death Mother institution where mothers are disenfranchised of their birth process; where they expect to be listened to and cared for but are at worst abused and at best ignored or neglected.

Certainly, an insistence on maternal instinct as entrapping a woman in a primary parent role is damaging for the entire family. Maternal instinct as deterministic of a constructed and gendered role is overused by a patriarchal ideology, and perhaps diminishes women's potential power in other spheres than the home, discounting the possibility of other instincts, talents, and desires she may possess. But it is important not to conflate maternal instinct with deterministic value. It is possible to have both: women valued outside of motherhood and a ubiquitous maternal instinct. We do not need to strip a woman of one of her essential potencies. Discounting a maternal instinct is pulling out the wrong roots, throwing the baby out with the bathwater.

Giving up one's previous identity, body, and life in a physical and psychical oneness with the fetus is an experience unique to the pregnant woman. The gestational, birth, and postpartum process has distinct lifelong implications for her instinctive relationship with her child, creating, as we have seen, both a sense of having two souls and the ambivalence of two dangers (Lowinsky, 2009). Although it is important to credit fathers with the instinctive capacity to provide nurturing love and caregiving activities, it is also important to acknowledge that mothers cope with an inherently bipolar maternal instinct in a society that tells them it is unipolar, all and endlessly loving, giving, and nurturing. For a father, or a male, to lay claim to a maternal-like instinct is rare, and society tells him his role is to love his children *without* sacrificing his other interests, pursuits, or identity.

The conversation regarding a maternal instinct fails to recognize that we are talking about two things that have been fused by patriarchy: women have a maternal instinct *and* there are constructions of motherhood that women are expected to perform. A woman's maternal instinct neither frees her nor saves her from being socially shamed, nor will its presence save children from further destruction. Holding onto an innate maternal instinct, among the plethora of all other instincts, emboldens an essential power saved for women alone. The patriarchal constructions of motherhood dismember the archetypal (psychological) birth–death bipolarity of the maternal instinct, crippling mothers' ability to integrate and consciously mediate the range of affective energies coursing through their maternal bodies. The expected performance of Virgin Mary is used by Western institutions to support male supremacy by glorifying this disempowerment of women and the maternal instinct/Great Mother archetype. But the solution to maternal infanticide is not to separate women from the fullness of their instincts or to shame them for not exhibiting the patriarchal fantasy of what a maternal instinct looks like.

Her maternal instinct is one thing a woman has that she does not have to purchase. Not all women can or want to conceive or adopt a child or access their maternal instinct, but it is available as the primordial energy of the archetypal Life–Death–Life Mother, inherent in the psyche of every woman. The Great Mother's bipolar nature is present in a woman's reproductive cycle, in which the potential for life is created and then bled away. The maternal instinct is a variation of the energies of the Great Mother, including those of the Death Mother, a dynamic that lives in potential in all women when initiated into motherhood. When a woman's self-image is tied to patriarchal ideals that devalue motherhood and objectify her, she can "lose a biological, creative image of herself" (Rand, 2016, p. 45). She can cease to value, trust, and advocate for her own experience and what she knows, including the ambivalence and presence of the Death Mother in her maternal instincts. "Her self-image, at a psychic level, must come to include grounded images of her own biological creativity, knowing that behind her stands the Great Mother who continually births the entire world" (45). If a mother has the support—the inner and outer resources—and opportunities to relate and engage fully with her own maternal psychology as it arises in her instincts, her lineage of mothers, and her mother complex, she can break the chains that bind her without killing her child or herself.

Note

1 This familiar nursery rhyme was written by an English colonist who observed the way American Indian women placed their babies in birch bark cradles suspended from the branches of trees, allowing the wind to rock the baby to sleep (Carpenter & Prichard, 1984).

References

Ainsworth, M. D., & Bell, S. M. (1970). Attachment, exploration, and separation: Illustrated by the behavior of one-year-olds in a strange situation. *Child Development, 41*(1), 49–67.

Ainsworth, M. D., Blehar, N. C., Walters, E., & Wall, S. (1978). *Patterns of attachment: A psychological study of the strange situation*. Erlbaum.

Almond, B. (2010). *The monster within: The hidden side of motherhood*. University of California Press.

Badinter, E. (1981). *Mother love: Myth and reality*. Macmillan.

Beer, C. (n.d.). Instinct: Behaviour. In *Britannica: Science and tech*. Retrieved August 7, 2023, from www.britannica.com/topic/instinct

Bowlby, J. (1968). *Attachment and loss. Vol. 1: Attachment*. Basic Books.

Carpenter, H., & Prichard, M. (1984). *The Oxford companion to children's literature*. Oxford University Press.

Conaboy, C. (2022). *Mother brain: How neuroscience is rewriting the story of parenthood*. Henry Holt.

Faedda, N., Baglioni, V., Natalucci, G., Ardizzone, I., Camuffo, M., Cerutti, R., &Guidetti, V. (2018). Don't judge a book by its cover: Factitious disorder imposed on children—report on 2 cases. *Frontiers in Pediatrics, 6*. www.ncbi.nlm.nih.gov/pmc/articles/PMC5915702/

Gilman, C. P. (1998). *The abridged diaries of Charlotte Perkins Gilman* (D. Knight, Ed.). University of Virginia Press.

Gilman, C. P. (2016). *The yellow wallpaper*. Wisehouse Classics.

Green, A. (2005). *The dead mother*. Routledge.

Gurton-Wachter, L. (2016, July 29). The stranger guest: The literature of pregnancy and motherhood. *Los Angeles Review of Books*. https://lareviewofbooks.org/article/stranger-guest-literature-pregnancy-new-motherhood/

Hart, P. (2018). *Mothers over Nangarhar*. Sarabande Books.

Howard, L. M., & Khalifeh, H. (2020). Perinatal mental health: A review of progress and challenges. *World Psychiatry, 19*(3), 313–327.

Hoyert, D. (2023). *Maternal mortality rates in the United States, 2021*. www.cdc.gov/nchs/data/hestat/maternal-mortality/2021/maternal-mortality-rates-2021.htm#:~:text=The%20maternal%20mortality%20rate%20for%202021%20was%2032.9,23.8%20in%202020%20and%2020.1%20in%202019%20%28Table%29

Husserl-Kapit, S. (1975). An interview with Marguerite Duras. *Signs, 1*(2), 423–434.

Jennings, K. D., Ross, S., Popper, S., & Elmore, M. (1999). Thoughts of harming infants in depressed and nondepressed mothers. *Journal of Affective Disorders, 54*(1–2), 21–28.

Jung, C. G. (1967). *The collected works of C. G. Jung: Vol. 5. Symbols of transformation* (H. Read, M. Fordham, & G. Adler, Eds., R. F. C. Hull, Trans.). Princeton University Press. (Original work published 1952). https://doi.org/10.1515/9781400850945

Ketter, S. (2021, June 3). *The story of Gypsy Rose Blanchard and her mother*. www.biography.com/crime/gypsy-rose-blanchard-mother-dee-dee-murder

Knight, M., Tuffnell, D., Kenyon, S., Shakespeare, J., Brocklehurst, P., & Kurinczuk, J. (2016). *Saving lives, improving mothers' care—surveillance of maternal deaths in the UK 2012–14 and lessons learned to inform maternity care from the UK and Ireland confidential enquiries into maternal deaths and morbidity 2009–14*. www.npeu.ox.ac.uk/mbrrace-uk/presentations/saving-lives-improving-mothers-care

Kristeva, J. (1985). Stabat mater (A. Goldhammer, Trans.). *Poetics Today*, 6(1–2), 133–152. (Original work published 1983)

Kristeva, J. (2010). *Hatred and forgiveness* (J. Herman, Trans.). Columbia University Press. (Original work published 2005)

Lowinsky, N. (2009). *The motherline: Every woman's journey to find her female roots.* Fisher King Press.

Marchiano, L. (2021). *Motherhood: Facing and finding yourself.* Sounds True.

Notley, A. (1998). A baby is born out of a white owl's forehead. In A. Notley (Ed.), *Mysteries of small houses: Poems* (pp. 38–39). Penguin Books.

Parker, R. (2005). *Torn in two: The experience of maternal ambivalence (New)*. Virago.

Plath, S. (1962). *Three women: A Poem for three voices* (T. Hughes, Ed.). Harper & Row.

Quindlen, A. (2001, July 1). Playing God on no sleep. *Newsweek*. www.newsweek.com/playing-god-no-sleep-154643

Rand, E. (2016). *Recovering feminine spirituality: The mysteries and the mass as symbols of individuation*. CreateSpace.

Rich, A. (1976). *Of woman born: Motherhood as experience and institution*. W. W. Norton.

Rose, J. (2014). Mother. *London Review of Books*, 36(12). www.lrb.co.uk/the-paper/v36/n12/jacqueline-rose/mothers

Sieff, D. F. (2009). Confronting death mother: An interview with Marion Woodman. *Spring*, 81, 177–199.

Sieff, D. F. (2019). The death mother as nature's shadow: Infanticide, abandonment, and the collective unconscious. *Psychological Perspectives*, 62(1), 15–34.

Stein, M. (1998). *Jung's map of the soul: An introduction*. Open Court.

Vesey-McGrew, P. (2014). *Passion, obsession, depression: Exploring dynamic images of the dark mother*. Lecture given at the C. G. Jung Institute, Chicago. https://jungchicago.org/blog/product/vesey-mcgrew-dark-mother-3gp/

Welldon, E. (1988). *Mother, Madonna, whore: The idealization and denigration of motherhood*. Routledge.

Winnicott, D. (1994). Hate in the countertransference. *Journal of Psychotherapy Practice and Research*, 3(4), 348–356.

Woodman, M. (1985). *The pregnant virgin: A process of psychological transformation*. Inner City Books.

Woodman, M. (2005). The eye that cannot see. *Spring*, 72, 31–42.

Chapter 8

Abandonment, Adoption, and Abortion

Infanticide is a rare outcome of an unplanned pregnancy. Significantly more prevalent, the Death Mother archetype is activated in potentially less-harmful ways via abandonment, adoption, or abortion. These alternatives can be considered sublimations of the Death Mother coursing through our society. Sublimations convert instinct (i.e., a mother's to end her child's life) into more socially acceptable forms (e.g., adoption agencies, Safe Haven laws, and abortion clinics). These practices, enactments of maternal finitude, may prevent the birth of an unplanned or impoverished child or provide a potentially safer life for a child, but they all devastate the mother–child line. Each woman who *voluntarily*[1] aborts or gives up her child is accessing—in her context, emotions, and motivations (however altruistic)—the Death Mother, an archetypal energy surfacing in times of unsentimental maternal subjectivity.

Currently in the U.S., it is estimated that annually there are around 20,000 private domestic adoptions in which a woman decides during or immediately after her pregnancy to terminate her parental rights and place that child for adoption. Legal child abandonment through Safe Haven laws is significantly rarer: 4,505 infants were surrendered nationwide between 1999 to 2021 (National Safe Haven Alliance Impact Report, 2021–2022). Abortion, with about 900,000 per year, has always been much more prevalent, even before Roe v. Wade granted constitutional protection for abortion (Sisson, as cited in Kelly et al., 2021). In comparison, in 2021 there were 31 neonaticides, with babies found in backpacks or discarded in dangerous locations. The total number of U.S. cases of maternal infanticide has remained relatively stable at around 250 per year.

Abandonment

Abandonment has historically been one of the most common actions of a mother who cannot care for her newborn, arising from an archetypal instinct toward survival and the preservation of what is most viable. Hrdy noted that most mothers did not, nor do they, have the luxury of loving every child they have. "There is no doubt that socially produced scarcity, unpredictable resources, Roman Catholic attitudes toward birth control, unreliable fathers and chronic feelings of

DOI: 10.4324/9781003412809-11

powerlessness—definitely political in origin—are implicated in the abandonment of infants" (1992, p. 11). Resources, safety, and timing are crucial: Human and other primate mothers may abandon a child when the circumstances for rearing them do not seem right, yet the same mother can lovingly and devotedly care for another child born in more propitious times. Younger mothers in bad circumstances are more likely than older mothers to abandon offspring, feeling confident that they will have other chances.

Abandonment of newborn babies was widespread throughout much of Western Europe over the past two millennia. In Middle Ages Rome, mothers could abandon their babies in a foundling wheel—a revolving wooden barrel lodged in a wall, often in a convent, that allowed women to deposit their offspring in secret. Eventually foundling homes were created, as much to save babies' souls through baptism as to save their lives. It's likely the mothers hoped and assumed these homes would place their babies with wealthier families, but it's estimated that most of the children died due to the horrid accommodations, circulating diseases, and poor care. Later critics referred to foundling homes as slaughterhouses, tombs, and legal infanticide (Kertzer & White, 1994). During this time, "for many Europeans . . . abandonment and infanticide were indistinguishable and interchangeable" (Kilday, 2013, p. 89).

In the 1980s, anthropologist Nancy Scheper-Hughes studied the culture of mothers in a region of northeast Brazil where disease, dire economic conditions, and high rates of infant mortality are prevalent. She noted that the mothers would distance themselves from babies who were unlikely to survive, allowing them to die from eventual malnourishment or illness. Some mothers believed that if their infants were born sickly, pale, or thin, their impending death was part of God's plan and purposefully neglecting the infant helped to facilitate this plan. These mothers lived in extreme poverty, were unable to bring their children to work with them, couldn't afford childcare, and had very limited access to healthcare. When mothers did bring their child to the local healthcare center, doctors prescribed sleeping pills and pain suppressants to stop the infant from crying, silencing the starving infant until it quietly died. Scheper-Hughes described a mother giving birth in one room, while one of her infants died of malnutrition in an adjoining room.

The child would be unceremoniously buried by other neighborhood children in an unmarked, unvisited grave. Women generally endured child death stoically, "with a kind of belle indifference that is a culturally appropriate response" (Scheper-Hughes, 1993, p. 429). Mothers were discouraged from displaying grief for their lost child because "The path [to heaven] is dark. A mother's tears can impede the way, make the road slippery so that the spirit-child will lose her footing, or the tears will fall on her wings and dampen them" (429). Although this form of maternal love may seem cruel by Western standards, Scheper-Hughes pointed out that it is a form of family survival.

Abandonment is not confined to economically dire conditions. I worked with a couple who were ecstatic to become pregnant, but then both had a shocked reaction to their newborn. They started to spiral with anxiety, one fueling the other, exasperated and at a loss as to how to connect with or calm their baby. After a few weeks of sleep deprivation and what the husband described as a "fantasy of turning back time," they arrived at the option of abandoning their child at a Safe Haven location. A snowstorm and temperature drop made the prospect of leaving their infant outdoors unfeasible, and the Safe Haven option was forgone.

The 2018 Spanish film *Sunday's Illness* follows the story of a daughter, Chiara, who was abandoned by her mother, Anabel, at age 7. When Chiara is 42, she seeks out Anabel, who is living in splendid wealth with a husband and daughter not much younger than herself. When the mother is asked by her current husband how she knows that Chiara is her daughter, she confesses, "I can feel her in me." The movie centers itself in the dim and haunting cabin where the women spend time together, circling a primal connection that has been thwarted. One film reviewer remarked:

> A broken, solitary woman with a history of drug addiction, Chiara drifts through the house like the ghostly recurrence of sins Anabel tried to bury long ago . . . . It may as well be a horror movie in disguise.
>
> (Kohn, 2018, paras. 4, 9).

In its examination of abandonment, the film reveals a mother who, when young, had been overwhelmed by her newborn, and was now a mother but also never a mother to Chiara. Chiara's pain is a mix of sadness, longing, and animalistic aggression, while Anabel reveals both fear and guilt, obvious marks left by the Death Mother archetypal act.

The U.S. has institutionalized support for the abandonment of infants. Safe Haven laws (also known as Baby Moses laws) decriminalize leaving unharmed infants in statutorily designated locations (i.e., a hospital, police station, or a fire station). The parent, typically the mother, is allowed to remain anonymous, shielded from liability and prosecution as long as the abandonment is done within 72 hours of birth in most states. The local child welfare department assumes custody of the infant, typically placing the infant in a pre-adoptive home while terminating the birth parents' parental rights. What began as a way to prevent extreme cases of child abuse, neonaticide, or infanticide has gained support, especially among religious conservatives who promote abandonment or adoption as alternatives to abortion.

During oral arguments in the case Dobbs v. Jackson Women's Health Organization, which overturned Roe v. Wade, Supreme Court Justice Barrett suggested that Safe Haven laws offered an alternative to abortion, with Justice Alito Jr. citing Safe Haven laws as, in the majority's view, obviating the need for abortion rights. What the Justices failed to point out is the rare use of Safe Haven practices—just 115 legal surrenders were made in 2021 (The National Safe Haven Alliance). The Justices also failed to note a mother's grief, emotional and cellular maternal bond, lactation, and postpartum depression, all of which likely make a Safe Haven option unbearable and keep the surrender numbers low.

Adoption

With the rise of legal repercussions for infanticide in the 18th century and the increasing collective moral conscience, empathy, and sensitivity toward children, abandonment shifted to nascent forms of adoption. "Putting a child up for adoption" originated from the orphan trains of the 1850s-1920s that took wayward street kids from the East to West Coast of the U.S., placing them on platforms along the train route for people to adopt. These were mostly Irish and Italian Catholic immigrant children, collected by a social welfare system attempting to convert them to Protestantism. In the early 1900s, legal and moral concern for the welfare of unprotected children was on the rise, and agencies began to pop up that stopped the trains and homed the children. In a short time, an industry of adoption was born.[2]

The history of adoption in the U.S. began with closed stranger adoptions, where a child's birth certificate was sealed and filed away. One of the motivations was to keep evidence of "bad blood"—such as deviance, race, or ethnicity—from being known to adoptive families, thanks to the Eugenics movement of the early 1900s. Another motivation was the widely accepted blank slate theory, purporting that once a child is detached from the biological mom, they are a blank slate, and the adoptive family can imprint upon them to make the child their own. In this sense, adoption reflects Death Mother energy that can sever, virtually as effectively as death, the mother line to the child.

Closed stranger adoptions were practiced in the 1950s during the "Baby Scoop Era," when high demand for building the suburban American family required the relinquishing of newborns from young pregnant unwed girls who were sent away to maternity homes to have their babies in secret.[3] This era resulted in one of the highest periods of adoption, the ramifications witnessed now as the Baby Boomer generation discovers previously unknown whole or half siblings who had been relinquished by their mothers. Although these meetings may be celebratory, the reunion between adoptees and their biological mothers tends to be more fraught. When an adopted child has found their biological mother's information, sought her out and met her, the reunion often perpetuates a deep sense of being unwanted and rarely brings the earnestly sought closure or experience of mother. One woman I know who discovered her biological mother has maintained pleasant, regular contact, whereas her sister, adopted from a different agency, has found only further heartache through her biological family. What might be considered an intervention to save unplanned babies from the enactment of the archetypal energies of the Death Mother, adoption often leads many women and their children into her grip (Glasser, 2021).

With adoption, literal infanticide shifts to psychological infanticide, institutionalized by the adoption industry. Jungian psychotherapist and adoptee Violet Sherwood wrote about psychological infanticide in cases of closed stranger adoptions that enact violence on "the truth of original being" (2021, p. 123). Sherwood emphasized the lie the adopted child lives, "denied its own mind and existence in a kind of living death" (123).

Same-race adoptions had long been the practice; eventually barriers to trans-racial adoption (TRA) were dropped, again largely due to demand. TRA has grown rapidly but remains controversial. There are more white parents who want to adopt than there are white children waiting for homes, yet children of color are less likely than white children to be placed in permanent homes. Legislative efforts to amend these discrepancies by promoting TRA have not significantly improved placement statistics (Jacobson et al., 2012). In parts of the U.S., adopting parents can receive a tax deduction if adopting an African American child, the highest population of chil-dren put up for adoption. TRA adds a severance of cultural/ethnic lineage/identity to the severance of the mother line in an adopted child, a new family co-constructed by the state but without biological or identifiable connections.

International adoption picked up in the 1970s and 80s due to shorter wait times for infants at lower costs, and increasingly celebrity mothers' choices for creating a family. Advertisements pull at the Good Mother and the infertile woman's heart-strings, asking her to save a malnourished child who otherwise will be deprived of education, at risk of being sex trafficked, conscribed as a child soldier, or forced into child labor. The international adoption business has been profitable for under-developed countries, with reports of nations such as Argentina, Honduras, and Thailand placing children in adoption after being purchased or abducted from their birth mothers.

> In Honduras . . . merchants pay teenage girls to get pregnant and monitor them to make sure they eat well and receive some kind of care. After the baby is born, $50 is paid to the birth mother in exchange for the healthy baby . . . . The lack of information on the circumstances involving the conception, birth, and the placement of a child poses a dilemma for women adopting internationally who have pro-choice views and yet quite possibly adopt from women who have little to no choice.
>
> (Khazan, 2021)

We can only imagine the effect this has on the adoptive/purchasing mother and what damage is done to the agency and subjectivity of the mothers who give up their child in these circumstances.

From the adoptions of the 20th century to today, young and poor birth mothers are seduced with false promises of money and/or continued contact with their child, or even immigration to a first-world nation. The adoptive mothers may know nothing of these circumstances and/or look the other way as the system exploits them, the birth mother, and the bartered children (Smolin, 2005).[4] In 1973, there was a huge drop in the rates of adoption when Roe v. Wade made abortion legal. It's likely there will be an increase in adoptions in areas of the U.S. where abortion is now unavailable, as the drive of Death Mother will continue to seek an outlet.

From a psychoanalytic viewpoint, adoption is often considered a murder of the merger between the biological mother and infant in the first year of life. Although the adoptive mother may be a safer option than the birth mother, the experience of this separation is psychological infanticide. In his article "Infanticidal Attachment," Kahr noted that psychological infanticide manifests as a relational style adjacent to disorganized attachment. He found the harm is created at a very early stage of life when the mother is severing her bond with the infant, who has not yet organized experience into a coherent identity. Woodman suggested that the Death Mother archetype may be experienced as early as in the womb by mother and child, when the fetus is not being welcomed into life, is unwanted, or is experienced as wrong in the womb (Sieff, 2017). Sherwood wrote, "The unwelcome fetus and unwilling mother form an infanticidal attachment centered on their shared experiences of helpless terror, and utilizing mutual survival strategies of dissociation that orient the child towards death rather than life" (2020, p. 11). The unwelcome child is born in a terror of annihilation, absorbed into his or her neurobiology and psyche. This internal experience of deadness, terror of being killed, feeling one does not exist, frozen states, and a murderousness or suicidality can continue long into adulthood. When unable to form an emotional bond with caretakers, the child's terror may express as violence, depression, psychosis, reactive attachment disorder, or in the high rates of murder and suicide among adoptees (Brodzinsky, 1990). Such symptoms are both protection from a world perceived as annihilating and a desperate attempt to communicate the inner experience of being held hostage by internalized murderers. As Sherwood observed, the inner world of the child victim of "psychological infanticide is haunted by the infanticidal introject," which is the relinquishing mother (2021, p. 15).

Shannon's Story

Shannon grew up in an abusive household; both parents were addicted to heroin and were regularly evicted from apartments, often living with other families. Shannon's mother was particularly violent toward her, whipping her for minor infractions or when her younger sister misbehaved. Shannon's mother told her that her own mother never loved her. The family culture purported that life is a struggle, you don't complain or have stress, and "you don't have a right to anything"—even love. Shannon attempted to protect her younger sister from drugs and their parents' addiction. During our interviews, Shannon remembered going without food and being hungry, with her father in and out of jail for selling drugs.

Her parents split up when she was in grade school and her mother moved them into her new boyfriend's apartment. The boyfriend began regularly sexually abusing Shannon, bringing her to the bed he shared with her mother, assaulting her while Shannon believed her mother was asleep. Shannon never told anyone, feeling she would get in trouble. She also believed it was punishment for looking like her father.

In her adolescence, one of Shannon's cousins approached her for sex and she "didn't know how to say No." They had a sexual relationship for the next year. Shannon had never received any sex education. At age 15 she became pregnant for the first time. Her mother refused to speak to her when she found out and her grandmother was irate, "more than she'd ever been." Shannon believed the father was her "8th grade sweetheart." She initially considered having an abortion, which was supported by her grandmother, but her mother wouldn't allow her to because it was a sign of shame, and she didn't want to "lose that fight." Shannon understood that she was being punished for "something she didn't do."

One day, while in her third trimester, Shannon heard her mother and aunt talking about how her father was in jail and "not coming home." Shannon became very upset as she had been close to her father. As she was crying, she began to go into labor. Her cousin checked to see how dilated her cervix was and told her, "You need to shave; you can't go into the hospital like that."

After giving birth Shannon regularly experienced a depressed state. She told herself she "always got the short end of the stick and always will"; "I must be a dingbat and a whore"; "I don't know how to stop being a bitch"; "I just need to endure this, I have nowhere else to go." Shannon began ruminating on death and suicide, thinking "death is not a bad thing." Shannon also never wanted her child to see her in that light. She told me she wanted him to know her as his "savior."

At 17, Shannon became pregnant again, then miscarried. Shortly after the miscarriage, she became pregnant again, which surprised her because she had been on the birth control patch. She did not want to be pregnant; she wanted her son to be her only child. Shannon considered abortion again, but she was afraid of the pain of the procedure, which she had heard from other women was "gruesome."[5] Considering adoption, Shannon found a relative who wanted the baby. Throughout the pregnancy the father of the fetus was agreeable to the adoption but when Shannon delivered the baby girl, he refused to give her away. Shannon initially felt no connection to this baby. When she cried, Shannon would think, "One of us has to go."

Shannon's 4th pregnancy happened when she was 19, when her children were 3 years old and 8 months old. At 24 weeks she began bleeding heavily; she believed it was because of the physical abuse from her boyfriend. She went to the hospital where they did an ultrasound and discovered the fetus was dead. Shannon said she did not know how to process that—she was sad but not sad. The doctor induced labor in her that night. She pushed the fetus out and they gave her a bucket for the infant. Her boyfriend's mother came to the hospital and told Shannon to look at the dead infant, but she didn't want to look. Shannon felt anger toward her boyfriend "because of all the stress that made me lose the baby." He was angry with her for losing the baby and being "inadequate." Shannon went into a deeper depression at that point; she felt resigned to a terrible life. She knew she had to keep going for her children.

At 20, Shannon became pregnant for the 5th time. Again, she did not want to keep this baby, but she did not consider abortion. She also was in numb resignation to the events of her life. Shannon said this pregnancy was very difficult. She had recurrent yeast infections, but her boyfriend accused her of having a sexually transmitted disease and cheating on him. At one point he pulled her pants down to see if she was lying. He then forced himself into her. After this she attempted to overdose with Tylenol. She "just wanted to sleep . . . . Why do I have to keep going through this? I have no family, I have nowhere to go, I have to keep dealing with this kind of stuff. I am humiliated." But she called 911 and was taken to the hospital, where she was admitted to the psychiatric unit for one week. She said the hospitalization "felt like a break." They attempted to medicate her, but Shannon refused because she was pregnant.

When Shannon went into labor the baby was stuck. The doctor told her, "We could take the baby out now and see how he does, or you could go to delivery and we could see which one of you lives." When he was delivered the infant was pale, he had significantly low oxygen to his brain, which caused developmental and cognitive delays.

At 21, Shannon became pregnant for the 6th time with the same boyfriend, this time with twins. She felt as if it was "the end of the world" and was in "disbelief." She reported, "I wanted to get hit by a bus. I felt like a fuck up. Every time I think it's gonna be okay, I get hit." Shannon didn't tell anyone. She again wanted to relinquish the babies. She tried to keep the pregnancy secret from her boyfriend, covering herself with baggy clothes and blankets to hide her stomach. Shannon called an adoption agency and met with a family. They agreed on an open adoption. Only Shannon's sister knew of the arrangement. At 25 weeks pregnant Shannon began bleeding and the doctor told her Baby A had died. Shannon was transferred to another hospital, where she was told to carry the nonvital fetus for 8 more weeks to keep Baby B alive. Shannon was "detached" from her body and the experience.

Her mom found out she was pregnant and told Shannon that she didn't want her to give him up for adoption. She said, "No one is raising our family." The night she went into labor her boyfriend, who now knew the situation, came to the hospital "raging like a lunatic." Shannon told him she wasn't in a position to have another kid. He screamed, "No one gonna have my kid!!" He had also found out that the adoptive couple was gay, and he didn't approve of that. They canceled the adoption and Shannon kept the baby, who was born prematurely. Shannon felt her lifelong primary doctor was "really disappointed in her." Shannon now had an infant (who she could barely name), a 1-year-old, a 3-year-old, and a 5-year-old. She felt as if she had failed them, "cheating all the children out of having a mother." Eight weeks after Shannon brought Baby B home she was arrested for the homicide of her newborn.

Sociologist Gretchen Sisson has studied the profiles of women who relinquish infants for adoption. Using data from various adoption agencies, she found that the birth mothers are typically over 30 years old, racially and ethnically diverse, have other children, and "lack the economic resources that would give them meaningful power over the options available to themselves and their children" (2022, p. 46). Like Shannon, women who put their children up for adoption are often "in double binds, sexually, culturally and economically. They are desperate mothers relieving their despair" (Sherwood, 2020, p. 112). Also like Shannon, they might be caught in their own infanticidal attachment from their mother. Also, most women who relinquish infants have made the decision to not keep the child long after the stage of pregnancy when abortion is possible, and often birth mothers will relinquish more than one infant for adoption over the course of their reproductive lives (Sisson, 2022).

A recent NPR podcast featured a woman who had given her infant up for adoption in her early 20s. This young woman, pregnant for the first time and living in a rural and poor area, visited a pregnancy help center that unbeknownst to her was run by an anti-abortion group. The adoption agencies they referred her to confirmed that relinquishing her parental rights would be the best thing for her and her child. This messaging reflects most contemporary adoption agencies that advertise to desperate pregnant mothers—give life, give unconditional love, your baby will know it's loved by two set-up parents—the underlying message is that abortion is a sin (Cradle of Hope Adoption Center, n.d.). Interviewed by NPR for their "Consider This" podcast, a woman who chose adoption reflected on her experience ten years later:

> The suggestion that abortion isn't needed because adoption is there makes it seem like this casual thing, like taking off a sweater and giving it to someone else, and just forgetting about it or moving on, and that's not what it is. It's this huge event that you do to yourself and your child and it changes you . . . . If I had the support then I absolutely would have parenting; when I contacted the adoption agency I was at the lowest point I had been. I was thinking about it . . . after I made the adoption decision and I was in the waiting room and the *Ellen Show* was on the TV . . . giving away cars and I thought, if I had a car I could do this . . . . I tried in the ways I knew how to make the situation work and it didn't work . . . . The social workers at the adoption agencies were really good at undermining my confidence as a parent. They never saw me as a parent; they saw me as someone who could provide a baby to one of their waiting couples . . . . When it happened and I was hit by this grief I never experienced before it threw me completely off. I didn't know what to do with my life anymore. After visits I would go home and sob. I cried until I busted blood vessels in my eyes. There was a period of time I would throw up; it was a reaction to leaving my child. It's been 7 years almost and I still feel that grief with me pretty constantly. Adoption has changed the way I parent. I had another child about 3.5 years ago and I feel like I will never be good enough to parent her.
>
> (Consider This from NPR, 2021)

Women who relinquish infants for adoption experience a specific and extreme type of grief. Although the process of adoption has become more humane, the mourning and the trauma of it does not abate. Studies of mothers who have given a child up for adoption are sparse, but there have been enough reports of similar experiences that they have been given the name *birthmother syndrome*: a combination of PTSD symptoms, unresolved grief, decreased self-esteem, perfectionism masking shame, impaired emotional development, self-punishment, "unexplained secondary infertility," and "living . . . various extremes" (Henney et al., 2007, p. 876).

A recent study reported that although many birth mothers reported satisfaction with their decision, the more time that had passed since the adoption, the less overall satisfaction some birth mothers felt (Madden et al., 2018, p. 128). With age, satisfaction with their decision also decreased, especially for women whose educational attainment was college or higher or who had relative financial success in their lives. In their study of 323 adoptions, Ge et al. found,

> Open adoption also helps to mitigate birth mothers' feelings of pain and loss, resulting in less destructive behavior and greater emotional well-being. Moreover, birth mothers who are involved in open adoption are more likely to feel assured of the child's welfare because the direct contact they have . . . In contrast, closed adoptions are viewed as confining; birth mothers often feel isolated, have unresolved feelings of guilt and self-blame, and feel uncertain of the well-being of the child . . . . [Open adoption] may not only alleviate the birth mother's grief, but also may contribute to her sense of pride regarding the decision.
>
> (2008, p. 529)

Like the haunting of the child by a shadow biological mother, the birth mother may feel a sense of someone who mourns for her or for whom she mourns. However, I also have witnessed mothers who found solace in their choice to relinquish a child to adoption. The solace comes from their choice for *life*, especially when abortion was thought of as a sin or a murder.

Relevant to this conversation is surrogacy, a quickly growing fertility assistance made popular by celebrities, which also complicates a mother–child line. Surrogacy, originally performed by slaves and concubines, is now a transaction reimbursed by ~50k, in which a woman's body is used as an instrument for another's goal. Surrogacy has been lauded as an empowering way for a woman to earn money and as an example, like sex work, of a woman's ability to exercise her rights over her own body. However, in the discussion there is often a denial of the cost to the maternal instincts of both women in the equation and a dangerous conflation of empowerment and commodification. Moreover, although commissioning mothers and their gestational surrogates have reassured themselves that the pregnancy is carried in a "fostering womb" with no genetic links to the fetus, the biology of microchimerism suggests the surrogate may be exchanging cellular material with that fetus, which may affect epigenetic changes to the expression of the child's genes.

> What has been overlooked is that new biosocial understandings of epigenetics, and more recently microchimerism, might demand a radical rethinking of the relation between a gestational surrogate, and the developing fetus and subsequent child. In both cases, the processes of gestation and birth clearly contribute much more than a nurturing environment and will persistently impact mother and child alike.
>
> (Shildrick, 2022, p. 11)

Microchimerism brings us back to the closing argument of the defense attorney in the film *Saint Omer* (Diop, 2023), previously presented in Chapter 3, who referenced the chimeric cells as providing evidence of the primal and primitive connection mother and child have, built into the very biology of their beings. Regardless of rationalized commodification in the case of surrogacy, the essential biology of mother and child is perverted permanently. In her implicatory book, *American Baby: A Mother, a Child, and the Shadow History of Adoption*, Glasser is clear that there always remains a bond between a biological mother and the child she relinquished to adoption. I would add that there may always be thread—no matter how invisible—between a surrogate mother and the baby she carried, between a mother and the infant she abandoned at a fire station, and between a mother and her aborted fetus.

Abortion

A quick internet search for the word *infanticide* produces pro-life and conservative Christian websites equating abortion to infanticide, a conflation that transforms a medical procedure into murder. The Christian conservative pro-life agenda reflects the bedrock of the U.S., in which the progress hoped for in the nation's founding was based on escaping rampant illness, poverty, oppression, and child mortality in the Old World. In 2015, Trump selected Mike Pence as his vice president largely due to his significant pro-life following. Pence's August 2023 statements on abortion—"I want to always err on the side of life . . . to restore the sanctity of life to the center of American law" —demonstrate the problem of pro-life polemics in their lack of familiarity with the actual lives of many contemporary American mothers and infants.[6]

Like abandonment and adoption, the procedure of an abortion gives a vehicle to the Death Mother archetype. As established earlier, at conception a mother has access to the collective unconscious of motherhood, a store of archetypal responses to mothering of every generation in every country and every religion. With the right circumstances, the Death Mother archetype can enter and have a legitimate place in the mother's field and be enacted in the form of abortion as a more effective and less harmful act than infanticide, especially in the form of legal, medicalized abortion. Abortion is, in fact, a sublimation of the Death Mother. The socially unacceptable impulse of infanticide is transformed into the socially acceptable (in most Western countries) act of abortion. Deprived of the option of legal abortion, the archetypal drive of maternal infanticide will too often turn to illegal, highly risky abortions.

Abortion is neither new nor unnatural; it has been practiced by humans for as long as we have records. There are many examples of mammals who induce abortions to avoid undue burdens to raising offspring when the conditions are unfavorable. In sharks and rays, when a pregnant female is stressed, such as during capture, they will reabsorb the fetus(es), recovering nutrients and eliminating the costs and risks of carrying the pregnancy to term (Adams et al., 2018). The tammar wallaby can pause a pregnancy for up to 11 months if she senses that she is pregnant too soon to provide for both the current and the next litter (Whelan, 2009). Pregnant female meadow voles, if they meet a new male early in a pregnancy, will reabsorb the fetus to become sexually receptive again. This sounds like a superpower but reflects the instinctual nature of mothers to manipulate a pregnancy for the good of the larger family system. In what zoologists refer to as a *postpartum abortion*, some mothers will eat their young after birth to assist the growth of the healthiest infants. Like the cannibalistic tendencies of evil witches in Grimm's fairy tales, a Death Mother can consume and absorb the child into herself, raising her own power and efficacy.

Although the behaviors of abortion and infanticide are considered by some to be unnatural, the inverse is evidently more accurate—these behaviors are natural and close to nature. Under duress, a human mother may fall back on instincts that resemble a mammal's. In this survival state, the psyche accesses the archetypal energies of the Death Mother held in the collective unconscious and available to a human mother as a way of ending life to save life. What may have been a lack of a fertile climate or a threat of nearby predators for a marsupial mother is now the poverty or domestic violence a modern mother faces when deciding to bring a baby into the world through her body. Other stressors such as a large family, medical disabilities, trauma (conception during rape, incest), substance-exposed fetus, and conditions of war largely inform these decisions.

In the premodern era, abortions were performed by using a cocktail of herbal remedies, uterine massage, insertion of foreign objects into the uterus, strenuous labor, climbing, falling, self-hitting, paddling, and weightlifting (Olasky & Savas, 2023), but were substantially ineffective and often involved considerable risk to the woman. Abortifacients are well documented, from Silphium used by the Greeks and Romans in classical antiquity to the bitter waters referred to in the Bible used by wives whose husbands suspected that they had been unfaithful. Various native and aboriginal societies used bloodwort, quinine, and blue cohosh, whereas American slave women used cotton bark root. (Boeck, 2013). Up until the 20th century, it was generally accepted that an abortion could be induced if it was prior to quickening, or when a mother first felt fetal movement. There were no laws that applied to abortions performed early in a pregnancy, as they were thought of as returning a woman's body to the state of menses. But in 1803, if an abortion was performed after the quickening, the punishment was the death penalty (Luker, 1984).

Approximately 18% of all pregnancies in the U.S. end in induced abortion by dilation and curettage (D and C) procedures or by Mifeprex, a medication to induce abortion. These procedures, if done legally, are generally safer than a live birth, but rates of complication and death are much higher for illegal abortions performed outside of regular medical facilities (Bearak et al., 2020). Women in their 20s have the highest abortion rates, whereas adolescents under 15 have the lowest rates. During 2010–2019, women ≥40 years old accounted for a relatively small proportion of reported abortions (3.4%–3.7%). However, the abortion ratio among women ≥40 years old continues to be higher than among women aged 25–39, likely due to the number of children already in the home. (Kortsmit et al., 2021).

Statistics also suggest that abortions are more common among those who lack financial and social resources or whose reasons for an abortion include rape, incest, fetal abnormalities, and threats to physical health. However, overwhelmingly, abortions are due to conventional motivations for family planning: not wanting another child because of life course issues, such as school or career; financial concerns; or relationship problems (being unmarried, not wanting a child with the father, or lack of support from current partner) (Bearak et al., 2020). An analysis of long-term abortion studies that considered women's reasons for abortion found "that the reasons described by the majority of women (74%) signaled a sense of emotional and financial responsibility to individuals other than themselves, including existing or future children, and were multi-dimensional" (Biggs et al., 2013, p. 2).

Gina's Story

Gina, referred to earlier, became pregnant when she was 13. She hadn't had any sex education, although her mother had told her to "never have sex" and her family had taught her never to discuss topics like sex. When her 18-year-old boyfriend Billy asked her if she wanted to have sex, Gina said yes, and she remembers lying down while Billy took her pants off and had sex with her. She stared out the window the entire time and "felt nothing." Billy began to talk to her about doing other sexual acts and she became confused, so she asked her friend what he meant. Her friend asked her if she was on the pill, and Gina said no. Her friend took her to Planned Parenthood, where she had a pregnancy test and discovered she was pregnant. Gina felt humiliated and didn't tell anyone.

When Gina's mother caught sight of her pregnancy one day while she was getting out of the bathtub, she said, "How could you do this to me?" She took Gina to the doctor to schedule an abortion. The doctor told them Gina was too far along for an abortion, which relieved Gina because she had begun to feel happy about the baby. She had seen a television show about a girl getting pregnant and her whole family coming together in happiness to help her raise the child. Billy fed this fantasy; he wanted her to keep the baby and promised they would be a family.

After Gina had the baby, Billy grew violent. He regularly accused her of being with another man—who, because of his suspicions, he had already badly beaten up. Billy would hit her in the face, chase her around the house, bang on doors in rooms she was hiding and threaten to break them down. Other people in the house would tell her she had to come out and calm him down. After the baby was born Gina said it was "open season," going from "bad to worse." Gina remembers no one intervening and the abuse becoming routine.

At 16 years old, Gina became pregnant again and had their child. A year later she became pregnant for a third time. Billy didn't believe the child was his and he didn't want her to keep it. Gina did not want to have an abortion, having even stronger feelings about it than with her first pregnancy, but Billy threatened, "You have an abortion, or I'll give you one." Gina had the abortion.

Gina said when she came back from the abortion the kids were all crying and the house was chaotic. She took the kids into the living room, made them noodles, and put them to sleep. Billy came in and wanted to have sex. Gina told him she had an "open wound" from the abortion, and he said, "Ain't nothing wrong with your mouth."

Lack of sex education, sexual abuse, and IPV can deprive women of control and choice related to their bodies and pregnancy. The research cited earlier suggests that the ability to choose abortion can be important to women's well-being. However, Gina's story also points to the fact that for a man, coercing an abortion can be part of his control of a woman and part of the woman's context in which she becomes both victimized by and blamed for male violence.

Deciding on Abortion

In the U.S., since the 2022 overturning of Roe v. Wade, we've experienced back-pedaling on a woman's right to make a choice about her pregnancy. With certain states decreasing access to abortion, those in my field expect women to turn to neonaticide and infanticide. Neonaticide has always been more common in rural communities where abortion was less acceptable (Jason, 1983). As a statistical profile, many women who seek abortions in the U.S. share the same profile of women who commit neonaticide: women of color under the age of 18 who are victims of DV and sexual violence, have an unplanned pregnancy, and lack resources and social support. Women who are in desperate conditions and are vulnerable to the effects of Death Mother energy will take desperate measures.

Unfortunately, the outcome of a lack of access to legal abortion can have a severe impact on the born children. Although many pro-life supporters and Christian conservatives point out these children wouldn't be alive if an abortion had occurred, there is evidence compiled over decades that suggests that when abortion was legalized violent crime was reduced by up to 47% and robbery by about 33% (Donohue & Levitt, 2001). It is uncomfortable to accept, but "unwanted children are at an elevated risk for less favorable life outcomes on multiple dimensions, including criminal involvement" (381). Graham Music, a psychotherapist who has worked extensively with trauma and addiction, posted on his website a blog that offers an astutely honest reflection on severely troubled adolescents and abortion:

> Some were conceived via sexual assault, even rape, or in drug and alcohol induced stupors or in atmospheres far from love. The loveless and often violence and drug fueled early lives too often show in their bodies . . . and actions. Other children are born in less worrying circumstances, but still not as wanted as we would hope, and this too has consequences . . . . Without abortion, not only is there more infanticide, there is more violence against all of humanity. Few can argue about the effects of not being well cared for . . . the evidence is clear.

For example, nearly half of the young prison population have been in the care system, most others have suffered some form of trauma and abuse.

(Nurturing Natures Webmaster, 2022, para. 1)

Roe v. Wade is about more than a contentious reproductive medical procedure or the effects on children; it is about the effects on women not being able to make imperative decisions that pertain to their health, that of their families, and the larger society. In fact, taking away the choice over her own reproductive capacity takes her out at her knees; it takes the decision belonging to her most potent power and gives it to someone else.

Debates that center around the experiences of a fetus are embedded with a mix of medical science, religion, and emotion that is rarely centered on the emotional experience of the mother, whose agency often is presumed to exist in her "right to choose." Without doubt, the individual experience of each aborting woman carries within it conscious and unconscious desire and/or regret to end potential life. However, women tend to be caught in the larger debate: shamed and accused of being heartless murderers on the one hand and expected (and perhaps expecting) to have few regrets on the other; thus one is rarely aware, including the woman herself, of her truer feelings regarding abortion.[7]. This again reflects the neglect of women's lived experiences and voices, in which sadness, regret, and even haunting can *coexist* with having made the best or needed choice. As such, the emotional side of abortion, as a trauma that requires tender care and recovery, is often overlooked. There are few places for a woman to share her feelings of loss, confusion, or regret. Even if an abortion was a choice, it is still a rupture of her bodily and primal integrity.

In the current literature, it is difficult to discern the psychological impact of abortion on women, and it largely depends on the publication. It's dangerous to the pro-choice stance if there are studies that prove abortions have a negative impact on women. In 2011, a British study claimed to have amassed the largest quantitative estimate of mental health risks associated with abortion available in the world literature (Coleman, 2011). This study concluded that women who had undergone an abortion experienced an 81% increased risk of mental health problems, about 10% of which were attributable to abortion.

However, the American Psychiatric Association task force found that women who had abortions experienced grief, sadness, anxiety, and depression after the abortion, but they did *not* attribute the abortion as the cause of their mental and emotional struggles. The researchers concluded that these mental health challenges would not have been different if the woman had remained pregnant and had the baby. In fact, their statement suggested the underlying cause of the mental health issue may relate to the cause for pursuing an abortion (Major et al., 2008).

The University of California, San Francisco's landmark Turnaway Study, often referred to in the abortion conversation, interviewed women 5 years after they had an abortion and found that more than 95% of these women reported that it was the right decision for them. Obstetrician and gynecologist Diana Greene Foster led the study because "the debate about abortion rarely focuses on what happens to the pregnant person" (as cited in Fost, 2022, para. 6). The study found there was no evidence of mental health problems among study participants following an abortion. It "also found that those who sought and received an abortion were more financially stable, set more ambitious life goals, raised children under more stable conditions, and were more likely to have a wanted child later" (Fost, para. 3). Women unable to have abortions because they were past the gestational limit suffered from adverse effects such as serious physical and mental health challenges, economic hardship, lack of support and insecurity, although they are likely to raise the child rather than choose adoption (Goldstein, 2022).

In her rebuttal of the Turnaway Study, human development researcher Priscilla Coleman (2022) claimed,

> In a study by Coleman and Nelson (1998), 38.7% of female college students voiced regret of their abortions in the first few years afterward. Similarly, Fergusson et al. (2009) reported that 32.7% of women aged 15–30 reported some level of regret (endorsing "somewhat" or "very much") in association with an abortion experience. Finally, Söderberg et al.'s (1998) study revealed 76.1% of women who aborted would never consider abortion again. This indirectly suggests some level of regret.
>
> ("Abortion and Mental Health in World Literature", para. 12)

It should be noted that Coleman's article was retracted without explanation by the journal in which it appeared.

What seems important to acknowledge is that although abortion can be a deeply emotionally disturbing event with mental health consequences, a woman should still be able to choose it. There are circumstances in which a *loving* mother may experience the arrival of a baby as a profound *disaster*; this is one of the underlying truths that is rarely spoken of out loud in the politics of abortion. We have no models or ways of understanding this paradox of emotion. If the Death Mother's archetypal energy—as depicted in Kali the Hindu Goddess of womb and tomb or the infanticidal slave fugitive Margaret Garner—is available to all mothers, and under certain conditions abortion may be the most adaptive option. The end goal of the destructive maternal force is annihilation, but it also can be an act that serves a greater purpose. Of my personal and clinical experiences, I have witnessed various reasons women have abortions, all of which are significantly valid and not without heartfelt consideration. Women have abortions because they have limits; an abortion is an expression of maternal finitude. Mothers have abortions so they can then be better mothers, so their existing children have more resources and more time with attentive care. Women have abortions because even in the modern era, the dyad of a mom and baby is not considered a family; they are deviant pods and unsupported. Women have abortions who were forced into prostitution, who live in destitution, who are teenagers and students. Women have abortions to refuse men, to reject his seed and his reckless colonization of their bodies: Abortion obviates his descendants. Women have abortions because they were raped; their fetus is a trauma object that they can't accept, and abortion is a way to take control over their bodies after sexual trauma.

I see my work as softening the binary between pro-choice and pro-life and between good and bad. Abortion is painful, women may regret it, it may haunt them, and it may also be the best choice for them, one they continue to report as good. This is the crux of unsentimental motherhood: making impossible choices and a life sentence of loss to allow someone or something else to live. This is what women have done. What mothers have done.

If the Death Mother, as the archetypal image of an instinct found both throughout nature and human history, must inevitably annihilate a child, providing mothers paths which result in the least possible damage enactsa sublimation. I believe Safe Haven abandonment, adoption, and abortion together as options serve as such sublimations. The first two leave more likelihood the child will survive (although research suggests it's often with harmful consequences to both child and society). Abortion prevents further harm coming from and to an unwanted child. Symbolically, we squash or murder potential life every day, both individually in not letting paths in our lives come to fruition, and collectively in war, discriminatory practices, and socioeconomic deprivation. As revealed here, the individual and collective (systemic) impact one another. In this nexus, not all children can live to their potential, and some must be aborted, abandoned, or adopted by others. But setting some potential life aside makes it possible for other lives to survive.

Notes

1 Forced abandonment, abortion, and adoption are acts of violence and control, and have been weapons of war and colonization.
2 Colonizing powers have used adoption to convert the children of indigenous populations in a violent destruction of family and cultures. In North America, Indigenous children were taken from their families and placed in boarding schools, then adopted into white families. In New Zealand, the Māori lost around 80,000 children to legal closed stranger adoptions with no way of accessing their ancestral roots (Ahuriri-Driscoll et al., 2023).
3 These practices mimicked the Irish Catholic homes abroad, where pregnant girls were sent until the 1960s. Later, mass graves of infants were found on the grounds (Subramanian, 2017).
4 It is important to differentiate these circumstances from adoptions that save a young woman in the dilemma of an unplanned pregnancy and fulfill an adoptive family's desire for a child.
5 Women have told me they didn't want an abortion because they "didn't want to see all the blood" or they "didn't want to see their baby pass that way," There is a general lack of knowledge regarding abortion in these communities.
6 Hinging on the use and meaning of the words *baby* and *fetus*, this debate obscures pregnancy as a part of a woman's body.
7 The same can be said for sex work, the legalization of which is often supported as empowering women's choice over their body. Often overlooked is the social and cultural context of sexual objectification that makes women's bodies instruments for others' use and ignores the psychological impact of context on women's opportunities and choices.

References

Adams, K. R., Fetterplace, L. C., Davis, A., Taylor, M., & Knott, N. (2018). Sharks, rays and abortion: The prevalence of capture-induced parturition in elasmobranchs. *Biological Conservation, 217*, 11–27.

Ahuriri-Driscoll, A., Blake, D., & Dixon, A. (2023). The paradoxes of closed stranger adoption in Aotearoa New Zealand. *Adoption Quarterly, 26*(3), 281–309. https://doi. org/10.1 080/10926755.2022.2156012

Bearak, J., Popinchalk, A., Ganatra, B., Moller, A.-B., Tunçalp, Ö., Beavin, C., Kwok, L., & Alkema, L. (2020). Unintended pregnancy and abortion by income, region, and the legal status of abortion: Estimates from a comprehensive model for 1990–2019. *Lancet Global Health, 8*(9), e1152–e1161.

Biggs, M., Gould, H., & Foster, D. (2013). Understanding why women seek abortions in the US. *Women's Health*, 1–13. www.ncbi.nlm.nih.gov/pmc/articles/PMC3729671/pdf/1472-6874-13-29.pdf

Boeck, B. (2013). Medicinal plants and medicaments used for conception, Abortion, and fertility control in Ancient Babylonia. *Journal Asiatique, 301*(1), 27–52.

Brodzinsky, D. (1990). *The psychology of adoption.* Oxford University Press.

Coleman, P. (2011). Abortion and mental health: Quantitative synthesis and analysis of research published 1995–2009. *The British Journal of Psychiatry, 199*(3), 180–186.

Coleman, P. (2022, June 17). The turnaway study: A case of self-correction in science upended by political motivation and unvetted findings. *Frontiers in Psychology.* Retrieved December 26, 2022, from www.ncbi.nlm.nih.gov/pmc/articles/PMC9247501/

Coleman, P. K., & Nelson, E. S. (1998). The quality of abortion decisions and college students' reports of post-abortion emotional sequelae and abortion attitudes. *Journal of Social and Clinical Psychology, 17*(4), 425–442. https://doi.org/10.1521/jscp.1998.17.4.425

Consider this from NPR. (2021, December 9). Why "abortion or adoption" is not an equal choice. *NPR.* www.npr.org/2021/12/08/1062401420/why-abortion-or-adoption-is-not-an-equal-choice

Cradle of Hope Adoption Center. (n.d.). *29 reasons women place baby for adoption.* https:// cradlehope.org/birth-mothers/29-reasons-why-women-place-baby-for-adoption/

Diop, A. (Director). (2023). *Saint Omer* [Motion Picture]. Dogo Digital.

Donohue, J. J., & Levitt, S. D. (2001). The impact of legalized abortion on crime. *Quarterly Journal of Economics, 116*(2), 379–420.

Fergusson, D. M., Horwood, L. J., & Boden, J. M. (2009, November). Reactions to abortion and subsequent mental health. *British Journal of Psychiatry, 195*(5), 420–426. https://doi. org/10.1192/bjp.bp.109.066068. PMID: 19880932.

Fost, D. (2022, June 30). *UCSF turnaway study shows impact of abortion access on well-being.* www.ucsf.edu/news/2022/06/423161/ucsf-turnaway-study-shows-impact-abortion-access

Ge, X., Natsuaki, M., Martin, D., Leve, L., Neiderhiser, J., Shaw, D., Villareal, G., Scaramella, L., Reid, J., & Reiss, D. (2008). Bridging the divide: Openness in adoption and postadoption psychosocial adjustment among birth and adoptive parents. *Journal of Family Psychology, 22*(4), 529–540.

Glasser, G. (2021). *American baby: A mother, a child, and the shadow history of adoption.* Viking.

Goldstein, D. (2022, August 6). Drop box for babies: Conservatives promote a way to give up newborns anonymously. *New York Times.* www.nytimes.com/2022/08/06/us/roe-safe-haven-laws-newborns.html

Henney, S., Ayers-Lopez, S., McRoy, R., & Grotevant, H. (2007). Evolution and resolution: Birthmothers' experience of grief and loss at different levels of adoption openness. *Journal of Social and Personal Relationships, 24*(6), 875–889.

Hrdy, S. (1992, August 30). The myth of mother love. *New York Times*, Sec. 7, p. 11.

Jacobson, C. K., Nielsen, L., & Hardeman, A. (2012). Family trends and transracial adoption in the United States. Adoption Quarterly, *15*, 73–87.

Jason, J., Carpenter, M., & Tyler, C. (1983). Underrecording of infant homicide in the United States. *American Journal of Public Health, 73*, 195–197.

Kahr, B. (2007). Infanticidal attachment. *Attachment: New Directions in Relational Psychoanalysis and Psychotherapy, 1*(2), 117–132.

Kelly, M. L., Westerman, A., & Handel, S. (2021, December 3). Sociologist says women are more likely to choose abortion over adoption. *NPR*. www.npr.org/2021/12/03/1061333491/ sociologist-says-women-are-more-likely-to-choose-abortion-over-adoption

Kertzer, D., & White, M. (1994). Cheating the angel-makers: Surviving infant abandonment in nineteenth-century Italy. *Continuity and Change, 9*(3), 451–480.

Khazan, O. (1921, October 19). The new questions haunting adoption. *Atlantic*. www.theat lantic.com/politics/archive/2021/10/adopt-baby-cost-process-hard/620258/

Kilday, A.-M. (2013). *A history of infanticide in Britain, c. 1600 to the present*. Springer.

Kohn, E. (2018, June 16). "Sunday's illness" review: Netflix's brilliant mother-daughter drama is like "hereditary" without the horror. *IndieWire*. https://indiewire.com/features/ general/sundays-illness-review-netflix-1201975415/

Kortsmit, K., Mandel, M., Reeves, J., Clark, E., Pagano, H. P., Nguyen, A., Petersen, E. E., & Whiteman, M. K. (2021). Abortion surveillance—United States, 2019. *Morbidity and Mortality Weekly Report, 70*(9), 1–29.

Luker, K. (1984). *Abortion and the politics of motherhood*. University of California Press.

Madden, E. E., Ryan, S., Aguiniga, D. M., Killian, M., & Romanchik, B. (2018). The relationship between time and birth mother satisfaction with relinquishment. *Families in Society, 99*(2), 170–183.

Major, B., Appelbaum, M., Beckman, L., Dutton, M., Russo, N., & West, C. (2008). *APA task force finds single abortion not a threat to a woman's mental health*. www.apa.org/ news/press/releases/2008/08/single-abortion

National Safe Haven Alliance Impact Report. 2021–2022. https://www.safehaven.to/wp-content/uploads/2022/07/2021-2022-Safehaven-Annual-Impact-Report-Final.pdf

Nurturing Natures Webmaster. (2022, June 28). *Wade and Roe, abortion. Some less mentioned (controversial?) impacts, like future crime, trauma and babies not loved* (Blogpost). https://nurturingnatures.co.uk/wade-and-roe-abortion-some-less-mentioned-controversial-impacts-like-future-crime-trauma-and-babies-not-loved/

Olasky, M., & Savas, L. (2023). *The story of abortion in America: A street-level history, 1652–2022*. Crossway.

Scheper-Hughes, N. (1993). *Death without weeping*. University of California Press.

Sherwood, V. (2020). The black sun: Symbol of the unwelcome child's annihilation terror in pre-natal infanticidal attachment. *Ata: Journal of Psychotherapy Aotearoa New Zealand, 24*(2), 11–27. https://doi.org/10.9791/ajpanz.2020.09

Sherwood, V. (2021). *Haunted*. Chiron.

Shildrick, M. (2022). Maternal-fetal microchimerism and genetic origins: Some socio-legal implications. *Science, Technology, & Human Values, 47*(6), 1–22.

Sieff, D. F. (2017, June). Trauma-worlds and the wisdom of Marion Woodman. *Psychological Perspectives: A Semiannual Journal of Jungian Thought*, 1–19. file:///C:/Users/writi/ Downloads/SieffD.F.2017Trauma-worldsandthewisdomofMarionWoodmanAuthors copy.pdf

Sisson, G. (2022). Who are the women who relinquish infants for adoption? Domestic adoption and contemporary birth motherhood in the United States. *Perspectives on Sexual and Reproductive Health, 54*(2), 46–53.

Smolin, D. (2005). Child laundering: How the intercountry adoption system legitimizes and incentivizes the practices of buying, trafficking, kidnapping, and stealing children. *Wayne Law Review, 52*.

Söderberg, H., Janzon, L., & Sjöberg, N. O. (1998, August). Emotional distress following induced abortion: A study of its incidence and determinants among abortees in Malmö, Sweden. *European Journal of Obstetrics and Gynecology and Reproductive Biology*, *79*(2), 173–178. https://doi.org/10.1016/s0301-2115(98)00084-0. PMID: 9720837.

Subramanian, S. (2017, March 3). *Nuns in Ireland buried babies and children in mass graves*. www.thenationalnews.com/world/nuns-in-ireland-buried-babies-and-children-in-mass-grave-1.87981

Whelan, J. (2009). *Maternal recognition of pregnancy*. Excerpta Medica.

Chapter 9

Interpreting the Act

In the absence of an understandable explanation of maternal infanticide a Rorschach is left, inviting projection. Uncovering the causes, conditions, and motivations of the infanticidal mother in the preceding chapters attempts to counter the projected narratives, and yet the act of a mother killing her child easily slips into the ineffable, defies the logic of cause-outcome. Still, interpreting the act—understanding its meaning—offers information mothers need.

Anthropology understands maternal infanticide as an evolutionary adaptation in the human struggle for existence. In *Mother Nature*, Hrdy suggested that the pressures that contribute to infanticide may be greatest in patriarchal cultures, where a mother is idealized and under intense pressure to give birth to children and nurture them with self-denying devotion.

> One of Hrdy's revelatory insights was that being a natural mother is not synonymous with unconditional love; rather, evolution has built flexibility into the way that mothers respond to their infants. Depending on circumstances, a mother may be fully committed to her infant, she may feel somewhat ambivalent, or she may abandon her infant to die. And all these emotional responses lie within our species' natural repertoire of behaviors.
>
> (Sieff, 2019, p. 20)

Daniela Sieff pointed out that evolutionary infanticide lives on in the collective unconscious and thus is available to a modern mother's instincts when the circumstances align. Five such circumstances affect a mother's infanticidal reaction to her newborn: (1) her ability to provide for her children, (2) social support availability, (3) the child's health and robustness, (4) the child's disposition toward receiving maternal care, and (5) the child's gender.[1]

Let's apply the first four to the cases of infanticide I've shared in previous chapters. (1) *The inability to provide*: Shannon had an extensive history of trauma and five children. She suffered severe postpartum depression with no family help, an abusive partner, and a part-time job at Burger King. Emotionally, physically, and financially she was unable to provide for her children. (2) *Lack of social support*: Gina lived in a hostage-like situation with her severely abusive boyfriend. He

DOI: 10.4324/9781003412809-12

rarely allowed her to see friends or family without his presence or permission, let alone get support from them. With her three children, Gina lived in an isolated state of survival with no social support. (3) *The child's health*: Astria's newborn was on a CPAP machine at home to assist his breathing after being in the NICU for several months. Similarly, Ruth's adopted toddler, born with fetal alcohol syndrome, had special needs. Both children were frail and required extra resources the mother didn't have. (4) *The child's disposition*: Leora's stepson had experienced his own trauma of witnessing sexual abuse at his mother's house, then acted it out on Leora's young daughters. His behavior triggered her PTSD and violent outrage. Moreover, he was not her biological child, she had a protectiveness toward her daughters, and he was an outsider.

Infanticide as an Act

When referring to *Act* in psychoanalysis, it is neither merely the voluntarily doing of a deed nor simply the motif of rising conflict, climax, and resolution in an event. Rather, an Act is a performance in which the subject "act[s] in conformity with the desire that is in [him or her]" without adhering to ethical, moral, or contextual boundaries (Lacan, 1986/1997, p. 314). The Act is distantly related to *acting out*, a Freudian concept in which the subject "loses himself" in his unconscious fantasies and effectively "relives [them] in the present with a sensation of immediacy, which is heightened by his refusal to recognize their source and their repetitive character" (Laplanche & Pontalis, 1973/1974, p. 4). Yet an Act is not rebellious, reactionary, or reckless; rather, in Lacan's terms and for my purposes when considering the infanticidal mother, the Act refers to an outright (whether conscious or unconscious) rejection of the symbolic contours in which the mother lives—language, norms, structures, and values—that comprise the social order. The Act is a subversion of that order, positioned outside its rules that determine good and bad, thus destabilizing the ruling order's symbolic coordinates.

Lacanian-Marxist philosopher Slavoj Žižek, addressing violent acts from historical genocides to Andrea Yates's murder of her children, wrote:

> Is there not something real/impossible/inexplicable about . . . these acts? Is it not that, as Schelling put it more than 200 years ago, in each of them we confront the ultimate abyss of the free will, the imponderable fact of "I did it because I did it!" which resists any explanation with psychological, social, ideological, etc. causes.
>
> (2001, para. 2)

Although Žižek's statement about free will feels dangerously exciting, she did not just "do it because she did it." She also did not do it because she had to or wanted to. Her Act has layers of meaning regarding her existence, with psychological and social implications and intentions. Her Act generates its own ahistorical possibility; it has the potential to affect all that came before it and all that comes after it. In the way that every infanticide is a *deus ex machina*—a story abruptly, unexpectantly ended—her Act is powerful in its surprise, impossibility, and irreducibility; it stops time and changes everything. Žižek suggested the presence of this meaning when he asserted that the insanity of the Act is a *rejection of the field of the symbolic code of Law* and can be partially attributed to the subject's decision to "strik[e] at himself, at what is most precious to himself" (Butler et al., 2000, p. 122).

At the end of Euripides's play, one of Medea's final lines reflects that precious striking:

> Give not one thought to thy babes, how dear they are or how thou art their mother. This one brief day forget thy children dear, and after that lament; for though thou wilt slay them yet they were thy darlings still, and I am a lady of sorrows.
>
> (as cited in Frisch, 1941, p. 180)

When Medea spoke this line, she'd already put her Act into motion. Here she is encouraging dissociation while also knowing lamentation will come. She names herself the "lady of sorrows," an uncanny precognitive nod to the Biblical "Mary Our Lady of Sorrows," who is aggrieved at the loss of her son, Jesus. Mary lamented, "Yea, a sword shall pierce through thy own soul also" (Luke, 2:34–35), as written circa 150 CE, more than 500 years after Euripides wrote *Medea*. In this way the Death Mother archetypal energies encompass both Mary and Medea in an overlapping experience of *mater dolorosa*—the mother who renounces the fleshly tie to her child and relinquishes him into the world and into death.

Right before the curtain closes, Medea with the corpses of her children is "borne aloft away from Corinth" in a golden chariot driven by dragons sent by her grandfather Helios, the sun God. Euripides saves Medea with a deus ex machina, as he commonly did in his plays to create a surprise ending, a twist that allows Medea to escape and live on, moving beyond the bounds of history into the archetypal. This move transfigures her into an image of the Death Mother and brings the Death Mother forward as both transcending and rejecting the field of ideological meaning tied to *mother* and *murderer* as well as the secularized reality of social or lawful punishment. Evans noted, "Medea does not escape the Law or suspend ideology, but rather casts them into the void along with everything else rejected by her statement's radical finitude: reconciliation, remorse, family, and subjectivity" (48). Žižek suggested that Medea's radical Act is unique in its ability to "out-violence Power itself" or "out-universalize universal Power itself" (as cited in Evans, 2007, p. 51).

Subverting the Code of Law

In 431 BCE, Pericles's Law codified marriage as the institution for preserving citizens' property and codified a woman's primary civic role as the (present or future) mother of citizen children. A woman was legally a daughter, then a wife, then a mother, with all authority in the household perpetually resting on its male head. The ongoing development of male-ruled societies during this time required the destruction or disempowerment of the Great Mother and Goddess worship (Relke, 1999). Within Greek mythology Goddesses, such as Hera, Athena, and Aphrodite, are yet honored and sacrificed to, but it is men who have taken all the power of decision-making and ownership. Women who do hold power—such as medicinal women or priestesses/oracles—become a threat to the increasingly patriarchal nature of early state-based societies, which were built on wars, power struggles, and territorial disputes (Given, 2008). Medea was such a woman. Erich Neumann suggested that Jason abandoned Medea because he was no match for her dangerous individuality. When Medea is left alone, shamed, and disillusioned by Jason's abandonment, she regresses to the archetypal energies of the Death Mother, who Neumann named the "Terrible Mother" (1994, p. 47). The question is: What in Medea's psyche and circumstances aroused the Death Mother's archetypal energies such that striking at what was precious to her and casting herself and her children into the void became the needed Act?

In the era represented in Greek mythology, as the social order was shifting from a matriarchal mentality—non-dominating and goddess-worshiping—to a war-prone, hierarchical, and patriarchal worldview, the collective psyche was also in a state of transition. The mythology from this period (e.g., Euripides, Sophocles, Ovid, Seneca, Aeschylus) is likely both consciously and unconsciously processing this transition. Within this context, it's easier to understand Medea's Act as not so much a personal reaction to Jason's betrayal, although that may have offered a trigger, but as a response to the loss of a feminine-honoring paradigm to a misogynistic life in which women had no agency. In the book, *Violence and Women: Exploring the Medea Myth*, Anita Chapman suggested,

> In the myth, as Euripides presents it, the failure is caused by Jason's regression and submission to the exclusivity of the patriarchal principle—the Old King. Medea, who not only represents the *feminine* but also the forces of Nature and Transformation, is profoundly incompatible with this regression. She reacts! She destroys and creates havoc. This is what the unconscious does when it is not heard or denied.
>
> (2020, p. 2)

If Medea is a symbol of the unheard or denied feminine, now acting out and getting our attention, it is imperative we accurately interpret her. It seems clear her Act is an outrage at the patriarchal system, and by behaving as a Terrible Mother she is a threat to patriarchy. In this symbolic interpretation, Medea reverses the ideal of Mary and rejects the position of Eve. She becomes the dark aspect of the feminine and the mother, ruling over life and death in a way that the dominating system is attempting to control. Medea is outraged, as many of the women of this era arguably were, by the displacement of goddess worship and the suppression of feminine instincts. The potency of this painful rageful cry can be felt in Zoe Caldwell's 1982 blazing and hypnotic performance as Medea on stage. At 21:30 of the televised version she appears in a possessed state, screaming to the Gods in agony after Creon, the "barking dog", exiled her. Slithering like a venomous snake, she hisses, "Women, it is a bitter thing to be a woman."

The ineffable Act of maternal infanticide requires an audience to go beyond their rational and linear paradigms—such as life is more important than death, a child outlives a parent, a mother is never a murderer— so as to understand the essence of the Death Mother and her power of death and transformation. Like Kali, she makes no sense. "Kali is perpetually destroying and at the same time creating—destroying in order to create, creating in order to destroy, death in the service of life, life in the service of death" (Woodman & Dickson, 1992, p. 16). Patriarchal culture, based on the Christian iconography of the spotless Mother and the resurrection of her Son, attempts to take death out of Mother, and yet she brings it inherently with her in miscarriage, menstruation, childbirth, and the mortality of the lives she births. The masculine prefers the linear progress of life from birth, rejecting the cyclical nature of life-death-life-death. The rational patriarchal paradigm seeks progress, mastery, and eternal life, creating a system based on a fear of death, as evident by the drastic attempts to thwart it. While the Western world is attempting to live youthfully forever, the infanticidal mother puts a stop to the denial of death at life's start: She embodies the ability to give and take life, death as part of life, destabilizing the order of progress and time. The Kali energy of the Death Mother breaks the illusion of progress and death-free life, perverts the advancement from animal to human behavior, from barbarian to civilized, establishing humans as mortal and limited beings—as animals.

The patriarchal cultivation of consciousness has an inner need to murder the mother, that is, as far as possible, to "negate, exclude, devalue, and repress the maternal feminine world which represents the unconscious" (Neumann, 1966, p. 100). The wholeness of the mother has been sacrificed in patriarchal culture, rejected as the unconscious is rejected, her inherent relationship with death and power seen as irrational, needing to be repressed and oppressed in women. In *Dancing in the Flames*, Woodman and Dickson elucidated the history and ramifications of the repressed maternal feminine, pointing out that although the patriarchal principle works hard to suppress the feminine out of fear, she reemerges in her repressed state, as unconscious shadow in a tragic and imbalanced mother capable of infanticide. Similarly, Massimilla Harris and Bud Harris stated, "When the feminine principle is repressed into our unconscious, it becomes part of our collective shadow, and this shadow projects itself as a longing, or even a demand, for power" (2015, p. xiv).

A Demand for Power

Although much progress has been made in women's rights, I have seen in my clinical practice with women that it is their powerlessness—enforced by men's violence, poverty, and systemic sexism related to parenting expectations and blame—that breeds the tragedy of infanticide.

Mary, after having her child, was victim to her husband's scrutiny—never getting it right, failing to keep her baby at a healthy weight. In her postpartum depression, the trauma of a man raping her resurfaced, in addition to the unrecognized loss of an abortion. Underlying her psyche was the experience of the sudden loss of an adolescent closeness with her father, when he betrayed the family and abandoned them to begin a life with another woman. Left and bereft, she believed the prospect of death for her and her infant was a better place.

Shannon grew up amidst domestic violence and drug use. Sexually assaulted by the age of 13, she had no sense of stability or safety. The father of her children was severely abusive toward her, from which she had one brief reprieve in a battered women's shelter, only to return to him a month later. By the time of her infanticide, she had 4 children, none of whom were planned, but her abusive partner insisted she continue to have babies and keep those babies instead of giving them up for adoption as she had tried to do. Shannon was suicidal, overwhelmed in hopelessness and powerlessness. Pushed beyond her tolerance, Shannon snapped. The tragic killing of her infant was the definitive act that ended their suffering.

Both Tally and Pam were born with birth defects for which they received little to no assistance. Pam had no contact with her father, and Tally's father had untreated bipolar disorder and regularly raged at the family. Because of both girls' vulnerabilities, they were recruited into inappropriate sexual relationships with older men. Tally and Pam began to have children with abusive men, to whom they became unhealthily attached and dependent. Neither woman worked outside of the home; they depended on state assistance and raised their children on their own. Both women had a child with special needs, adding to the excessive toll of childrearing in impoverishment, with little support, their own disabilities, and constant threats of violence. For Tally, like Shannon, the stress culminated in hitting a tolerance threshold and a lack of control over a violent response to a crying infant. For Pam, the number of children in the home outweighed the availability of resources, physical and intellectual; thus the weakest child, the one living on a breathing machine due to his prematurity, passed away in his sleep.

Lissette, also born with cognitive deficits, was bullied as a child, and then experienced sexual trauma from coyotes who brought her over the border from Guatemala. Once she arrived, her host "brother" bullied her and sexually assaulted her. When she became pregnant, she went into a psychotic state of denial. She had been raised in a strict Catholic home and was deeply ashamed. Isolated and trapped, living under the legal radar, Lisette had almost no options. These are mothers who are screaming into the void that they've been damaged, degraded, forgotten, taken advantage of, and misused.

These women's Acts are the cry of Kali. Women are acting out of powerlessness in their lives, breaking free of roles they are trapped in. Infanticide is an escape from the mundane daily tasks, an urgency to rise with Medea out of the concrete and literal into something bigger and symbolic.

The Good vs Bad Mother

The split between the good and bad mother requires the parts of the feminine perceived as negative to be repressed. These parts then tend to fester and are apt to Act out. The archetypal Death Mother is our culture's primary symbol of this split-off part of the wounded feminine principle; infanticide is her Act, meant to gain our attention.[2] Because of this split, the dark mother is often projected onto the class of mothers who are Othered by race and class in the West. Actively working to repress their negative maternal feelings, mothers often join the projection of "bad mother" onto women deemed inferior to them, perpetuating the collective cultural image of bad mothers as poor, non-White women. The White mother gets to say, "I'm not like that," and the mother of color or impoverished mother acts as the catchall to hold unwanted aspects of motherhood.

I witnessed this in my work with an American Indian mother. During her court proceedings, she stood in handcuffs before a courtroom overwhelmingly filled with White people. All her life, this woman had been disadvantaged due to her impoverished upbringing on one of the poorest reservations in the Midwest. In addition, she had been abused for most of her life by men, first by her father and then her husband, and had been homeless several times when attempting to live off the reservation. Her position in society had brought her to a predestined position: as a container for all that is uncivilized and crude in American society.

Many mothers who killed their children are very good mothers. Among the infanticidal mothers with whom I have worked are women who love children and had longed to be a mother, who adopted children, delivered newborns, or taught preschool. These are women about whom others say, "She loved children, all she wanted was to be a mother, her kids meant everything to her." These perfect mothers often have denied their negative maternal feelings, their ambivalence, hate, and fear toward their children. Because of the intense energy put toward "good mothering," there is a buildup of negative feelings in the unconscious. These dissociated feelings form an autonomous force charged with repressed energy that has the potential to Act. The Act breaks through maternal pressures and expectations, announces the mother's limits, and shatters her good mothering.

Von Franz suggested that certain women, who are bothered or annoyed by their child's needs and the mundane routine of baby caring yet cannot admit even to themselves that they hate the child or resent the child, will overcompensate. Rather than accepting that they may both love *and* hate their child, they read books on how to bring up children and model their behavior thus. The denial, devaluation, and dissociation of this negative maternal consciousness is partly responsible for activating the Death Mother. Her archetypal energy acts from the unconscious, such that a mother's resistance to her authentic negative feelings may cause her "to drop the child, for no reason—an unconscious murder act" (1993, p. 96).

Without an ability to hold the tension or maintain balance between the positive and negative experiences of motherhood, both individually and collectively, the Death Mother is activated. In this way, infanticide is a transgressive Act, an event in the world meant to bring the Death Mother out of the shadows toward psychic balance, an attempt to heal motherhood. Just as a dream has the purpose of healing the whole and ushering individuation, it is the same for the Act of infanticide. It is a recurring nightmare that repeats itself until consciousness has been brought to its potent encounter and the psyche is able to integrate it. By bringing attentive awareness to maternal destruction, it is possible to recover the maternal toward women's choices, experiences, and generative capacities, while also accepting the mother's destructive potential.

The Rage

Medea as Death Mother was consistently described by Euripides as animalistic. He emphasized her "bull-like" glare in protecting her children (Konstantinou, 2012, p. 131), and alternatively referred to her as prey: "Yea, God hath hunted thee, Medea, forth to the foam of a trackless sea" (431BCE/1906, p. 22). Later in the play, Jason says to Medea, "You are a lioness, not a woman, with a nature more savage than Scylla the Tuscan monster!" (as cited in Konstantinou: 132) Which Medea accepts; bereft and maligned, she has turned from being preyed upon to her predatory instincts.

Any animal, if beaten and trapped long enough, will respond with violence. Even a submissive and friendly animal will act out if they experience pain, illness, hunger, or other underlying medical conditions, or if they are repeatedly pushed past their tolerance, especially when earlier warning signs are ignored.

> It turns out man's best friend has a dark side. An estimated 30–50 Americans are killed by dogs each year. Unfortunately, many of these attacks are carried out by dogs that were mistreated by humans in their past.
>
> (Cutolo & LaBianca 2022, "Dogs", para. 1)

If an animal is in captivity for long periods of time, it may exhibit destructive and repetitive behaviors, like grinding its teeth, bobbing its head, hitting its body against walls, or swimming in circles. An animal's brain will change in captivity. When animals—including humans—are reduced to the experience of pain and fear and the struggle to survive, they rely on their instincts.

Many infanticidal mothers have been cornered physically by a violent partner, by suffocating isolation, and/or by poverty. Trapped in fear, the anger and outrage Medea-turned-predator showed toward Jason, his family, and the patriarchal system at large is akin to clinically what is often referred to as *snapping*—acting violently after prolonged mistreatment and toxic stress.

The law of the conservation of energy states that the energy in a system remains constant so that when energy enters an equivalent amount must be discharged. This also applies to violence. When its energetic force lands on a woman from a male abuser, an equal energetic force must respond from her. Most of the time she is likely to discharge energy in acts of self-harm, such as substance abuse, cutting, or suicide attempts, but sometimes it gets unconsciously acted out on another. Although this may be her abuser, it is more likely someone weaker than her, such as a pet or a child.

> Disappointment, broken promises thwarted expectations, insult and humilia-tion, the feeling of being trapped and stuck on top of alienation, exile, poverty, dependency and the loss of personal dignity and opportunity. These are the ele-ments that can combine to incite in a woman anger, violence and the impulse to destroy. She can act it out or turn it against herself. There are many different ways a woman who feels betrayed, rejected and abandoned can destroy her future, her own as well as the future of her children.
>
> (Chapman, 2020, p. 151)

Blowing past a human mother's boundaries by placing superhuman demands on her begins a stockpiling of dynamite sticks within her, ready to ignite when her tolerance or finitude has been fully crossed or triggered.

The idealization of Mother and the ensuing societal pressures are internalized by contemporary mothers. With unrealistic expectations to be an All-Good Mother and her needs and body devalued, the human mother loses her sense of self.

> With only the light side of the mother archetype developed, we lose the ability to be reflective of feminine wholeness. The unreflected mother goddess archetype displays unchecked charity, giving herself to everyone and every situation; thus she becomes the great whore.
>
> (Rand, 1997, p. 48)

The psyche of human mothers can be ruptured by the expectations imaged in the Christian ideal of the Virgin Mother and the ways in which patriarchal culture demands that she gives herself—her sexuality, procreativity, labor, and needs. Without an ability to say no, infanticide becomes the Act that does it for her. With no room to acknowledge and adhere to maternal finitude, she can get caught in the chaos of the Death Mother. In the profound unfairness of the Western maternal mandates,

> mothers may unconsciously project rage toward their children in subtle ways, however the rage isn't really toward the children. The rage is toward the patri-archal culture that requires women to sacrifice and utterly deplete themselves in order to mother a child.
>
> ("Recognize the Roles of Sacrifice and Rage", para. 1)

Maternal infanticide is a perverse way of establishing a distinct sense of the bound-aries between herself and others, including her child. In "Medea and Mothers Who Kill," Kate Smith-Hanssen noted that mothers who become overidentified with their children in maternal solicitude can experience a psychotic merging with the child, not knowing where one begins and the other ends. The only way out is to kill the child part. That way a woman can emerge liberated from her material nonexistence and invisibility as a self into a radically free being. Anna Motz, a British forensic psychoanalyst who worked for many years with violent women, suggested:

> Infanticide is a tragic act of violence which can result from a tremendous fear of social stigma, feelings of total helplessness in relation to an unplanned baby or a range of complex psychological factors which result in an almost psychotic panic, in which killing seems the only solution, particularly when the baby is newborn and has not yet been recognized by the mother as a separate human being.
>
> (Motz, 2000, p. 131)

The Shame

Rage is often a response to shame. In a 2020 piece titled "The Rage Mothers Don't Talk About," Minna Dubin writes, "Mothers are supposed to be patient martyrs, so our rage festers beneath our shame." Feelings of ambivalence, fear, or repulsion toward her baby quickly evoke fear and self-loathing in a mother, as their internal world doesn't match the maternal ideal. These feelings are thus kept in the shadows, hidden even in psychotherapy offices. Women who are struggling with motherhood or experience periodic hatred for their child typically feel they are deficient and bad, possibly even monstrous (Baraitser & Noack, 2007; Myers, 2017). Such beliefs constitute shame—a deep, visceral, and insidious conviction that one is essentially flawed and inadequate. Living with shame can be intolerable. Mothers meet the Death Mother and her infanticidal aspects in the frightening energy of their hostile feelings and/or behaviors toward their child. Her inner dialogue, conscious or unconscious, is *I'm getting it all wrong, I am bad, I am useless*. Then, as she pushes her child off the chair: *See how bad I am*.

> Maternal shame leaves women isolated in an emotional wasteland. Terrified to expose their supposedly inhuman inadequacy to both themselves and others, mothers strive to deny and dissociate their feelings, thus becoming alienated from themselves (and, of course, from their children). In this place, there can be no transformation or healing.
>
> (Sieff, 2019, p. 29)

When mothers feel they must withhold and suppress their negative or ambivalent maternal feelings, their experience of isolation increases. Although the concept of loneliness conjures an image of the elderly person living alone, unkempt, and perhaps desperate—not a woman surrounded by children and family and pets—loneliness in mothers is a paramount and under-acknowledged experience. About 69% of mothers are classified as lonely, seven points higher than the rate of loneliness among fathers. (Panchal et al., 2023). It is not necessarily social isolation that contributes to loneliness, although that is a part of it. According to sociological research, the factors that contribute to loneliness include "personal inadequacies, developmental deficits, and unfulfilling intimate relationships" (Arimoto & Tadaka, 2021, p. 2). Analytical traditions further the definition of loneliness to include: an inability to express oneself to others. In his memoir *Memory Dreams and Reflections*, Jung described a sentiment that resonates with motherhood: "Loneliness does not come from having no people about one, but from being unable to communicate the things that seem important to oneself, or from holding certain views which others find inadmissible" (1961/1963, p. 426).

The experience of maternal shame has increased in a society that has put mothering on capitalistic steroids. According to psychotherapist and parent Rozsika Parker, mothers are feeling much "more judged and policed by society as well as judging themselves harshly" (as cited in Benn, 2006, para. 20). Parker, asserting that shame is the most salient emotion she sees in her work, observed that mothers have the awful sense of not measuring up in the modern world of success-based parenting:

> [A mother] feels the judgmental eyes of the world upon her with particularly shame-inducing force. Every year her child is publicly examined and every year she feels implicated in the results. It's as if her mothering is being awarded an A* or a U.
>
> (Parker, as cited in Benn, para. 21)

Any person burdened by intolerable feelings of disavowing shame may have compulsive thoughts and feelings about ridding themselves of whatever is activating their shame. For mothers, that can mean ridding themselves of the child. Parker reflected, when the mother's "shame mounts . . . soon the child is perceived as nothing more than a guilt-inducing, hateful persecutor" (as cited in Benn, para. 13).

In 2000, Josephine Stanton and her colleagues in Auckland, Australia interviewed women who had been arrested for infanticide. Almost all the interviewees spoke to the cultural idealization of motherhood and their resulting feelings of failure. In another similar study, impoverished mothers who had been diagnosed with depression revealed that their explicit and implicit narratives of psychological distress most often involved anger, frequently imagined in violence toward their children (Kruger et al., 2014). In this study, through the course of collecting and analyzing narratives, Kruger et al. found that depression obscured the women's anger at having to mother in adverse conditions. They suggested that the participants were "frustrated with trying to live up to idealized notions of motherhood in impoverished contexts" (461). They found that the participant's thoughts were melancholic, self-defeating, murderous, and violent in reaction to the idealization of motherhood bearing down on them. In her analysis of this study, Jacqueline Rose pointed out, "They felt they had failed because they lashed out at their children but they lashed out at their children because they felt they had failed" (2018,

p. 187). Within the dark and lonely experiences of failure and shame in isolation, the grounds become fertile for rage and violence.

The Revenge

Akin to Euripides' depiction of Medea as scorned and vengeful, infanticide as revenge is a theory commonly propounded in the media. In constructing and representing the infanticidal mother, news articles communicate the essential message: *She did it to get back at her husband/boyfriend.* Recent examples include: "Woman Spitefully Texts Photo of Dead Toddler to Baby's Father During Fight" (*Essence*, 2020), "Mom Accused of Killing Baby with Teaspoon of Salt to 'Get Her Husband Back'" (Tribune Media Wire, 2016), "Va. Mom Who Killed Daughters in Plot to Exact Revenge on Husband, Then Called to Tell Him, Gets 78 Years" (*People*, 2023), "Gresham woman kills 2 young children, herself in midst of custody battle" (*The Oregonian*, 2021).

The revenge theory makes three baseless assumptions: A woman feels she cannot live without a man, that a man is more important to her than her child, and that the child is excessively sacred to the man.

It is a familiar narrative: the violence toward the child is a manifestation of the weak and needy character of a woman, delusionally dependent on her husband for attention and attachment, and so desperate for attention from him that she would use what's most sacred to her to retaliate. In 2004, Lois Pomplun was convicted of reckless homicide in the death of her 9-month-old daughter. An article on her case reads, "Law enforcement officials believe [she] had a history of suffocating the girl in order to gain attention from her husband" (Graff, 2004, para. 24). Lois also happened to be born with fetal alcohol syndrome, was one of 10 children, and was adopted as an infant. Her adoptive mother died when Lois was 9, and Lois suffered "severe depressive episodes" most of her life. The reality of Lois' life begs the question: Did Lois want attention from her husband, or did she want to be left alone?[3]

Euripides' narrative, that Medea was abandoned by Jason and was mad, enraged, and ashamed, so the suitable revenge was to kill their children, is suspicious. Not only because Euripides is a man and Greek myths have been interpreted and propagated from a male point of view in service of patriarchal structures, but because I have come to know the infanticidal mother and I have yet to meet one who has expressed feeling scorned. The hypothesis that women kill their own children to get back at their wayward husbands is a construct born of a sentiment found in the 1697 play *The Mourning Bride*, written by British playwright William Congreve (2011). His play popularized the belief in the vengeful woman in its often-quoted lines from Zara in Act III, Scene II: "Heav'n has no rage, like love to hatred turn'd, Nor hell a fury, like a woman scorn'd."

This quote, burned into our collective psyches, constructs the irrational, furious, mad woman who is capable of abhorrent destruction when her husband betrays her. In 1969, forensic psychiatrist Phillip Resnick included "the revenge theory" as one of five basic motives in maternal filicide. However, more recent theorists such as Cheryl Meyer and her coresearchers, who work, study, and write on maternal filicide, dropped it as a category in their 2001 book, *Mothers Who Kill Their Children*.

Perpetuating the revenge theory does two things: (1) It further pathologizes a woman as irrational, crude, and crazy, and (2) It solidifies her psychological and physical status as subordinate to and dependent on man. The historical patriarchal construct of a scorned woman is a way to trap and belittle her rage as being about *abandonment by a man*; thus, the court of popular opinion judges infanticide as a grotesque overreaction of a woman's feelings, instead of seriously considering what she is so angry about.

Meanwhile, fathers are "more likely to kill [their children] out of revenge towards a partner or former partner in the context of family separation" (Buiten, 2021, "Why Men Commit Filicide", para. 1) or as a result of "fatal physical abuse" (Leveille & Doyon, 2019: "Results", para. 1). In such cases, children are treated as an instrument of retaliation (typically when an abused mother leaves the father[4]) and are killed in a deliberate attempt to cause the partner to suffer. This type of violence often occurs after a series of acts of abuse have been committed by the male perpetrator toward the mother and the children (Bourget & Bradford, 1990; Lewis & Bunce, 2003; Liem & Koenraadt, 2018).[5] Thus, it would seem interpretations of maternal infanticide as revenge are actually projections of a man's psychology onto women.

There is an element of revenge in the Death Mother, but it is as Von Franz wrote, as death's revenge against life. In this regard, "nature is sometimes harsh, severe and cruelly revengeful. There is neither judgment nor rule, but the revenge of the dark aspect of the feminine nature goddess" (1993, p. 39). The revenge of the feminine nature acting through maternal infanticide is an attempt to restore justice. It is not revenge toward an unruly husband, but toward a tribe of men who have made the rules that imprison her. In mythology this energy is sometimes referred to as the Furies, Greek Erinyes, or Eumenides, who have been said to be the daughters of Gaia and Nyx (Night). They are thus known as dark feminine (sometimes as sisters) who live in the underworld and ascend to earth to take revenge on the negative masculine (Graves, 1988). They are "vengeful ghoulish bloodthirsty goddesses who wish to avenge the maternal blood" (Stone, 2014, p. 327).

According to Von Franz, nature rectifies masculine law in a complementary way, which can be seen from the outside as ugly. She gave the example of the infant animal who wants to be fed by his mother for too long, taking up space from the other infants, thus the mother gives the child a harsh bite to stop him. This functioning of the feminine rule of balance is not recognized in Christian patriarchal civilization. Instead, law is based on "just" punishments, doling out equal punishments for equal offenses. In 1993, Von Franz suggested there will be revenge from nature because "White man's civilization is contributing to overpopulation, so there will be a virus with mutations or an atomic bomb" (41). Such is the cyclical nature of Mother Earth. If humanity creates an excess, "the dark side of nature appears asserting its claim on the child" (37).[6]

The Abandonment

Early experiences of abandonment from central relational figures set a deep frac-
ture in attachment patterns for adults; without treatment, these wounds will be
enlivened in self-sabotaging or destructive ways. Relational patterns can be set
according to these attachment traumas creating contexts of violence and shame that
overwhelm their ability to cope. Mary (mentioned earlier) experienced a closeness
with both of her parents growing up, especially her father. Mary played softball
throughout her childhood, with her dad often being her coach. Long hours of car
rides, dinners, and post-game chats filled her sense of self. But when Mary was in
high school, she discovered her father had cheated on her mother. He suddenly left
the family and created a new family with another woman. Having been abandoned
by her longed-for father, Mary predictably struggled in relationships with men,
often allowing herself to be taken advantage of or intensely attaching herself to
destructive men. When her husband began ruthlessly criticizing her and aligning
himself with his own mother, she was again the victim of abandonment, but this
time it overwhelmed her psyche. Mary, now imprisoned for ending the life of her
child, seems to be stuck in a world in which she is both victim and perpetrator.
While she consistently speaks of her lost father and husband, and the troubles the
world has dealt her, she also expresses regret and remorse for the ending of her
child's life.

Motz noted some women would be "emotionally detached from her offence,
presenting herself as a victim of violence and rejection rather than as aggressor
herself" (2000, p. 121). She reflected on the role of abandonment in one of her client's stories:

[She was] enraged by her own abandonment, by her husband, son and at a
deeper level, her own mother. In fantasy she became the abandoned infant whose
depressed mother had neglected and rejected her. She powerfully projected
these feelings onto the baby who became the embodiment of the unwanted,
demanding and completely helpless child.

(120)

Motz included several case studies in her book, *The Psychology of Female Violence: Crimes Against the Body*, most of which echo the cases I have seen:

In the cases of women who kill their children there is a conflict between the
desire to have children and the fear of motherhood, which may reflect a complex
relationship between them and their own mothers, in which feelings of rivalry,
envy, anger and deprivation may be evident. The mother who cannot bear to
hear her infant scream may be rejecting or assaulting it because she wanted the
baby to contain her despair and feels unable to perform that maternal function
herself. Again this may relate to abuse, neglect and trauma in her own experiences in childhood, which dramatically interfere with her own relationship

with her children. DeMause (1990) suggests that infanticidal mothers have had highly inadequate child-rearing experiences and have harsh punitive superegos that demand punishment of their strongest wishes including their wish to be a mother.

(2000, p. 127)

Importantly, Motz's research points to maternal subjectivity as an interplay between past and present in the mother, in which a mother's historical relationship with her mother is present and even activated in her relationship with her child. This directly implicates the infanticidal mother's *mother* in her parenting and in her infanticidal Act. If there is a significant wound in the early relationship with her mother, disorienting pain and rage may be invoked in a new light in her new existence as mother. "The ultimate object of revenge is their own abandoning mother, as identified in themselves and then in their extensions, their babies" (Motz, 2000, p. 120). Motz wrote of her client,

The offense served several functions for Dawn, first, through the temporary annihilation of the hated aspects of herself; second, through the fantasized revenge on her mother and actual revenge on her husband; third, to draw her own alienation and despair to the attention of the paternalistic psychiatric and custodial services. It also communicated to the world her symbolic ownership and control of Gabriel [the child]. Her request for containment and a "place of safety" was expressed through the infanticide, and tragically it was only through this act that her needs for psychiatric treatment were met. She did not feel able to ask for help in her own strangled voice and needed to gain some sense of power through her own capacity for destruction. In the past she had used threats about her own suicidal intentions to gain entry to the psychiatric services.

(118)

Estela Welldon, a psychoanalytic researcher and clinician who wrote extensively on severe female pathology, also found that women who committed infanticide were experiencing the psychotic pain of abandonment from their own mothers. What Welldon called *perverse mothering* refers to a significant psychic disruption that can occur in the tension of meeting a child's needs as an adult woman while being prompted to separate from one's own mother. These disruptions lead to a feeling of "intense hatred" toward the mother, although it may be unrecognized (1992, p. 9), and can result in acts of hostility toward her own body or the body of her baby, both extensions of the maternal body.[7]

Both Motz's and Welldon's points touch on the salient experiences that I have seen in women who've had a postpartum crisis. In the 4- or 6-hour or 3-day interviews I conduct, I am listening for the most wounded parts of a woman and the traumas that brought her to her current state. Oftentimes her sense of grief, abandonment, and shame from her own mother has not been spoken about to anyone before as to blame one's mother, especially in African American cultures, is often taboo. Yet that tends to be where the pain began which fueled her violent act. In the forensic cases I've presented, there are many examples of broken maternal bonds. Several of the mothers described being shamed by their mothers, such as Shannon and Ruth. Even in the retelling of the story, years later, there is a concern in having "disappointed" their mothers.

This maternal pain surfaced with Denise, who shot and killed her landlord 8 weeks after she delivered her child. As a child Denise experienced sexual assault from her stepfather, then had an early teenage pregnancy by a classmate. She attempted to conceal that pregnancy, as she wanted to keep the child and raise it herself, but her mother discovered the pregnancy and insisted she have an abortion. Denise refused but her mother forced her, and as she was already in her third trimester the abortion was an extensive 3-day traumatic event. Denise went on to have several abusive relationships, another traumatic sexual assault, and became a mother to five children. We met after she was arrested for killing her landlord, who was attempting to sexually assault her in the presence of her 8-week-old. The piece of her story that was the most emotional for her, that took the most out of her and was the longest for us to get through, was her abortion—her mother wound. Denise had never resolved that loss for herself. She had wanted that baby and it felt like it was stolen and killed inside of her, against her wishes. She had not forgotten or forgiven her mother. That event went on to inform all her other choices and contributed to a depressive shame in her sense of self. This was the most wounded part of her. Never discussed and never treated, it ended in deep depression, isolation, violence, and a prison sentence.

A daughter who has a broken or damaged connection with her own mother may suffer with an inability to mother herself. Woodman identified the presence of the Death Mother in a woman as a state of being unloving and unmothering toward herself, inherited from her own mother and often leading to addictions, destructive relationships, or eating disorders. In her desire to have a baby—to "have someone who would love her"—a mother may be looking for the fullness, warmth, and value that she did *not* receive from her mother and cannot manage to create for herself. In these instances, the mother is usually headed for disappointment, as unrealistic expectations and conflicted and unwanted feelings often overtake the mother who has not learned to value her needs and mother herself.

S. Alease Ferguson and Toni King described how this experience of longing for mother is more acute in African American girls. The trauma in the mother–daughter bond has been precipitated by the inability of many African American mothers to be wholly present for their own daughters while they cared for other people's children in diverted mothering, suffered impoverishment, or lived in violence. Ferguson and King pointed out:

> When the very promise of the mother–daughter bond rings hollow and beyond reach, albeit in plain view, such unfulfilled striving for relational wholeness with the mother can drive the developmental urge for maternal connection and ultimately self-connection, underground. In a racist society, this leaves Black

daughters particularly vulnerable. The daughter struggles with unmet mother needs that play out at a level resembling the stage of infantile rage . . . The result is a form of alienation from the feminine soul-self that plagues a girl's development, ruptures the mother-daughter bond, and threatens vitality one or more spheres of the adult daughter's life.

(2014, p. 180)

In this way, the Act is a cry for help, both in her personal relationships and to the wider culture. At first it begins as a longing typically ignored and suppressed within her, then it becomes a screaming demand. Unmothered mothers can be incredibly independent and self-sufficient women, having essentially raised themselves and possibly younger siblings. They often have lived a life without allowing themselves the disappointment of depending on another. One woman I spoke to described being in a state of postpartum psychosis and literally screaming for someone to help her. With her infant just days old, she pleaded with her husband to not leave for work and with her mother-in-law to spend nights with her. Eventually, when she knew that her psychosis was escalating, she insisted on being taken to the hospital. Even at the hospital, because she appeared "high functioning," they sent her home. This woman became increasingly unwell and began plotting the death of herself and her child. It was only in her truly volatile and deranged behavior that the husband took her back to the ER. Later, she and I talked about how "crazy" she had to become to get help. Although there is a myth that strong women don't need help or are difficult to help, these women need help. Their extreme competence can come crumbling down upon them in the absence of inner and outer maternal scaffolding.

These stories speak to the longing a woman has for her mother. Rebecca Saunders pointed out in her book, *Lamentation and Modernity in Literature, Philosophy, and Culture*, that when a person experiences trauma their psyche regresses to an infantile state. This infantile state is the pre-libidinal position of primary identification prior to ego separation and subject–object relationship governed by bonding to mother. Essentially, this translates to: When something awful happens, you want your mom. The psyche may assess that in a deprived state of unhappiness, whether it be isolation, abuse, or psychosis, what is required is the induction of a trauma that will return one to an infantile, dependent, and cared-for state. In other words, infanticide is paradoxically a trauma-filled Act trying to bring the new mother closer to her lost and missing mother or maternal within herself. The trauma returns the victim to a moment of dependency on the mother, a state of passive subjection to the feminine and to the original mother rupture.

The Madness

The Death Mother archetype and postpartum psychosis are forms of madness akin to hysteria, the original female trouble. Hysteria is no longer recognized as a medical disorder, but was treated routinely for hundreds of years in Western Europe as a female malady of the uterus (the term *hysteria* stems from the Greek cognate of uterus), with symptoms such as "overdramatic or attention-seeking behavior . . . fainting, sexual desire, insomnia, fluid retention, heaviness in the abdomen, irritability, sexually forward behavior, and a tendency to cause trouble for others" (Maines, 1999, p. 23).

Like hysteria, psychosis is known to manifest in women in significant transition periods in life that are accompanied by drastic hormonal changes and rites of passage: namely, puberty, childbirth, and menopause. It seems that because a mother has a uterus, the ability to reproduce a child, the breasts to feed that child, and the primal instinct to keep that child alive, she has a distinct type of madness. Women-specific pathologies like postpartum psychosis are baffling to Western science. Like female madness and hysteria, they tend to be dismissed as evil at worst, nonsense at best.[8]

Psychosis, as understood from an analytical perspective, is the result of a severe personality disturbance in which there is marked regression in ego control. The delusions and hallucinations are ideas, concepts, beliefs, and images from the unconscious that, without ego control, burst forth into consciousness as a waking nightmare (Jung, 1961/1963).[9] A simplified explanation is that the ego identifies with the emerging unconscious content, the bizarre beliefs, and is enveloped into the delusion.[10] Most women I've met who have experienced postpartum psychosis describe being in and out of the delusion, at one moment believing they have to leave the country because a giant holocaust is occurring, evidenced by the construction trucks around the block; in the next hour being able to feed her children, change them, sing to them, and gently put them to sleep while planning the next night's dinner.

Psychosis can put us in touch with deeper and earlier forms of the archetypal feminine, the hidden consciousness of the dark engulfing void—both creative and destructive (Sherwood, 2021, p. 202) —thus opening a primitive expression of violence long suppressed from consciousness. These may be the long-buried negative and destructive maternal taboos. For many mothers, the regression into psychosis is ripe for violence.

> Moreover, for these individuals (in themselves vulnerable to stress due to disease characteristics), the accumulation of emotional and physical stress associated with parenting plays an important role in sudden and catastrophic failure in the psyche of an already weakened self. For each of these patients, as part of their personality disorder is the repressed rage that is violently released by his psychosis.
>
> (Almeida & Vieira, 2017, p. 186)

For women who experience postpartum psychosis, only a fraction (4%) of them will commit infanticide, and it tends to be those with illusory beliefs that are focused on the child. She may hear voices telling her to sacrifice the child in the name of God, or that the infant is an alien. Sometimes, in psychosis, the Act is not designed to sacrifice the baby, but to save it from a fate worse than death; this is *altruistic infanticide*. It is an Act dependent on personal ethics and justice outside the Law. We see this historically in slave mothers who killed their children to save them from the horrors of abuse and enslavement. This represents a sentiment that is repeated over and over in present-day infanticide narratives and it is squarely located in a maternal instinct.

The Subversion

French post-structuralist feminists have long interpreted the madwoman as subversive. They have argued that because patriarchal rules and institutions have situated women/mothers as hidden in domestic, submissive, and caretaking roles, it is only an act of madness that subverts these rules and systems by which women have been defined. Irigaray suggested the hysteric's response to her life is making way for her voice and her message (Chisholm, 1994). A woman's hysteric language does not make rational sense in masculine forms of logic and reason; it is messy, circular, incoherent, and nightmarish. Hélène Cixous saw the hysteric as a revolutionary, in the sense that she is "the typical woman in all her force" because she "resists the system" not by directly contesting patriarchy, but by making her protest known indirectly through her hysteria (Dane, 1994).

Yet like Susan Ayres, I ask, "Can we argue that the psychotic mother, like the hysteric, makes her protest known indirectly—a protest, for instance, to the difficulties of mothering, to her oppression within the patriarchy, and to her own loss of self and speech?" (2006, p. 112) In a 2014 article in the *Washington Post*, journalist Fredrick Kunkle examined the explanation of infanticide as committed by a woman who, because of her lack of access to traditional power sources, i.e. financial, physical, or gender status, is left to use the object of her child as a means to obtain that forbidden power. In other words, the transgression of infanticide is the only power available to a mother. Moreover, if women had a longer tradition of belonging to the power structure their attitudes toward men and children would not be governed as they are by fear and rage. This is seen in Medea,

> [who] is intensely threatening to the Greek patriarchal society by killing her children. She expresses what is usually seen as male power, that is the right of the father to reject. A woman must kill a child in order to take this active position. Medea empowers herself when she has power over life and death. Medea rejects the bondage when she kills her children, she dissolves the last bond between her and Jason. She is again virginal in that she depends on no man anymore. Empowerment and autonomy seem the key terms in this transformation.
>
> (Morgane, 2010, p. 11)

For the African American mother, subversiveness is even more layered, protesting not merely the prevailing social conditions endangering the Black mother–child dyad, but also the White middle-class Christian ideal that shapes the constructions of motherhood. As Dorothy Roberts persuasively argued, "The cherished icon of the mother nurturing her child is also imbued with racial imagery . . . . And even today, society views Black mothers as outside the class labeled 'ideal mothers'" (as cited in Ayres, 2004, p. 335). The infanticide in Toni Morrisson's novel *Beloved* is subversive in that Sethe's radical Act makes it true that the dominant forces have no power over her baby; only her insanity does, and the baby's "death is the price paid for freedom" (Martinez, 2009, p. 5).

The Act of infanticide definitively rejects the pious all-nurturing image of Mother in favor of the dangerous mother, invoking the figures of Lilith and Medea, completely replacing an angelic image with mythical mother-monsters. The renunciation of the Virgin Mary's possession and power over maternity effectively dismantles the Christian model of motherhood for all women of every culture, race, and religion.

It is a tentative leap to imagine the psychotic mother, like the hysterical woman, experiences madness as a protest and an attempt to subvert the status quo of modern womanhood and motherhood; in fact, this image of a psychotic infanticidal mother as a subversive woman is troubling. It is irresponsible and discompassionate to assert that a mother's greatest tragedy is a liberatory act of heroism. Not one of the women I've met reported that they committed their act for a revolutionary cause, although many have noted it was in response to larger systemic issues oppressing them. So should we view infanticidal mothers, like Shannon, Pam, or Gina, as empowered actors or as victims of their circumstances? Ultimately, Ayres purported that the hysteric does not have actual subversive potential because mental illness, including hysteria and psychosis, silences these mothers.

> While some might believe that Yates, Laney, and Diaz [mothers who committed infanticide] indirectly protested their overwhelming super-mom responsibilities, such as home-schooling children—and in Yates's case, being almost always pregnant or breastfeeding—these mothers do not come across as figures of empowerment. Although these responsibilities of mothering factored into their mental state, these psychotic mothers were not empowered, they were silenced. We can view them as subjects of empowerment only if we completely ignore the reality of their mental illnesses.
>
> (2006, p. 112)

Similarly, French feminist philosopher Catherine Clément questioned the claims of empowerment in hysteria. Unlike Cixous, Clement did not see the hysteric as revolutionary because the hysteric woman has not been effective. Rather, "she herself is the place where everything is turned back against her; she is paralyzed by it, physically or otherwise, and thus loses her impact" (Eagelton, 1991, p. 129). Almost all the women in the U.S. who have committed infanticide have lost their civic freedom.

It is possible the response to the infanticidal mother's Act is where it loses its power of subversion. It is her incarceration, her headlines, and her permanent position as *bad* or *mad* that maintain the status quo of motherhood. By knowing their actual stories directly, without appropriation, mitigation, or projection, the protest may be better understood and thus more impactful. The subversive potential is best enacted when their subjectivity and voices are heard because each story told by these speaking subjects has something to say about motherhood.

For Mary, she drowned her infant with her love. Triggered by abandonment and hurt, she transferred all her love and vigilance into her child, ultimately removing him from a hurtful world, bankrupt of possibilities. Ruth had a shaming father and an alcoholic mother and was violently abused by boyfriends; she suffered late miscarriages but adopted a child from foster care. When she could no longer contain her rage at her entrapment in abuse and deprivation, she snapped at her baby. Leora was protecting her daughters when she attacked her stepson (vicariously her younger sexually abused self from her sadistic predatory father). Gina was never taught that a man who loved her didn't beat her, but she never beat her children, yet she couldn't keep her abusive partner from beating her baby or the courts from convicting and imprisoning her for his actions. To hear these women's stories, something gets stirred in the listener, a sense of expanded awareness and knowledge about what it means to mother under these circumstances. This shift in our consciousness is the subversive change for which we can hope.

If we attend to the infanticidal mother's story, she encourages us to take seriously the plight of mothers trapped at home and tortured with intrusive thoughts of bringing harm to her baby, as well as to the inheritance of maternal trauma in racism and oppression as revealed in Morrison's *Beloved*. We also understand how the infanticidal mother serves as an outlet for the excess of victimization and violence a woman's psyche holds. Unbound by social, personal, or political constraints, she performs a dangerous Act of utter freedom. In my work, as I get close to her desperately free act, I feel its vibration and at the same time the dense immoveable presence of unmitigated grief that shackles her feet.

Notes

1 Of the cases I've worked on, most of the victims have been male, echoing research that has found in industrialized Western nations more than half of infanticidal victims are male (Porter & Gavin, 2010), but are likely unrelatable to anthropological findings.

2 The repression of the feminine principle also happens in men. In Western patriarchal societies most men experience feminine qualities as foreign or shameful.

3 In *Touched Out: Motherhood, Misogyny, Consent and Control* (2023), Amanda Montei outlines the deep desire mothers have to be left alone to take back their bodies from their children and husbands, although it's difficult to do as it's generally stigmatized as narcissistic, selfish, or immoral.

4 A well-established factor that precipitates male violence is a partner leaving or communicating their intention to leave the relationship (Dziewa & Glowacz, 2021).

5 Even males who commit filicide are sometimes described as suffering from a "Medea complex."

6 We may also consider the Death Mother archetype in the service of natural revenge in light of fertility assistance, increasingly used by families in the West. Historically, if a mother couldn't conceive, her only option was to accept and mourn her condition, and perhaps adopt. But now women can override these natural limits with IVF and

surrogacy, thwarting what "mother nature had in mind." Thus, it may be that abortion and infanticide reestablish the balance.

7 In "Dancing with Death," Welldon created an informative graph of the destructive and perverted drives that range from Munchausen by proxy to child pornography.

8 Anti-Christian, 2nd-century pagan philosopher Celsus declared that Mary Magdalene was "a hysterical female . . . who . . . likely, wanted to impress others by telling this fantastic tale, and so by this cock-and-bull story to provide a chance for other beggars" (Schaberg, 2004 [2002], pp. 84–85). Generations of envisioning, prophetic, and poetic women have been dismissed as hysterical.

9 In 1907 while at Burghölzli Hospital in Zurich, Jung drew an association between the content of dreams and the content of hallucinations and delusions (See Jung, 1909/1974).

10 My early work was with schizophrenia and psychosis (See Laufer, 2010).

References

Almeida, F., & Vieira, D. (2017). Profiling in violent crimes: The perpetrator and the victim in cases of filicide. In W. Petherick & G. Sinnamon (Eds.), *The psychology of criminal and antisocial behavior* (pp. 167–209). Academic Press.

Arimoto, A., & Tadaka, E. (2021). Individual, family, and community factors related to loneliness in mothers raising children less than 3 years of age: A cross-sectional study. *Women's Health, 21*(1), 1–11.

Ayres, S. (2004). The silent voices of the law. In M. Meyer (Ed.), *Literature and law* (pp. 21–36). Texas A&M Law Scholarship.

Ayres, S. (2006). Newfound religion: Mothers, God, and infanticide. *Fordham Urban Law Journal, 33*, 335.

Baraitser, L., & Noack, A. (2007). Mother courage: Reflections on maternal resilience. *British Journal of Psychotherapy, 23*(2), 171–188.

Benn, M. (2006, October 27). Deep maternal alienation. *The Guardian.* www.theguardian.com/lifeandstyle/2006/oct/28/familyandrelationships.family2

Bourget, D., & Bradford, J. M. (1990). Homicidal parents. *The Canadian Journal of Psychiatry, 35*(3), 233–238.

Buiten, D. (2021, January 19). Men and women kill their children in roughly equal numbers, and we need to understand why. *The Conversation.*

Butler, J., Laclau, E., & Žižek, S. (2000). *Contingency, hegemony, universality: Contemporary dialogues on the left.* Verso.

Chapman, A. (2020). *Violence and women: Exploring the Medea myth.* Chiron.

Chisholm, D. (1994). Irigaray's hysteria. In C. Burke, N. Schor, & M. Whitford (Eds.), *Engaging with Irigaray* (pp. 264–283). Columbia University Press.

Congreve, W. (2011). *The works of William Congreve* (Vol. I). Oxford University Press.

Cutolo, M., & LaBianca, J. (2022, November 28). 22 animals that are deadlier than sharks. *Reader's Digest.* www.rd.com/list/animals-that-are-deadlier-than-sharks/

Dane, C. (1994). Hysteria as feminist protest: Dora, Cixous, Acker. *Women's Studies, 23*(3), 231–255.

DeMause, L. (1990). The history of child assault. *The Journal of Psychohistory, 18*(1), 1–29.

Dubin, M. (2020, April 15). The rage mothers don't talk about. *New York Times.* www.nytimes.com/2020/04/15/parenting/mother-rage.html

Dziewa, A., & Glowacz, F. (2021). Getting out from intimate partner violence: Dynamics and processes. A qualitative analysis of female and male victims' narratives. *Journal of Family Violence, 37*, 643–656.

Eagelton, M. (1991). *Feminist literary criticism.* Routledge.

Euripides. (431 BCE/1906). *The Medea of Euripides* (G. Murray, Trans.). Oxford University Press.

Euripides. (431 BCE/n.d.). *Euripides' Medea* (C. A. E. Luschnig, Trans.). file:///C:/Users/writi/OneDrive/Desktop/medea.pdf

Evans, C. (2007). Medea's family reunion: The Lacanian act & aphanisis as a challenge to liberal humanism. *Cinephile: The University of British Columbia's Film Journal, 3*(1), 47–60. https://doi.org/10.14288/cinephile.v3i1.197827

Ferguson, A., & King, T. (2014). Dark animus: A psychodynamic interpretation of the consequences of diverted mothering among African-American daughters. In P. Bueskens (Ed.), *Mothering and psychoanalysis* (Ch. 6.). Demeter Press.

Franz, M.-L. V. (1993). *The feminine in fairy tales* (Rev. 1st ed.). Shambhala.

Frisch, M. E. (1941). *The Medea of Euripides and Seneca: A comparison* [Master's Theses]. 180. https://ecommons.luc.edu/luc_theses/180

Given, J. (2008). Constructions of motherhood in Euripides' Medea. In S. Constantinidis (Ed.), *Text & presentation* (pp. 42–54). McFarland Press.

Graff, D. (2004, July 30). Woman is sentenced to 35 years in death of child. *Watertown Daily Times*.

Graves, R. (1988). *The Greek myths*. Moyer Bell.

Harris, M., & Harris, B. (2015). *Into the heart of the feminine*. Daphne.

Hrdy, S. (1999). *Mother nature: Natural selection and the female of the species*. Chatto & Windus.

Jung, C. G. (1963). *Memories, dreams, reflections* (A. Jaffe, Ed., R. Winston & C. Winston, Trans.). Vintage. (Original work published 1961)

Jung, C. G. (1974). *The psychology of dementia praecox* (A. A. Brill, Trans.). Princeton University Press. (Original work published 1909)

Konstantinou, A. (2012). The lioness imagery in Greek tragedy. *Quaderni Urbinati Di Cultura Classica, 101*(2), 125–141. www.jstor.org/stable/23347423

Kruger, L.-M., van Straaten, K., Taylor, L., Lourens, M., & Dukas, C. (2014). The melancholy of murderous mothers: Depression and the medicalization of women's anger. *Feminism and Psychology, 24*(4), 461–478.

Kunkle, F. (2014, September 27). What makes mothers kill their own children? *Washington Post*.

Lacan, J. (1997). *The seminar of Jacques Lacan: The ethics of psychoanalysis (Book VII)* (D. Porter, Trans.). W.W. Norton. (Original work published 1986)

Laplanche, J., & Pontalis, J. (1974). *The language of psycho-analysis* (D. Nicholson-Smith, Trans.). W. W. Norton. (Original work published 1973)

Laufer, B. (2010). Beyond countertransference: Therapists' experiences in clinical relationships with patients diagnosed with schizophrenia. *Psychosis: Psychological, Social and Integrative Approaches, 2*(2), 163–172. https://doi.org/10.1080/17522430902736893

Leveille, S., & Doyon, L. (2019). Understanding the motives behind male filicide to better intervene. *European Review of Applied Psychology, 69*(2), 73–81.

Lewis, C., & Bunce, S. (2003). Filicidal mothers and the impact of psychosis on maternal filicide. *Journal of the American Academy of Psychiatry and Law, 31*(4), 459–470.

Liem, M., & Koenraadt, F. (2018). *Domestic homicide: Patterns & dynamics*. Routledge.

Maines, R. P. (1999). *The technology of orgasm: "Hysteria", the vibrator, and women's sexual satisfaction*. Johns Hopkins University Press.

Martinez, I. (2009). Toni Morrison's *beloved*: Slavery haunting America. *Journal of Jungian Scholarly Studies, 4*(3), 1–28.

Meyer, C., Oberman, M., & White, K. (2001). *Mothers who kill their children*. New York University Press.

Montei, A. (2023). *Touched out: Motherhood, misogyny, consent and control*. Beacon Press.

Morgane, J. S. (2010). *Interpreting Medea*. GRIN.

Motz, A. (2000). *The psychology of female violence: Crimes against the body*. Routledge.

Myers, A. (2017). *Blessed among women?* Oxford University Press.

Neumann, E. (1966). Narcissism, normal self-formation, and the primary relation to the mother. *Spring*, 81–106.

Neumann, E. (1994). *The fear of the feminine*. Princeton University Press.

Panchal, N., Saunders, H., Rudowitz, R., & Cox, C. (2023, March 20). The implications of COVID-19 for mental health and substance use. *KFF*. www.kff.org/mental-health/issue-brief/the-implications-of-covid-19-for-mental-health-and-substance-use/

Porter, T., & Gavin, H. (2010). Infanticide and neonaticide: A review of 40 years of research literature on incidence and causes. *Trauma, Violence & Abuse*, *11*(3), 99–112.

Rand, E. (1997). *Recovering feminine spirituality*. CreateSpace.

Relke, D. M. A. (1999). *Greenwor(l)ds*. University of Calgary Press.

Resnick, P. J. (1969). Child murder by parents: A psychiatric review of filicide. *American Journal of Psychiatry*, *126*(3), 325–334.

Rose, J. (2018). *Mothers: An essay on love and cruelty*. Farrar, Straus and Giroux.

Saunders, R. (2007). *Lamentation and modernity in literature, philosophy, and culture*. Palgrave Macmillan.

Schaberg, J. (2004) [2002]. *The resurrection of Mary Magdalene: Legends, apocrypha, and the Christian testament*. Continuum. ISBN 978-0-8264-1645-2.

Sherwood, V. (2021). *Haunted: The death mother archetype*. Chiron.

Sieff, D. F. (2019). The death mother as nature's shadow: Infanticide, abandonment, and the collective unconscious. *Psychological Perspectives*, *62*(1), 15–34.

Smith-Hanssen, K. (2009). Medea and mothers who kill. *Spring*, *81*, 165–176.

Stanton, J., Simpson, A., & Wouldes, T. (2000). A qualitative study of filicide by mentally ill mothers. *Child Abuse & Neglect*, *24*(11), 1451–1460.

Stone, A. (2014). Psychoanalysis and maternal subjectivity. In P. Bueskens (Ed.), *Mothering and psychoanalysis* (pp. 325–342). Demeter Press.

Welldon, E. V. (1992). *Mother, Madonna, whore: The idealization and denigration of motherhood*. Routledge.

Woodman, M., & Dickson, E. (1992). *Dancing in the flames*. Shambhala.

Žižek, S. (2001, October 1). *Reply to Marco Mauas*. www.lacan.com/mauasr3.htm

Part III

What She Needs

Chapter 10

Obviation and Antidote

When the field of psychiatry, and especially the field of law, address maternal infanticide we stagnate—always shocked, always wondering why. There is a general failure to act preventively on early warning signs and intervene more dramatically. For example, in 2014 there were several incidents of maternal infanticide in the same county of Maryland: Zakieya L. Avery in January, Frances Lyles in June, Sonya Spoon in September, and Catherine Hoggle in September. Two of the mothers had sought psychiatric services for postpartum psychosis. The media reacted to each event with shock and horror, yet there were more to come within 6 months. "The larger lesson, if any, is that medical officials should have acted on warning signs earlier and intervened more dramatically" (Kunkle, 2014, para. 38).

Although more urgent attention to mothers' mental health and treatment of postpartum symptoms is crucial, it is not sufficient. If we don't move the conversation beyond a woman-specific issue—a problem that needs to be corrected *inside* the woman—we repeat the pattern of mother blaming, and we miss the comment infanticide is making about our society. By singularly focusing on the question "What is wrong with this mother?" we miss the question: *What is wrong with a society that creates a deadly mother?* In the way I have conceptualized the infanticidal mother, I have found the concepts of obviation and antidote to best serve her. Obviate means to not only anticipate and prevent an action, but to make that action *unnecessary*. Antidote refers to a cure that uses the cause as cure: *The madness cures the madness.*

Obviation

Can we shift the landscape of motherhood enough that infanticide is obviated as a necessary Act? When we put the infanticidal mother in the role as the speaking subject to whom we listen and attempt to understand, we start on a path of obviation. Her stories tell us that some of the remedies require attending to the systemic oppression under which she lives, including racism, sexism, classism, rape, and domestic violence. Addressing these can go a long way in relieving her of the excess burdens in which she is trapped. Social scientists have offered a range of

DOI: 10.4324/9781003412809-14

assessments of and solutions to these structural problems that are beyond the scope of my research, but here I highlight what is most pertinent to mothers.

Reevaluating the Social Contract

The Social Contract, written by Jean-Jacques Rousseau in the 18th century, continues to be one of the defining texts of modern political philosophy. Designed to balance governmental authority and individual liberty, *The Social Contract* became an essential treatise establishing moral and political rules of behavior in accordance with Western patriarchal ideals. Both *The Social Contract* and the U.S. Constitution were drafted by men and for men during a time when women weren't considered rational enough to hold power, own property, or make decisions regarding the public. Within Rousseau's *Social Contract* is an unwritten sexual contract, in which women are objects to be controlled and used. British feminist and political theorist Carole Pateman identified the sexual contract as perpetuating a power difference between men and women, in which womanhood is controlled in all manners by men. Although in contemporary society there is largely an assumption that women are equal to men, in various contracts between men and women, she is a subordinate. In *The Sexual Contract*, Pateman cut through the polemic that places female prostitution under the liberating slogan, "Our bodies, our choice." She argued that sex work and surrogacy must be considered within their sociopolitical context. In both, a woman is not making an object to sell; rather, in keeping with patriarchal objectification of her, she is using her body as that object. She added that with the increasing use of surrogacy, men gain even more power and freedom to use women's bodies as they wish.

Pateman argued that the unwritten social and sexual contract needs revising, with women as authors rather than contractual objects. Similarly, feminist authors, such as Lisa Baraitser, Petra Bueskens, and Fanny Söderbäck among others, have promoted a new maternal ethics, in which a mother is a subject in her own right and her maternal perspective is privileged. If women's voices and lived maternal experience shaped the social/sexual contract, the oppression of mothers trapped in unrealistic expectations and the privileging of men and male authority would be largely obviated. This is an essential point of discussion for the purposes of the infanticidal woman, as power imbalances within the home provide the breeding ground for violence, a premise that is essential to address if we hope to make infanticide an unnecessary outcome.

Restructuring Parenting

The modern structure of parenting leans more heavily on the mother in every aspect. The mother conceives, carries the pregnancy, delivers the baby, nurses the baby, and her body regulates the baby's body. She researches care for the child, arranges for care providers, cleans the home, administers medicine, and takes the calls from the child's school. She also gets the abortion, she goes through the intrauterine insemination, she cleans up the miscarriage, and she shows up at the adoption interview. Then, overarchingly, she is responsible for her child's failings.

Psychosocial theorist Lisa Baraitser, who has dedicated much of her work to studying dimensions of care, has pointed out that in modern neoliberal language, *parenting* suggests mothers and fathers are on equal footing and assumes they both possess equal parenting knowledge, but the reality is women perform the vast majority of childcaring roles, and they are the ones held accountable for the child.

> It is especially the poorest and most disadvantaged mothers who are inevitably the most intensively regulated, as well as held the most responsible for the reproduction of social ills, including the very social disadvantage they find themselves in. The depiction of the deviant lone mother responsible for societal collapse through male juvenile delinquency is especially prevalent, harnessed relentlessly in periods of social unrest.
>
> (de Benedectis, as cited in Baraitser, 2014, p. 482)

Shifting the accountability of childrearing to include the inseminating father has the potential of radically shifting the trajectory of motherhood. If parenting was understood by men, women, and the state as a reverent duty to which one desires access and in which one has the privilege and honor of participating, parenting would become better supported, financially and socially, and more egalitarian. If there was an ethics centering parenthood written into the contract of moral and political rules of behavior, employers and institutions would invest more focused energy into social supports for motherhood.

Inversely, all the women I have worked with have lived in a dynamic with the father of their children in which he at times "babysits." This is true of women patients in my private practice and women in my professional circles. Paternal parenting is referred to as if it is aberrant, special, or worse, a favor. Because the father is working outside of the home, childcare is something extra he does. His role with the children is often described with an eye roll and a wink: "When he watches the kids all bets are off," because he is a "fun" dad who doesn't know the children's friends, where the clean soccer socks are, or how to make dinner. With dad it's McDonald's or cereal, homework isn't done, and teeth aren't brushed. If this comment were reversed—"When mom watches the kids all bets are off!"—we'd be sincerely concerned for the safety of those children, because bets can't be off for a mother. This is also true for households in which women are working as many, if not more, hours outside of the home, indicating the cause is less about economics than one may presume and more about the social/sexual contract.

When mothers entered the workforce with more regularity, daycares cropped up to take in their children, combined with messaging from social workers beginning in the 1970s that early intervention and early schooling is healthy for parents and children (Mortimer et al., 2018). Although much of this care is beneficial and promotes health and growth for families, in its institutional nature it has tended to prioritize efficiency and routine over spontaneity, creativity, or privacy, and it does "not replace love" (Bueskens, 2014, p. 22). Additionally, the idealizing of childcare outside of the home created "the inverse of the earlier dictum of 'biology is destiny' imposing compulsory motherhood on women" and "was tangled up with the anti-maternal strands in feminism, and each gave the other reinforcement" (22).

In *Reproduction of Mothering*, Chodorow, who pioneered the analytical examination of motherhood, found that mothers reproduce motherhood through their daughters, whereas fathers turn away from parenting to maintain dominance and avoid emotional vulnerability—both aspects of patriarchal male identity. Chodorow advocated for the model of shared parenting among the sexes and highlighted the significance of supporting mothers. She suggested that if the elusive father could become more visible and more participatory in family life, the imbalance in which males are perceived (and inculcated) as subordinately emotional than females would disappear. Reexamining Chodorow's theories on motherhood and emphasizing Chodorow's attention to the psychosocial creation of maternal subjectivity, Bueskens noted how parenting arrangements "reproduce our primordial debt to and dependence on women" (2020, p. 10). She added,

> Exclusive maternal care created self-sacrificing women and counter-dependent men who resented and refused women's authority. Both Chodorow and Dinnerstein conjectured that shared parenting would undermine industrial-capitalist patriarchy at its core, by knocking out its socio-economic, familial and unconscious foundations.
>
> (10)

Equitable parenting would relieve mothers of contemporary culture's impossible demands that she both work and fulfill patriarchal expectations of mothers. It would allow women an increased and enhanced sense of agency. If all the physical and emotional unpaid tasks of parenting were equally shared, she would be able not only to participate more fully in the public sphere, but in herself. She could find outlets outside of the home in which to release her anger; moreover, she could find ways to express herself creatively and sexually. Importantly, with her subjectivity stimulated she would be able to shift some attention away from baby, alleviating an imbalance and isolation that cultivates maternal solicitude, or too much mothering. The stagnant feminine energy with its repressed Death Mother energies would be less explosively trapped, festering underneath her identity as the Good Mother.

Redefining Manhood

What makes the greatest difference for the state of motherhood and the expression of the Death Mother energy is a shift in male violence toward women. A decrease in males forcibly or irresponsibly impregnating women would radically impact rates of abortion, adoption, abandonment, and infanticide. Eliminating male sexual violence toward women and use of women (including sex workers) as sex objects would drastically change the landscape to one the Death Mother would find much less fertile. The absence of male violence and the presence of fathers who act responsible for conception, contraception, and childrearing would ameliorate three primary forces behind infanticide: unplanned and unwanted children; children and their mothers facing profoundly inadequate physical and emotional resources; maternal desperation and hopelessness in the face of abuse and coercive control and isolation.

Research has found that men are more likely to have multiple children, with multiple women, and fail to take responsibility for them, especially if

> they had their first sexual experience at a young age, if they fathered their first child at a young age, and if they were neither married to nor cohabiting with the mother of their first child at the time of the child's birth.
>
> (Logan et al., 2006, para. 1)

Intervention during a first pregnancy, for both mother and father, could be effective in safeguarding that pregnancy and childrearing and preventing further unplanned pregnancies. For example, for every pregnancy, if it's safe for the mother, the father could be required to attend a birth control consultation with the local hospital in a legally mandated and federally funded program, serving the best interest of the government to save expenses that accompany unplanned pregnancies. This way any man who impregnates a woman, including illegally or forcibly, is forced to address his role in insemination, conception, pregnancy support, maternal support, and child support, and would be required to follow a plan as to how he will meet those civic demands.

Additionally, there is a need to involve males in preventing teen pregnancy, something the Urban Institute, a non-profit social equity research organization started in the 1960s, has long attempted to implement. Through the course of their work, the Urban Institute has found that success requires community support, males educating males, starting young, and "redefining manhood" to stress "taking responsibility for one's family and community" (Sonenstein et al., 1997, p. 75).

The difficult task of involving fathers as responsible for their own primal activities, including aggression, sex, and procreation, is long overdue. The effects of the culturally accepted aphorism "boys will be boys" promulgates the disconnect between their actions and responsibility for the consequences, a dissociation that contributes to countless broken relationships between fathers and their children and that reflects a broken relationship between men and themselves.

It is encouraging to note that when Roe v. Wade was overturned, vasectomy procedures increased by 30% and even higher rates of vasectomies were found in states where abortion was especially restricted. Additionally, men's voluntary contraceptive consultations increased by 18% from May through September 2022 compared to the same period in 2021 (Wilson, 2023). It appears that without the alternative of abortion (as other forms of birth control are not 100% effective and could also be banned by states), vasectomies became a more desirable option. With a woman no longer having a choice about being pregnant, the burden of birth control shifted and was picked up a bit by men. It makes sense, because vasectomies are one of the most reliable and cost-effective forms of contraception available, with almost none of the side effects or complications of female-oriented birth control methods, such as tubal ligation, hysterectomies, and hormonal contraceptives. A vasectomy involves a quick outpatient surgical procedure that cuts the tubes that carry sperm. It is rarely painful or extensive. Yet men taking responsibility for procreation continue to underperform women's contraceptive behaviors. Roughly 5 to 6% of men between 18 and 45 have gotten vasectomies, as opposed to roughly 20% percent of women aged 15 to 49 who have had their tubes tied (Zhang & Eisenberg, 2022). Journalist Alisha Haridasani Gupta reported, "One reason men have steered clear of vasectomy as a form of voluntary birth control was, experts said, a traditional concept of masculinity—one that prized virility and the ability to get a woman pregnant" (2022).

It is this traditional concept of masculinity that prohibits men from being reproductively responsible citizens. Virility, defined as manliness and sexual drive and associated with power, is threatened when a man feels humiliated and can quickly shift to violence. In patriarchal psychology this is excused, as virility and aggression are said to be biologically tied and thus men's "everyday violence" and sexual misconduct are expected, though there are numerous cultures in which this is not the norm (hooks, 2004, p. 55).

Since I have been in reproductive health, I have had many conversations with men in which the topic of vasectomies results in avoidance and then defensiveness. Recently, a 57-year-old man, in response to my question about a vasectomy, jerked back in his chair, then looked away, said "But I may not be done siring yet," and waved his hand across the room. His gesture and archaic language spoke to a primal and archetypal instinct to create progeny or a tribe, an instinct that is perhaps threatened by the idea of his potency being surgically removed. Yet, if men are not able to face that moment, tolerate that loss, and sublimate that virile energy into their current families and lives, the weight continues to be placed on the woman and their children.

Recognizing Maternal Finitude

Mothers also have a responsibility in equalizing parenting burdens, but it is a more insidious problem impacted by and requiring awareness of the expectations on the feminine. In the current construct of mother, based on the idealized image of Mother Mary, mother is saying "Yes" to everyone. She is endlessly available, mandated to sacrifice, a bottomless container.

> Women must learn to say "No" when necessary, rather than play the role of the overly available whore-mother. Saying "No" to inappropriate conception means that the woman must be in active relationship with the dark side of the goddess who can kill, bring on depression, and destroy endless possibilities by setting boundaries and natural limits.
>
> (Rand, 1997, p. 48)

This command to mothers is meant not to blame her but to give her permission to access an unsentimental part of herself. Maternal finitude, understanding there are limits in maternity, is essential to obviating the causes and conditions that birth infanticide. This requires saying "No," when physically possible, to unprotected intercourse that may end in an unplanned/unwanted pregnancy, which would obviate much of the need for infanticide, abortion, and adoption. Helping women come to terms with their ability to say "No," and then raising their daughters and sons to understand these limits, would help reproduce a mothering that is more sustainable (Chodorow, 1999).

Creating Maternal Spaces

Most mothers have had the experience while at the park with their children of becoming bored and fidgety, perhaps feeling guilty for not being more engaged with their child. The mother may respond by edging home or by over-focusing on the child—micromanaging their safety or their behavior with other children. She is caught in a dance of wanting to be fully present with her child and herself as a mother, while also wanting not to be there at all. Whereas if a mother goes to the park with another mom, friend, or relative, she is more relaxed, and she can allow the children to play freely and enjoy adult conversation. These are the maternal spaces where mothers can provide each other a chance for the discreet sharing of confidences. Mothers together can create spaces like these for the acknowledgment of their dark maternal feelings where they have the possibility of safely sharing their struggles, fears, and fantasies of killing their child. Evangeline Rand (1997) wrote of the crucial importance of such sharing:

> All thoughts, deeds and memories that carry shame, guilt or anxiety, and all unacknowledged desires, demands and expectations, must be fully expressed, related to and shared with another person. Something happens when these things pass through our larynxes that no amount of thinking about it can do.
>
> (1997, p. 87)

This is especially true of the mother, standing alongside another mother at the park. As she hears herself describe her harrowing morning, her marital injuries, her dread of the night, the incessant crying, and the burning rage, she may obviate a need to act it out. "The heat/energy liberated in this self-expression eventually dries out the complex and purifies it of its unconscious contamination. Eventually the archetypal realities will be more clearly able to express themselves without feeling muddled up in personal affect" (88).

For a mother to share these taboo feelings, she must be aware of them. Often mothers begin by focusing on the perennial hardships that the child creates for them, the messy eating, sleeping, toilet training, and skin problems, but if she can tolerate some of the focus on herself, or find the space in which to do it, she can get closer to harnessing her emotions to prevent them from gaining control of her. On this Roszika Parker was adamant in her encouragement of women:

> A mother needs to know herself, to own up to the diverse, contradictory, often overwhelming feelings evoked by motherhood. It doesn't matter whether she stays at home, goes out to work, is partnered or single. Only a mother who can face her own inner turbulence can make sense of her child's. It's only by accepting that at times you are a bad mother, that you can ever be a good mother.
>
> (As cited in Benn, 2006, para. 25)

Mothers create rituals for one another, such as the baby shower, where women intentionally come together as a predictable and contained event marking a woman's transition into motherhood. Perhaps more meaningful are rituals such as the 40 days of confinement with other women *after* the birth, which is practiced in Muslim, Latin, and Hindu cultures. This is an enveloping of the new dyad within the arms of the women in the community, which could help a new mother ease into the extreme changes of having a child, allowing her to ground and locate herself in her new identity. Within Aboriginal and Torres Strait Islander cultures, new mothers observe a traditional practice called yarning circles, during which they gather with other mothers to share their experiences and receive support during the postnatal period. Sometimes midwives in Australia will facilitate or encourage the circle, where a passing on of knowledge is invaluable to new mothers (Walker et al., 2014). Rituals such as these could help to mitigate the emotional isolation of motherhood.

> The lack of effective rituals in postpartum leads to feelings of alienation and distress. There should be some sort of communal acknowledgment however, simple but consistent like group rules like she always gets a card or she always gets flowers or she always gets a coin. Harriet Rosenberg points out that in kin based communities women who adhere to customary postpartum rituals do not experience postpartum depression, a phenomenon that she identifies as a structural problem of industrial society.
>
> (Davis-Floyd, 2003, p. 43)

Making Structural Changes

There are structural changes that need to happen in the U.S. in order to reduce the occurrence of infanticide, which I will briefly outline here. First, modeling the legal reaction to infanticide on other countries, where the response is to treat it as a mental health crisis. Britain's Infanticide Act and Canada's Infanticide Law have both been successfully keeping the rates of infanticide down and caring for women. A second is mandatory paid maternity leave. As of 2023 the countries requiring the longest minimum paid maternity leave are Bulgaria (58.6 weeks), Greece (43 weeks), and the United Kingdom (39 weeks), compared to 12 weeks in the U.S. In these countries, and many others, having a baby is not treated as an unwanted intrusion on work productivity; women are more cared for, and there is a lower infant mortality rate (World Population Review, 2023).

The third is the federal legalization of abortion. With access to abortion at all stages and under any circumstances, the number of unplanned pregnancies and unwanted children is greatly reduced. The fourth is upgrading the laws and punishment around domestic violence, including providing education and residential rehabilitation for abusers. The fifth structural change is enforced education and training of law officers and attorneys on postpartum psychosis, including firsthand accounts of survivors, maternal subjectivity, such as one talk at Chicago's Bluhm Legal Clinic by a woman who survived her 30-year imprisonment for neonaticide:

> I suffered from depression my whole life . . . Postpartum depression is [anxiety], guilt, shame, discomfort, a number of things that many people face and don't know they are going through this . . . No woman carries their child for nine months and wakes up and decides to kill her child. There's a mental break, and the criminal justice system needs to look into it more and not just lock women up and throw away the key.
>
> (Griffin, as cited in "Bluhm Legal Clinic Event," 2022, para. 6).

Psychosis as an Antidote

A clinical approach to treating and obviating maternal infanticide requires attention to the symptoms of the Death Mother, such as psychosis. Certain mid-century clinicians such as Jung, but also R.D. Laing, Harry Stack Sullivan, and Frieda Fromm-Reichman, treated psychotic patients by listening to and analyzing their psychosis, with little to no use of medications. It is an intuitive approach that requires a leaning into the madness, as opposed to simply eradicating it. In the spirit of this approach, the delusions are both the poison and the cure, making the psychotic content of one's delusions and hallucinations the antidote.[1] In continuation from the discussion of madness in Chapter 9, an examination of psychosis as curative requires analytic listening to mothers who are experiencing psychosis. Jung believed that once we understand the code or message hidden in the psychotic content, we could then put together the chain of events that led to the emergence of psychosis. Jung queried:

> Why is the mind compelled to expend itself in the elaboration of pathological nonsense? Our new method of approach gives us a clue to this difficult question. Today we can assert that the pathological ideas dominate the interests of the patient so completely because they are derived from the most important questions that occupied him when he was normal. In other words, what in insanity is now an incomprehensible jumble of symptoms was once a vital field of interest to the normal personality.
>
> (1914/1960a, para. 362)

One of my thesis projects in graduate school was, in the spirit of Jung's approach to psychosis, a makeshift documentary. I interviewed homeless psychotic people while handing out cigarettes on the streets of San Francisco. My hypothesis: There is meaning in the incoherencies of psychosis. In my decoding of the screeching and ramblings I recorded, I heard anguish and confusion of lost people trying to find their way. Eventually I gave it the canny title *Intelligible Unintelligibles* and showed the short film to kindly friends and family. My attempt to document unintelligible ramblings as a meaningful code that held the answers to their suffering was rough and inexpert. Sherwood captured this significantly better in her book *Haunted*:

> By discovering the patterns by which we are living, we have the means to know how to heal. As Patricia Berry (1982) put it, the therapy of archetypal psychology is akin to the maxim "like cures like": "that is, we treat it with itself—by deepening it, expanding it (so that it is no longer so narrowly fixated), and by giving it substance, body (so that it can now begin to carry what it is trying to express).
>
> (2021, p. 20)

A stunning novel that came out recently, *Trust* by Hernan Diez, follows the story of a woman who spends time in the Bad Pfäfers sanitarium in Switzerland in the 1930s. Her psychiatrist Dr. Frahm purported the theory that symptoms, disease, and cure were three in one—that the incoherent ramblings of a patient were the symptoms of the disease of psychosis *and* the cure to that disease. These were patients of the early 20th century who were kept in a sanitorium before the age of antipsychotic medications. Diez depicts Dr. Frahm's treatment approach:

> Rather than containing Mrs. Rask's free-flowing rants and redirecting them into the realm of normalcy (or gagging her with sedatives), he said, he wished to encourage her monologues. She could not stop talking because she could not stop trying to explain her illness—and her desire to understand her illness was, to a large extent, the illness itself. If he listened and taught her to listen, they would find that her never-ending rant was full of ciphered instructions.
>
> (2022, p. 86)

The idea that the psychotic process is the psyche trying to heal itself and that within it are opportunities for personal growth is a wholly positive approach that runs counter to the illness paradigm in contemporary psychiatry. Modern-day treatment modalities, such as medication management and skills building, have been effective in reducing psychotic symptoms, yet the underlying mechanisms are rarely approached, an oversight that may be consequential for the patient. I can't help but imagine a mother in a state of postpartum psychosis, safely contained in a turn-of-the-century hospital in the mountains of Switzerland, being able to share her psychosis with an intuitive doctor, who might recognize the mother as trapped in an inexpressible and impermissible mortal struggle with the Death Mother as both her savior and her enemy.

In the groups I facilitate with mothers who have experienced postpartum psychosis, the women generally stay away from discussing their psychotic experience. There are many reasons for this, one being that as facilitators we remind participants not to share too much graphic detail of their trauma, so as not to trigger anyone else's PTSD symptoms. Although this suggestion has a significant purpose in the group setting, my tendency is, as Jung's was, to make space for and listen closely to the recounting of the psychosis. At times women will share the narratives of their delusions, and there does seem to be some relief in her when she does. Occasionally, we have been able to use the content of her delusion story to decipher and interpret meaningful pieces that she may be able to integrate into her life. This method—like cures like or the disease is the cure—is almost exclusively more effective when the individual is no longer psychotic. When I meet with women it has typically been months or years since her last psychotic episode, and only if she is able to tolerate the memories of her psychosis is she able to analyze it. For actively psychotic patients, and for the homeless friends I made in San Francisco, interpreting the psychosis as it is happening is an exceptionally harder task. But for the women I have been able to work with, in groups and individually, to examine their psychotic thinking from a safe distance allows them the opportunity to be curious about the unconscious material that was breaking through into consciousness and discover if it has a relevant message for them.

As to why psychosis would occur for a woman after she delivers a baby, amidst all the other times it could happen, it likely has something to do with her hormonal, physical, and emotional vulnerability in that perinatal period. This could be considered what Jung called an abaissement "or slackening of the tensity of consciousness" (1950/1969, para. 213):

> *Abaissement du niveau mental* can be the result of physical and mental fatigue, bodily illness, violent emotions, and shock, of which the last has a particularly deleterious effect on one's self-assurance. The *abaissement* always has a restrictive influence on the personality as a whole.
>
> (para. 214)

This relaxation of ego strength permits more unconscious material to be present, and when the ego is not able to withstand the emergence of the unconscious content it is presented with, the psyche progresses further into psychosis (Jung, 1939/1960c, para. 520). Jung's suggestion is that the unconscious material coming forward should be seen and interpreted, as it is likely laden with archetypes and rich meaning (para. 528). He further suggested that the meaning of the psychotic content is compensatory—not only is it indeed an aspect of the patient (as opposed to something that is coming from the outside of her), but it's an aspect that has been relegated to the unconscious (1914/1960b, para. 449) —and and this is an important premise for most of Jung's work, the content of the psychosis/unconscious is often attempting to make up for deficiencies in the patient's life or personality (1914/1960a, para. 347).

In the murky boundaryless time of pregnancy, childbirth, and postpartum a woman is shifting from being one to two—her body is shared by another and her identity transforming, along with her senses and perception of time. It is a time when her ego has entered a new stage and is finding its way in a new land, and in this period of abaissement, it is a time when she is vulnerable to psychosis. If a new mother is isolated or not in a community of women that can usher her through this rite of passage with comfort and ritual, it is of little surprise that her ego might be unable to assimilate primitive psychic material—especially given the innate eruption of feelings that are culturally taboo, eruptions that at this crucial time of deep change can lead to a psychotic episode.

For the women I see, both in groups and individually, it is an important coping mechanism to set aside their psychotic experiences as a bizarre psychiatric crisis that they'd rather forget. There is a frightening fracturing of the psyche during the time of psychosis—a loss of trust in the stability of one's own mind, one's sense of reality, and in the relation of self to other that requires a tender and attentive recovery period. Often there is a significant crash from the mania and adrenaline of psychosis into a severe depressive episode that can last months. It typically takes about a year for a woman to feel recovered, although a sense of instability may linger for years. Support groups during this time can be exceptionally helpful. Within the groups there is often an immeasurable relief and a significant reduction of shame in knowing they are not alone. Some of the profound healing comes from the opportunity to be in a position of listening, understanding, and helping other mothers by the grace of their own trauma. This sublimation transforms their hurt, fear, grief, and resentment into service for other women.

When a woman is interested, I attempt to help her understand her psychosis in the context of her personality, social circumstances, personal history, and biochemistry. There are clear links between early life adversity and psychosis later in life (Sideli et al., 2020). Childhood trauma and a woman's neurochemistry may cause a dormant or untreated disorder, such as Bipolar, to manifest when triggered by stress and lack of sleep in the perinatal experience. I understand psychosis *both* as contributed to by a neurochemical blueprint *and* as a meaningful rupture of the ego boundary between consciousness and the unconscious due to a vulnerable period. It's important for the purposes of this text that depth psychological, developmental, and biochemical understandings are being held and accounted for.

Many women report frequent and abrupt waxing and waning episodes of postpartum psychosis (see Chapter 1), which makes the identification and harnessing of psychotic symptoms difficult. Jung also recognized this coming and going of psychosis, suggesting it is due to certain stimulants or topics that touch on the patient's delusions, activating the psychotic narrative again, but without which she is in a coherent state and there are "no difficulties" (Jung, 1907/1960, para. 202). The fact that in one hour she may seem normal and in the next hour appear "crazy" is often used against her in court, as if some rational moments mean there is no diminished capacity. A prosecutor is quick to point out "She's not psychotic now!" and that indeed she was malingering.

The infanticidal urge or behaviors in psychotic mothers tend to be singular, focused, and absolute in their conviction (i.e., "I knew it had to be done and I would do it"). Many women report a sense of the act being predestined. In 1953, John Weir Perry, a Jungian analyst who worked at a residence for psychotic patients where they could be treated without medication, referred to the experience in psychosis of a drama that was meant to play out (also see Laufer, 2010; Perry, 1990). Thus, the theater of the delusions is not driven by an actual desire of a mother to kill her actual child, but a sense that she is playing a part in a much grander mission. She has been given her script as a command from a higher authority and has adopted the utmost determination to play her part. There is little to no ambivalence reported in psychotic episodes. Often this storyline is about a focused attempt at saving herself, her baby, and her family from impending apocalyptic destruction.

The Numinous Function of Postpartum Psychosis

At times there is a strong religious presence in the content of psychosis, often emerging as a narrative of spiritual warfare. The mother is caught with her child in the contest between God and the Devil; she is persecuted by malevolent beings, controlled by spiritual entities, or has delusions of mortal sin or, inversely, of grandiosity. This reflects the studies done on general populations of schizophrenia, in which most psychoses contain some religiosity (Hartog & Gow, 2005; Mohr et al., 2010). The idea that psychosis and divine inspiration are closely related is an old and recurrent one, as in many traditional societies psychotic people may be seen as visionaries or mystics and sought out for their special insights and abilities.

Not all people who are psychotic with a background of religious practice will have religious delusional content, and not all patients with religious delusional content will have a history of religious practice or belief.[2] Instead it seems to manifest autonomously, perhaps per the need of the patient. One way to explain the presence of religious themes in psychosis is what Jung called the "religious function"—a drive for a relationship between the personal self and a transpersonal source of power and meaning. Jung suggested that access to this religious function is through the unconscious:

> The unconscious is the only available source of religious experience. This is certainly not to say that what we call the unconscious is identical with God or is set up in his place. It is simply the medium from which religious experience seems to flow. As to what the further cause of such experience might be, the answer to this lies beyond the range of human knowledge. Knowledge of God is a transcendental problem.
>
> (1905/1970, para. 565)

Because the unconscious is a source for the religious function, it makes sense that religious themes are present in psychotic episodes. The psychotic content erupts when a person is distressed or vulnerable and thus their religious function—their meaning-seeking function—may arrive in search of a connection to a higher power to create a healing mythology. The psychosis arrives to remythologize:

> The religious myth is one of man's greatest and most significant achievements, giving him the security and inner strength not to be crushed by the monstrousness of the universe . . . . Just as it provides an inner locus of authority, a religious orientation to life gives us inner strength, perseverance and a sense of purpose.
>
> (Jung, 1952/1967, para. 343)

In a 2001 talk on madness and religion, Jungian analyst Thomas Patrick Lavin stated,

Religion is a psychological necessity and can deliver us from uneasiness. Religion is an experience I have of me, in which I find inside of myself me, and more of me, and it heals and it saves; and that's called Divine. It is *more* of the same quality of the self, and in a crisis a person can make contact.

During the postpartum period, when one's entire life is in flux, messages of healing, growth, and comfort are necessary to sustain a transformation. This is true in other major transition times for women such as puberty and menopause, which are also times her mental stability is ruptured and often in crisis. The postpartum period for a woman naturally puts her in touch with greater life-giving forces, which take her to the edge of her possibilities. An expansion of self is required when one is initiated into motherhood. It is possible psychosis is attempting to offer spiritual content and meaning to a new mother as her psyche is in the most significant heroine's journey of her lifetime.[3]

Amelia is a woman who experienced postpartum psychosis. She had a strong history of Catholicism and when her psychosis took off quickly after birth, it centered on herself and her baby as "saviors of the world." This woman had 9/11 trauma and much of her delusion included terrorists taking control. A constant feeling of not being safe and a simultaneous feeling of "I'm supposed to help" possessed her behavior. She went up to strangers and said, "Peace be with you" and "Jesus loves you, don't be scared," all the while believing that the world was ending. At one point she believed her baby could walk on water. Eventually she believed she was a prophet and she needed to die to save the world, which meant sacrificing herself and her baby. With help from her family, she was hospitalized and medicated, but in her recovery process she also went to church and went on church retreats with her husband. She has remained a practicing Catholic but told me, "If I get too religious, I might become psychotic." Amelia's religious psychosis brought her in closer touch with her spiritual practice, and into a "more clear role in the position [she] holds in her family and her community." For Amelia to come to these insights, for the psychosis to be an antidote, it was necessary to connect the rational ego in a meaningful way with the psyche's overwhelming nonrational, mythical content.

The Transcendent Function of Postpartum Psychosis

If the ego can tolerate the emergence of unconscious content, space can be held for the work of the transcendent function, another of the core concepts of Jung's model of the psyche. The transcendent function is the process of integrating the psyche's conscious and unconscious contents into a third position, in the service of psychic change and development (Jung, 1928/1966, para. 368). The transcendent function enables a transition from one psychological attitude to another, forwarding the process of individuation toward greater wholeness. This requires coming to terms with and integrating unconscious content. For some women I've met, they have been able to examine their psychosis in hindsight, allowing for their unconscious material to be brought into consciousness, which has given them access to repressed feelings and a more holistic sense of self.

One such woman is Tracy, who was a teacher and described herself as a highly competent person. She had grown up with a "very difficult mother who downplayed everything." Tracy had distanced herself from her mother, but when it was time for the baby to be delivered her mother talked her way into the delivery room and the nurses had to escort her out. Tracy's psychosis started at the hospital. She remembered feeling "uncared for," confused, and vigilant. Her husband "didn't like blood" so was not regularly present. Tracy had a "burning thought" that lasted throughout the psychosis: "I gotta find a person who's gonna help me." Once she and the baby were home, she began to lose executive functioning. She couldn't cook or care for her child and wanted to be hospitalized again. She eventually took herself there and reported suicidality so that they would keep her. While she was there, she wouldn't talk to her mom or husband when they visited, trusting only her mother-in-law to care for her and her newborn. Tracy's psychosis broke open her psychological defense of being competent and self-sufficient. She projected the incompetence she feared onto the people around her, criticizing everyone at the hospital—no one was helping her, no one was doing it right. Her psychosis finally sank her into the helplessness she feared such that even her basic needs—hygiene, eating, sleeping, speaking, participating—had to be taken over by others. Eventually she emerged from her psychosis in a new state, neither unerringly competent nor helpless, and from this place she was able to mother her son.

Abby, another woman whose psychosis started during labor and delivery, had also been working to keep her mother from "intruding," while at the same time she said her mother-in-law "had her back all the time, she got it." Abby had a harrowing experience with psychosis, for which eventually she got treatment, and during her recovery she worked with a therapist to unpack her childhood, which "was the piece that had been missing." Abby told me that going through postpartum psychosis opened her mind, that she "saw everything like a wash, saw the trauma, saw the people pleasing I was doing, saw how I made myself little, how I wasn't my full self." Abby told me that she now feels like a "completely different person, the 2.0 version." The psychosis had "taken the logical part of my brain and I got to do whatever I wanted to do," which freed her up to see parts of herself that had been buried.

Competency and perfectionism are common themes I hear from women who have experienced postpartum psychosis. One woman reported that, while most of her life she experienced disruptive anxiety and perfectionism, since her experience with postpartum psychosis and her subsequent treatment, she has been relieved of the fear and disturbing need for control that she had been struggling with. Similarly, another woman told me before the postpartum psychosis she held "rock core beliefs that I need to have this all together. I need to keep this quiet. I need to look like I have it together. I need to be perfect, appear as perfect." Since the psychosis she has "given myself more grace." Several women spoke of the postpartum psychosis bringing them into confrontation with these underlying mental health issues, including unresolved trauma such as sexual assault, abusive parents, or toxic relationships that had never been addressed. The buried parts of themselves were now getting the attention they needed in therapy. These are all examples of the way bringing the unconscious to consciousness has allowed for a transcendent function that has expanded her experience of herself and facilitated her individuation.

Notes

1 It's likely the first antidote was used by Mithridates VI (135–63 BC), the king of Pontus, who had conquered several territories including Colchis, today's Georgia, where the inhabitants produced plant extracts that were thickened into a poisonous concentrate which, when highly diluted, could be used medicinally. Historical records point to the Colchian medicine woman Medea as mixing poisons and medicines from local plants and herbs including autumn crocus, hemlock, and belladonna. Medea's name appears in Greek and Latin literature as a late Bronze Age (1200 BCE) priestess, in the ca. 750 BCE writings of Hesiod, and through the era of the Roman Empire, 625 BCE to 476 CE. However, the nature of the sources makes it impossible to know if Medea was actually a historical woman, though in Apolonius's 3rd-century BCE *Argonautica* he calls Medea *polypharmakon*, which is translated to *enchantress* but means *skilled in many herbs*. Medea's older sister Circe was also competent in the art of healing and likely Medea's mentor, teaching her how to treat wounds with roots and grasses, including the Argonauts wounded in the battle. Eventually Ovid and Euripides presented the downside of Medea's transformation from human to witch by showing how she uses the good reputation she had won in order to accomplish horrific deeds (Norton, 2006).
2 A study of psychotic patients of religious and non-religious background did not find any difference in the severity of religious delusions across the two groups (Peters et al., 2004).
3 To be clear, I'm interested in the religious content of delusions as purposefully healing, not using religion to heal from the mental health crisis of psychosis.

References

Baraitser, L. (2014). Maternal publics: Time, relationality and the public sphere. In P. Bueskens (Ed.), *Mothering and psychoanalysis* (pp. 473–496). Demeter Press.

Benn, M. (2006, October 27). Deep maternal alienation. *The Guardian*. www.theguardian.com/lifeandstyle/2006/oct/28/familyandrelationships.family2

Berry, P. (1982). *Echo's subtle body: Contributions to an archetypal psychology*. Spring Publications.

Bluhm Legal Clinic Event Highlights Illinois Resentencing Statutes and Their Impact on Black Women. (2022, May 6). https://news.law.northwestern.edu/bluhm-legal-clinic-event-highlights-illinois-resentencing-statutes-and-their-impact-on-black-women/

Bueskens, P. (2014). Introduction mothering, feminism, psychoanalysis, psychotherapy and sociology: Intersections and antinomies. In P. Buesken (Ed.), *Mothering and psychoanalysis* (pp. 1–72). Demeter Press.

Bueskens, P. (2020). *Nancy Chodorow and the reproduction of mothering: 40 years on.* Palgrave Macmillan.

Chodorow, N. (1999). *The reproduction of mothering.* University of California Press.

Davis-Floyd, R. (2003). *Birth as an American right of passage* (2nd ed.). University of California Press.

Diaz, H. (2022). *Trust.* Riverhead Books.

Gupta, A. H. (2022, August 12). "Snip snip hooray": Vasectomies among the young and child-free may be rising. *New York Times.* www.nytimes.com/2022/08/12/well/vasectomy-contraception-abortion.html

Hartog, K., & Gow, K. (2005). Religious attributions pertaining to the causes and cures of mental illness. *Mental Health, Religion and Culture, 8,* 263–276.

hooks, b. (2004). *The will to change.* Washington Square Press.

Jung, C. G. (1960a). The content of the psychoses (R. F. C. Hull, Trans.). In H. Read, M. Fordham, & G. Adler (Eds.), *The collected works of C. G. Jung: Vol. 3. Psychogenesis of mental disease* (pp. 153–178). Princeton University Press. (Original work published 1914). https://doi.org/10.1515/9781400850921.153

Jung, C. G. (1960b). On psychological understanding (R. F. C. Hull, Trans.). In H. Read, M. Fordham, & G. Adler (Eds.), *The collected works of C. G. Jung: Vol. 3. Psychogenesis of mental disease* (pp. 179–193). Princeton University Press. (Original work published 1914)

Jung, C. G. (1960c). On the psychogenesis of schizophrenia (R. F. C. Hull, Trans.). In H. Read, M. Fordham, & G. Adler (Eds.), *The collected works of C. G. Jung: Vol. 3. Psychogenesis of mental disease* (pp. 233–249). Princeton University Press. (Original work published 1939). https://doi.org/10.1515/9781400850921.231

Jung, C. G. (1960). The psychology of dementia praecox (R. F. C. Hull, Trans.). In H. Read, M. Fordham, & G. Adler (Eds.), *The collected works of C. G. Jung: Vol. 3. Psychogenesis of mental disease* (pp. 1–151). Princeton University Press. (Original work published 1907). https://doi.org/10.1515/9781400850921.1

Jung, C. G. (1966). The relations between the ego and the unconscious (R. F. C. Hull, Trans.). In H. Read, M. Fordham, & G. Adler (Eds.), *The collected works of C. G. Jung: Vol. 7. Two essays on analytical psychology* (2nd ed., pp. 121–241). Princeton University Press. (Original work published 1928). https://doi.org/10.1515/9781400850891.121

Jung, C. G. (1967). *The collected works of C. G. Jung: Vol. 5. Symbols of transformation* (H. Read, M. Fordham, & G. Adler, Eds., R. F. C. Hull, Trans.). Princeton University Press. (Original work published 1952). https://doi.org/10.1515/9781400850945

Jung, C. G. (1969). Concerning rebirth (R. F. C. Hull, Trans.). In H. Read, M. Fordham, & G. Adler (Eds.), *The collected works of C. G. Jung: Vol. 9, pt. 1. Archetypes and the collective unconscious* (2nd ed., pp. 113–147). Princeton University Press. (Original work published 1950). https://doi.org/10.1515/9781400850969.113

Jung, C. G. (1970). On the psychological diagnosis of facts (R. F. C. Hull, Trans.). In H. Read, M. Fordham, & G. Adler (Eds.), *The collected works of C. G. Jung: Vol. 1. Psychiatric studies* (2nd ed., pp. 219–221). Princeton University Press. (Original work published 1905)

Kunkle, F. (2014, September 27). What makes mothers kill their own children? *Washington Post.*

Laufer, B. (2010). Beyond countertransference: Therapists' experiences in clinical relationships with patients diagnosed with schizophrenia. *Psychosis: Psychological, Social and Integrative Approaches, 2*(2), 163–172.

Lavin, T. P. (2001, February 3). *Madness, religious experience, and the wisdom to know the difference.* Lecture given at the C. G. Jung Institute, Chicago.

Logan, C., Manlove, J., Ikramullah, E., & Cottingham, S. (2006). Men who father children with more than one woman: A contemporary portrait of multiple-partner fertility. *Child Trends*. www.fatherhood.gov/research-and-resources/men-who-father-children-more-one-woman-contemporary-portrait-multiple

Mohr, S., Borras, L., Bétrisey, C., Brandt, P.-Y., Gillieron, C., & Huguelet, P. (2010). Delusions with religious content in patients with psychosis: How they interact with spiritual coping. *Psychiatry*, *73*, 158–172.

Mortimer, R., McKeown, A., & Singh, I. (2018). Just policy? An ethical analysis of early intervention policy guidance. *American Journal of Bioethics*, *18*(11), 43–53.

Norton, S. (2006). The pharmacology of mithridatum: A 2000-year-old remedy. *Molecular Interventions*, *6*(2), 60–66.

Pateman, C. (1988). *The sexual contract*. Polity Press.

Perry, J. W. (1953). *The self in psychotic process*. Spring Publications.

Perry, J. W. (1990). *The far side of madness*. Spring Publications.

Peters, E., Joseph, S., Day, S., & Garety, P. (2004). Measuring delusional ideation: The 21-item Peters et al. delusions inventory (PDI). *Schizophrenia Bulletin*, *30*, 1005–1022.

Rand, E. (1997). *Recovering feminine spirituality*. CreateSpace.

Rousseau, J.-J. (2019). *On the social contract* (D. Cress, Trans.). Hackett. (Original work published 1762)

Sherwood, V. (2021). *Haunted: The death mother archetype*. Chiron.

Sideli, L., Murray, R., Schimmenti, A., Corso, M., La Barbera, D., Trotta, A., & Fisher, H. (2020). Childhood adversity and psychosis: A systematic review of bio-psycho-social mediators and moderators. *Psychological Medicine*, *50*(11), 1761–1782.

Sonenstein, F., Stewart, K., Lindberg, L., Pernas, M., & Williams, S. (1997). *Involving males in preventing teen pregnancy: A guide for program planners*. www.urban.org/sites/default/files/publication/70406/307327-Involving-Males-in-Preventing-Teen-Pregnancy.PDF

Walker, M., Fredericks, B., Mills, K., & Anderson, D. (2014). "Yarning" as a method for community-based health research with Indigenous women: The Indigenous women's wellness research program. *Health Care for Women International*, *35*(10), 1216–1226.

Wilson, M. (2023, April 6). *Permanent contraception and restrictive abortion laws*. www.komodohealth.com/insights/permanent-contraception-trends-in-vasectomies

World Population Review. (2023). *Maternity leave by country 2023*. https://worldpopulationreview.com/country-rankings/maternity-leave-by-country

Zhang, X., & Eisenberg, M. (2022). Vasectomy utilization in men aged 18–45 declined between 2002 and 2017: Results from the United States national survey for family growth data. *Andrology*, *10*, 137–142.

Chapter 11

The Transmutation of the Infanticidal Mother

A reconceptualization of mother, in all her forms and on her terms, is long overdue. The split concept of the good vs. bad mother is not only dangerous for mothers and children; it hurts all who are forced to repress the dark feminine.

> In our rapacious, speeding society, the archetype of the mother is not alive and does not preside over the rites of harvest, decay and renewal. No mother mourns the loss of the maiden soul, nor restores her rituals and forms of worship to humankind. This archetype has been buried in the archives and dusty libraries of academia and in the dry realms of the church dominated by spirit.
>
> (Rand, 1997, p. 28)

For the Mother archetype to be alive she must be able to experience and embody the full range of her capacity, both creative and destructive. Women's submersion in an idealization of maternity must be alleviated even for those women who are not mothers. Men must accept the debt of life, body nourishment, and social existence they owe the mother, and in that acceptance work against the illusion that she has no self-agency in the matter (Irigaray, 1978). She must be allowed to exist in a space beyond the split of pious vs malevolent, where her *natural* negativity, finitude, and failings can be integrated. This type of response is required from legal, medical, and scientific institutions as well as from an individual's self-perception. Each time a mother kills her child, we are asked to face the destructive potential in all our mothers, and thus in ourselves.

> Seeing the Mother as purely tender and benign cuts us off from her (and our own) full being, as much as imagining her as either purely transcendent or purely immanent. The Mother is death, terror, horror, agony, hurricane, disaster as well as every marvelous and kind power. Learning how to adore her in her terrible as well as her benign aspect is the only way . . . of entering her total bliss, serenity, and power.
>
> (Harvey & Baring, 1996, p. 156)

DOI: 10.4324/9781003412809-15

This perspective asks us to "embrace all aspects of the Mother and so of the universe and life" and to refuse "to identify with only those aspects that keep the ego happy" (156). We are asked to be a little less blinded by self-interest to admit the subjectivity and agency of mothers and the conditions with which they struggle.

Transmutation

The transmutation of the infanticidal mother equals the embodiment of the Great Mother, who is capable of both giving and taking life. Evolutionary science describes transmutation as occurring when, in order to survive, an organism has to go to the margins, reject its constraints, and change so significantly that its former way of living is impossible. The alchemists of the 18th century relied on this principle of transmutation in their work of turning lead into gold—a metaphoric process for the transmutation of human experience into something greater, such as self-knowledge, wisdom, or spiritual gold. Jung recognized that the work of the alchemists corresponded to a process of psychological individuation or the becoming of a whole person. The psychic stages were analogous to the physical processes imagined by the alchemists (Nigredo, Albedo, Citrinitas, and Rubedo; in psychological terms, Confession, Illumination, Education, and Transformation). Alchemical transmutation requires the dissolution of the ego identity in the illumination of the ego-transcendent Self. It is a confrontation with the reality of the shadow, a process that transforms shadow qualities rather than releases them. For example, destructive impulses are transmuted into warrior-like aggression. In the case of the murderous mother, if her psychotic and violent rage is made conscious it has the potential to be transmuted into a powerful maternal passion. The mother becomes a transformed organism, with a passionate maternal voice and choices that speak to her needs, her child's, and the greater good. As in the sealed temenos of alchemy, this requires a safe container or space in which to meet her psyche.

However, the infanticidal mother's Act has largely remained unconscious; she is completely identified with the shadow and no longer the same organism. Unable to continue to live the way she was—in poverty, violence, abandonment, madness— she went to the margins of morality, rejected the constraints, and changed at such a level of significance that made the former way of living impossible. Her sense of self dissolves. She is often no longer a mother nor a citizen; her identity is taken away. The only way such a woman's transmutation can be rescued toward evolutionary change is if her condition is brought to the light. If we can look squarely at a mother's murderous, rageful impulse to destroy and allow it to exist, then it can move from the literal to the metaphorical or symbolic.

Transforming a mother's impulse to kill her children from a literal action into a reflection on her soul is paramount. Then the depth and range of a mother's feelings can be enacted on a much larger stage, in a richer, more imaginative theater. The prospect of killing her children no longer needs to be the only hope for an unhappy other and the solution to all her problems. Rather, a mother's emotions can be deepened through a connection to a psychology that recognizes the dangerous power of the mother's dark side. As she moves through motherhood, a mother can then have the opportunity to be continually reborn, half-human and half-divine, bringing her dark and murderous feelings to a mythological altar instead of the corpses of her literally sacrificed children.

(Smith-Hanssen, 2009, p. 170)

Jung recognized that all humans have the capacity to do horrible things. Paradoxically, *familiarizing* ourselves with our destructive dark potential and *responsibly accepting it* as part of us is the best way to ensure that we do not unconsciously act out.

> It is a frightening thought that man also has a shadow side to him, consisting not just of little weaknesses and foibles, but of a positively demonic dynamism. The individual seldom knows anything of this; to him, as an individual, it is incredible that he should ever in any circumstances go beyond himself. But let these harmless creatures form a mass, and there emerges a raging monster; . . . so that for better or worse he must accompany it on its bloody rampages and even assist it to the utmost.
>
> (Jung, 1943/1966, para. 35)

The text of this book has followed the mother on her bloody rampage, from her entrapment to her rage to her madness in the hopes that, as Woodman and Dickson suggested, the treasure is recovered through encountering the chthonic devourer, the dark side of the Great Mother. By going into the forest and meeting the ancient witch, we move beyond the "immature" either-or/good-or-bad stage of development into the "both/and world" (Woodman & Dickson, 1997, p. 49). In Jung's terms, this work is at the deepest level of the somatic unconscious which brings to consciousness the subtle body. This is the gift of the Death Mother archetype who shatters the illusion that there is only an all-good or all-bad mother or self. She brings us to the heart of the paradox of life itself and helps us birth the bliss of nondual acceptance, which is the Mother's archetypal essence and her gift of freedom to anyone brave enough to consent to being torn apart by her (Harvey & Baring, 1996).

To move beyond the duality, we must accept that mothers have the capacity, and at times interest, in killing their children; and our mothers, at some point, had murderous feelings toward us. If we can expand motherhood to include aggression and rage, we obviate the need for a mother to act it out. If a mother cannot accept her negative mothering, can't admit her hate for her child, can't openly despise her child and her trap in a lifetime of mothering, she has an unredeemed negative side within her and it gives her the sense she can't trust herself or act authentically. Through the integration of the shadow of the mother archetype, we embark on a journey toward a more holistic and authentic expression of the mother within ourselves, and our larger womanhood. As Rand wrote, "True hope is embedded within death's dark and somber shroud" (1997, p. 53). It is this material in the dark cave that requires our engagement.

> Challenging the sentimental idealism that surrounds "mother" can help women to understand their ambivalence in a more human context . . . . Although in today's world, in many countries, her children will survive, they would not have done so throughout most of our evolutionary history, and the mother's ambivalence may, in part, reflect this deeper history. Once a woman begins to understand this broader reality, she can start to deconstruct and integrate the shameful feelings of indifference or hostility that she sometimes feels for her infant, while fostering the kind of self-compassion that sets the stage for genuine change in both her internal and external worlds.
>
> (Sieff, 2019, p. 29)

In practice, this requires the clinician to be able to hold the taboo feelings of a mother. Often when I teach, I'm asked, "How do we actually help suffering moms?" I suggest clinicians invite their client's ambivalence. By giving love, adoration, *and* shame and rage space, the suppressed feelings are less likely to build, lurking with potential to act out on something or someone. If the clinician's capacity and performance of rage is slightly larger than what she suspects the mother's rage is, the mother will know her rage is safe there. For instance, I'll say, "Gosh, sometimes I just wanted to wring my kids' necks," giving the murderous desires a stage where they can play out metaphorically, emotionally, freely. "Naming and working is transformative, it takes the archetypal pattern out of unconscious repetition. Engaging with the Death Mother archetype helps activate and strengthen the warm and nourishing inner mother we all need" (Sherwood, 2021, p. 65).

The full complexity of the mother is a woman whose creativity has not been stifled, and the vital flow of her generative energies is available to be consciously used. Women with positive outlets, who have shaken a fixed definition that had obstructed their ability to be free, are able to be accepting of all forms of themselves. A woman in this process of individuation has the ability for murderousness, but it doesn't have to leak out of her in unconscious, harmful ways.

In alchemy, a final stage is often referred to as coagulation, the process by which a liquid, typically blood, solidifies. This stage involves the complete unification of polarities: spirit and matter, body and soul, masculine and feminine, to form a single whole. At this stage, maturity is achieved in which the opposing forces between matter and spirit, inner and outer, good and evil are balanced and there is harmony. In effect, it is the birth of a new being. As a mother walks through the tension between being sacrificial for her children and feeling repulsed by her children, if her self-awareness is raised enough to perceive that both are possible at once, and they are in balance, she may achieve a maturity that allows her some harmony.

The Power and Passion of Motherhood

A whole mother, the Great Mother, is found in the integration of the Virgin Mary and Lilith: a compassionate, loving, earthy, sensual, fierce (potentially violent), fallible woman—a woman of multitudes. Kristeva used a phrase that captures this alchemical energy: *maternal passion* (2005, para. 1). Maternal passions—sexual, wild, fierce, loyal, protective—are the gifts of ancient mothers that instruct our maternal subjectivity as a place of healing and transformation. It is our responsibility how we cradle it and how we deliver it to our daughters.

Women do not need to siphon "mother" off from their identity in order to be an empowered agent in step with men, as a woman's powerful potentiality can be found in her reproductive nature: "A woman's activity is of a different kind, attuned to inner bodily processes, developing a self-contained intensity of feeling that furthers intimacy" (Ulanov, 1971, p. 150).

Magnifying the importance, but lack of reflection on maternal passion, Kristeva noted, "Feminine fertility and pregnancy not only continue to fascinate our collective imagination, but also serve as a sanctuary for the sacred" (2005, para. 2). She described maternal passion as the nonrationality of maternal love, the flow of emotions toward the fetus, baby, and child which include attachment and aggression, love and idealization. Rather than a sublimation of the destructive energy of the Death Mother instinct, *maternal passion* embodies a dynamic place of integration that Kristeva insists we embrace. Maternal passion reclaims the qualities of hysteria, "the shortness of breath, fainting, nervousness, sexual desire, insomnia, fluid retention, heaviness in the abdomen, irritability, loss of appetite for food or sex, sexually forward behavior, and a tendency to cause trouble for others" (Maines, 1999, p. 23). At times the emotional messiness, veering from exaltation to melancholia, can reach "the point of 'maternal madness.'" Working through the "indestructible hold" of this madness gives way to maternal passion, "a 'cycle of sublimation' where the mother positions herself by differentiating her newborn from herself" (Kristeva, 2005, p. III para. 1)

Bueskens wrote that when the Mother was sequestered and institutionalized inside the home during the Industrial Revolution, her full potential was stolen from her; that is, she lost some blood and bone (2018). Like Bueskens, I argue for her stolen unique feminine—her subjectivity, intuition, bias, preference, also sexuality, determination, ferocity, pain tolerance—to be taken back. In our advancing medicalized gender-diverse society, doing away with maternal instincts, even semantically, academically, or scientifically, robs Mother of essential and potential power; she is much more powerful if she keeps it. As Hélène Cixous points out, although women's generative capacities are forced, controlled, and regulated through patriarchal relations, the ability to give birth is eternally empowering, akin to artistic creations that bypass the dualistic split of nature from culture. Cixous asserts that maternal generative capacity is the source of culture, art, and text. Thus, if maternal subjectivity is privileged, a society has the potential to be highly generative.

Centering and valuing Mother and her eternal mysteries of the birth and death cycles helps to recover powerful capacities in all people (Bueskens & Brock, 2020; Greer, 1999; O'Reilly, 2016). When the intuitive, unmitigated, unsentimental, animalistic maternal instincts are integrated, one can *see what is*, discerning and acting without self-incriminations, the way an integrated mother slices through the unnecessary distractions and nonsense, which may seem insensitive, but is honest. Von Franz noted that in fairytales when the witch tells the young girl to sort the grains and spin the thread, her commands contain the exacting mother energy of "ethical discrimination" (1993, p. 190). The girl is required to make unsentimental decisions, picking out the useful from the useless. Sort it out! The witch's demand slices through, gets to the heart, shreds the veil of pretense, and speaks what's needed in our world of false equivalencies.

Recently my son and I went to the zoo, where a baby zebra had been born in the preceding weeks. As we spiraled our way through the lions and flamingos, we found a large crowd standing along the fencing of the zebras' pen. Once we were able to squeeze in to get our view, we were able to see what at first struck us as peculiar. There was the baby zebra, stick-like limbs in a soft pile around a fluffy head with faded stripes lying under a tree, with another adult zebra only a few feet away, motionless, staring directly at this baby. Another adult zebra wandered around the pen and munched on grass. What we quickly realized was that this frozen and concentrated presence was the mother, her gaze did not waver from her child. My son and I commented on her ferocity; we could sense an intense energy coming from within and without the mother; she wasn't to miss, or to give away to the crowds, one small movement of her new baby. As we left the zoo that day I remembered that several years prior, we had been at the same zoo. It was still early morning after we dropped off his sister at kindergarten. He was at the age, maybe 2 or 3, when, although he could walk, he wanted to be held, so as we walked and noted the animals, he floated up and down from my arms. We were happy, marveling at the seals, and then the lions, spending time in front of the monkeys' cage. A woman approached us, a stranger, she was about 20 years older than me. She said, "You and your son, this is very special, I can see your connection so clearly. Shall I take your picture so you have this moment to remember?" With the photo it was imprinted for me: that tangible energetic field between mother and child, sometimes so strong it is visible to others.

A mother's passion may be an ineffable sensation she has not only in relation to beings she created in her body, but the larger energetic field that surrounds them. The maternal body is the feminine body in its most terrifying form: "that which does not respect borders, positions, rules" (Kristeva, 1982, p. 4).

Passion contains many things, a powerful enthusiasm, uninhibited desire, ecstasy, an intense drive toward one's deep interests, a feeling that nothing else exists. Passion is also suffering, most famously as the *Passion* of Christ—Jesus's arrest, trial, and execution by crucifixion. Mary's passion is her mother-love, sacrificial faith, and divine hope that helped her tolerate his execution. Kristeva referred to maternal passions as more than self-sacrificing energy, as the place of passionate violence and sexuality at "the crossroads of biology and meaning" (2005, para. 1). Mothers are the "cornerstone of today's civilization, a civilization which has lost its points of reference" (para. 4). Although maternal passion is sublimated into love for her progeny, a mother has an intense creative energy grander than the child born to her.

A good friend of mine told me of a time she was lying awake in a hotel bed, in a room with her sleeping children. She was suddenly filled with an immense, inexpressible feeling of warmth, pride, and fulfillment, her mind and body bursting with power. This maternal passion was her natural primal essence that had no past or future but originated, surrounded, and emanated from her and her children in that moment. The intensity of a mother's passion is bigger than the sum of its parts, the bursting sensation of it so devouring and engulfing it is largely suppressed. This is love as it really is: "a fire of tongues, an escape from representation" (Kristeva, 1985, p. 145).

Symbols

In Jungian psychotherapy we often work with symbols, as they are effective containers for holding the tension of conflicting or opposing forces. Much like an archetypal image, a symbol gives access to a larger sensation or experience. Jung suggested there is diverse symbolism that comes from the collective unconscious and includes such forms as a revolving wheel or the zodiac, the petals of a magnificent flower, or a serpent eating its tail. Symbols are worshiped, symbols are used as tools, symbols are hung on walls, symbols are also often woven into the background of contemporary society, and they largely go unnoticed. The symbol contains a union of opposites, the light and dark, the shadow and consciousness, and the potential for wholeness. When working with such rigid dualities as virgin/whore or mother/witch, which are buried in the collective unconscious, finding a strong enough symbol is effective in the process of transmutation.

A search for a whole female icon is perennial, as women have no metaphysical representations in the Christian God-image, and we largely lost our access to goddess culture. Whereas Protestantism has no female symbols, Catholicism has the Virgin Mary as a symbolic representation of femininity, but it's grossly incomplete as it encompasses only the sublime and light aspects of the divine feminine principle and therefore does not express the whole feminine principle. Von Franz (1993) wrote and spoke on this suffering fate of the Mother goddess, her sexuality siphoned off by Christianity, and the fruitless search for the female icon, now buried and bitter as the old witch stirring her potion and casting her spells.

There are symbols of the Divine Feminine that have crossed several cultures of the Middle East and West but have not made it to the U.S. The Sumerians called this great woman Ninmah, the Egyptians called her Isis, the Greeks called her Athena or Sophia, and the ancient Hebrews called her Asherah, the Woman of the Tree. These are a few leftover symbols, faded in our collective unconscious, that are worth uncovering and breathing life back into if we are to reclaim the dark feminine and integrate the Mother archetype.

Isis is a maternal symbol grounded in earth and reality, not immaculate martyrdom, originally an ancient Egyptian Goddess whose worship spread throughout the Greco-Roman world from 2465–2325 BCE. Isis was known as a Great Mother who greeted all Egyptians by calling them *my children*. She was the divine mother of Horus the Pharaoh; the image of him on her lap is a familiar Egyptian statue, archetypally linking her to the popular images of Mary with Jesus on her lap. In the story of Isis and Horus, Osiris, a beloved King of Egypt, was killed by his envious brother Seth. Isis revived Osiris from the dead by making love to him, during which she became impregnated with Horus, thus considered the son of God. Eventually Isis, with her cunning, helped Horus win the throne from Seth. A cult following of Isis spread throughout Egypt and parts of Africa. She is portrayed as a dark shade of Black and severely beautiful, known as a virgin deity since she was able to magically conceive a son, making her a mother goddess. Providing for and protecting her son, she is a symbol of maternal sacrifice and devotion. Her maternal aid was invoked in healing spells to benefit ordinary people, and she was believed to help the dead enter the afterlife.

Figure 11.1 Erzulie Danto Painting Black Madonna Voodoo Art by Magdalena Walulik (2016). Reprinted with permission. ©2015 Magdalena Walulik/ Artmajeur.com

Similarly, a senior spirit in Haitian Vodou named Erzulie Dantò is known as the divinity of love, has a dark complexion, and is maternal in nature. She is known as fiercely protective of her children as well as wild, aggressive, and difficult to control. She is considered a "hot" spirit.

One popular Haitian song dedicated to Dantò elicits images of the Virgin Mary and Medea:

> Seven stabs of the knife,
> seven stabs of the sword
> Hand me that basin,
> I am going to vomit blood,
> the blood runs down.

Dantò's strength and endurance is so vast that she can sustain seven stabs and still hold a basin and vomit blood. These are symbols of mothers giving life and taking life; they are impressive, not frail martyrs, and hold the tension between aggression *and* nourishment.

Black Madonna

The Black Madonna is closely tied with both Isis and the Virgin Mary, as it is believed she first became known to the West when the crusaders brought back to Europe treasures from the East, including exquisite statues of the Black goddess Isis, which were enshrined as the Black virgin. Throughout Europe in the 12th and 13th centuries devotion to her spread, as small shrines were set up in her honor.[1]

> She was revered in an underground way—the blessing of the crops in the field, the blessing of pregnancy and childbirth, the dark excesses of sexuality and delight in the mysteries of the boy, and the wisdom that can be experienced in lovemaking.
>
> (Woodman & Dickson, 1997, p. 28)

The birth of the Black Madonna was influenced by the predominance of the Marian cult and a preoccupation with the idealized woman, typically symbolized by the white Mary, generating the psychological need for a compensating element, such as the earthy Black Madonna (Woodman & Dickson, 1997). They suggested that the emergence of the Black Madonna in the Middle Ages was indicative of people unconsciously reaching for an image of a deeper, more potent Feminine. As Jungian analyst Ean Begg wrote, "The Black Virgin is a Christian phenomenon as well as a preservation of the ancient goddesses and compensates for the one-sided conscious attitudes of the age" (2018, p. 131). Although she is costumed as Mary, the Black Madonna is the recovery of the powerful ancient goddesses that were confined in repression by the patriarchal paradigm.

Woodman wrote about the recurrence of the Black Goddess image in her analysands' dreams, described to her by individuals around the globe. She interpreted these unconscious encounters with the Black Madonna as the harbingers "of a new paradigm of inclusiveness here at last, to tame the patriarchal lust for power and control that has brought us 'to the brink of extinction'" (Awaken, 2022, para. 6). Woodman suggested the Black Madonna was a symbol of the redemption of matter, the intersection of sexuality and spirit, and the loving biological tie to the body, fertility, and babies.

Of great significance to the Black Madonna, the words *black* and *wise* are almost indistinguishable in Semitic script; in addition, darkness is associated with the unknown and the repressed sides of life. Placing the word *black* with the word *virgin* or *madonna* conjures deeper resonances. It is the darkness of the Black Madonna that symbolizes her depth and points to the earthly feminine wisdom of the Great Goddess and the cycles of life and death. Mary's white purity signifies her chastity, and the Black Madonna's darkness points to her sexuality. Whereas the pale madonna is often depicted lovingly embracing the baby Jesus, the Black Madonna stands alone or holds the Christ-child with noble austerity. The Black Virgin is an archetypal rebellion, a recovery of the deep, wise feminine lost to the past.

> Developing a relationship with the tyrannizing killing feminine . . . struggling towards wholeness, women can finally bring value to the totality of mother and recognize that, without blackness, there can be no conscious creation and order.
>
> (Rand, 1997, p. 49)

The Black Madonna is associated with the unknown repressed side of femininity, thus intimately tied to the integration of shadow materials. Bringing a Black Madonna statue into one's presence introduces a deeper container for a fuller range of maternal passions, positive and negative, and a step toward understanding the whole mother.

Woodman suggested the Black Madonna "somehow carries the energy of the Black spirituals as sung by Blacks—passionate, rooted in suffering, lusty, singling the tragedy in the ordinary, imponderable, subatomic depths" (Woodman & Dickson, 1997, p. 9). It's an important connection, as the icons and shrines of the Black Madonna are incredibly rare in the U.S., yet the U.S. has the highest population of Black mothers who commit infanticide. Without a symbolic container for the intensity, resilience, history, power, and passion of the Black mother, the negative archetypal possession of the Death Mother is more apt to act out.[2]

If destruction is transmuted into passion, the effects on a mother may release a breadth of positive emotional effects. Ulanov described this transformation as

> feelings of being caught up in a creative process, feelings of excitement, zest, vitality, or being inspired and called out of oneself by something of compelling, life-giving value. There may be an opening to new insights, or a changing of the

shape and texture of one's life or relationships. One may lure or inspire others to new feats or new insight. One may enjoy a sense of the playful and unexpected. One may find that one can risk exposure to forces beyond one's control and with a sense of expectation rather than fear.

(1971, p. 160)

This is the maternal subjectivity that Kristeva called for and that every mother deserves. The infanticidal mother has no container for her maternal madness or her psychosis. She is caught in the intersection of oppressions and split off from the Good Mother.

Reclaiming mother's voice of dark death and all that has been excluded, slowly we begin to feel in our bodies the truth of the eternal sense of the Self. Such a paradoxical self-image, with a thousand names, is the mother who is dead yet still lives, an indestructible eternal figure which cannot be harmed by the changes of life. She is the virgin at the centre of the earth and the enfeebled, exhausted old woman. She is matter knowingly embracing psyche in creative paradoxical tension. She is an intimate of feminine self-hood. Now the dark mother can have her rightful place in the home of the flesh and blood and we hear the fertilizing truth from her.

(Rand, 1997, p. 55)

There is hope and possibility by becoming familiar with long-suppressed or underappreciated archetypes, such as the Black Madonna, Kali, Isis, or Lilith. These female identities all hold destructive, creative, and sexual powers. This archetypal energy embodies a dark feminine mystery, a feminine with less sentimentality, a mystery that cannot be explained, a deeper understanding of life, in favor of life but in an unsentimental way; earth herself, she gives and takes.

In the End

In the end, Medea escaped to Athens on a chariot drawn by winged Dragon-Serpents, which she had received from her grandfather, the sun-God Helios. She is saved by the Gods, who Jung suggested are the transcendent principles that regulate the laws of nature and transformation of the psyche. Thus Medea, as an archetypal image, remains alive, available to contain the shadow of the modern mother. Medea deserves to be known on her terms and in all her forms as a passionate—not vengeful—mother, who lives beyond the Law.

Medea is highly skilled in the art of alchemy and can revitalize dead and mutilated flesh. She is well versed in the cycles of creation and symbolizes three transitional phases of a woman's life from birth to development, to maturity and reproductivity, into decline and death. Her origins are gynocentric, reaching back to a pre-patriarchal period when female potency was revered as a source of empowerment. Early mythic narratives reveal Medea as an earth goddess, who embodies the energies of the earth, sky, as well as the underworld. Hence, she is often connected to the archaic pattern of sacrificing the king to ensure the fertility of the land associated with matriarchal societies and ceremonies. Yet, over time, the myth of Medea has adopted a dichotomous world view that de-emphasizes her life-giving propensities.

(Rivers-Norton, 2020, p. ix).

Modern-day society creates a calamitous tension with the Death Mother archetype in its attempt to eradicate it—by shame or punishment—rather than accept the unresolvable nature of an archetypal drive. If we begin with acceptance that the infanticidal drive is inherent to human nature, cannot be eradicated, and serves an evolutionary and beneficial purpose, we might also be able to see that humankind has need of the death mother, honor her with avenues of expression, and heed her messages of needed change.

When the Death Mother archetype is activated in mothers and comes to the surface, it may be the archetypal image that the moment requires: A woman is seized by it, simultaneously expressing her lived experience and a deeper, mythic archetypal process that informs it. By being seized and compelled to unconsciously act out this powerful archetypal force as infanticide, her Act seeks to correct the foundation of Motherhood and reestablish vital creativity. An infanticidal mother is a threat to patriarchy, as apparent in media and law enforcement persecutory attitudes toward her. Reversing the ideal of Mary and rejecting the position of Eve, Medea stands as the shadow aspect of the modern mother, ruling over both life and death. When the extreme of the idyllic mother, a self-sacrificial maternal love associating obedient devotion to a patriarchal God, is leveled by the infanticidal mother, we find ourselves at the balance of the Great Mother and the human mother, at maternal love without guarantees (Kristeva, 1985).

How many times will our headlines need to announce the recurring nightmare of maternal infanticide before we believe it is not about someone else? As we bring her out into the light of our awareness, we free ourselves to live the full range of the feminine in both women and men. The Death Mother archetype, the one who burns with aggression, is a strong negative energy that can be transmuted into maternal passion (including collective care for mothers by ending the oppressive forces they face) and a changed concept of womanhood and motherhood. The event of killing a child is an attempt to make society whole by recognizing the oppression of the mother in her subjugation to men who bear no accountability, to capitalism's failure to recompense her, and to the idealization of motherhood that dismisses her struggle. The anguish of motherhood calls attention to the unspeakable debt that culture and society owe the maternal body—a debt that is denied in rampant male violence against women—including pregnant women. The murderous mother is screaming, *let me not be trapped here.* To listen to and heed her is to begin the transmutation into a new era.

Notes

1 Investigations into the origins and meanings of the Black Madonna include evidence of discoloration of Virgin Mary statues due to fire and the problems of appropriation by a White Western audience (Moss & Cappannari, 1953).
2 Long-unrecognized potency of African women has been recovered in some of the new research on the "Eve Gene," otherwise known as "Mitochondrial Eve," which traces the matrilineal descent of all humans to an African woman who lived an estimated 200,000 years ago. In the modern day, only Black women possess the mitochondria DNA that contains all possible human variations (African, Asian, European, Middle Eastern, etc.).

References

Awaken. (2022, December 28). *The emergence of the Black goddess—Marion Woodman.* https://awaken.com/2022/12/the-emergence-of-the-black-goddess/
Begg, E. (2018). *The cult of the black virgin.* Chiron.
Bueskens, P. (2018). *Modern motherhood and women's dual identities: Rewriting the sexual contract.* Routledge.
Bueskens, P., & Brock, S. (2020). Matricentric feminism: Abjection and disruption. *Hecate: Interdisciplinary Journal of Women's Liberation, 45*(1–2), 13–22.
Franz, M.-L. V. (1993). *The feminine in fairy tales* (Rev. 1st ed.). Shambhala.
Greer, G. (1999). *The whole woman.* A.A. Knopf.
Harvey, A., & Baring, A. (1996). *The divine feminine: Exploring the feminine face of god around the world.* Conari.
Irigaray, L. (1978). The sex which is no one. In P. Foss & M. Morris (Eds.), *Language, sexuality and subversion* (pp. 161–172). Feral.
Jung, C. G. (1966). On the psychology of the unconscious (R. F. C. Hull, Trans.). In H. Read, M. Fordham, & G. Adler (Eds.), *The collected works of C. G. Jung: Vol. 7. Two essays on analytical psychology* (2nd ed., pp. 1–119). Princeton University Press. (Original work published 1943)
Kristeva, J. (1982). *Powers of horror: An essay on abjection.* Columbia University Press.
Kristeva, J. (1985). Stabat mater (A. Goldhammer, Trans.). *Poetics Today, 6*(1–2), 133–152.
Kristeva, J. (2005). *Motherhood today.* www.kristeva.fr/motherhood.html
Maines, R. P. (1999). *The technology of orgasm: "Hysteria", the vibrator, and women's sexual satisfaction.* Johns Hopkins University Press.
Moss, L. W., & Cappannari, S. C. (1953). The Black Madonna: An example of culture borrowing. *The Scientific Monthly, 76*(6), 319–324.
O'Reilly, A. (2016). *Matricentric feminism: Theory, activism, practice.* Demeter Press. http://www.jstor.org/stable/j.ctt1rrd8b4
Rand, E. (1997). *Recovering feminine spirituality.* CreateSpace.
Rivers-Norton, J. (2020). *The tragic life story of Medea as mother, monster, and muse.* www.cambridgescholars.com/resources/pdfs/978-1-5275-4130-6-sample.pdf
Sherwood, V. (2021). *Haunted: The death mother archetype.* Chiron.
Sieff, D. F. (2019). The death mother as nature's shadow: Infanticide, abandonment, and the collective unconscious. *Psychological Perspectives, 62*(1), 15–34.
Smith-Hanssen, K. (2009). Medea and mothers who kill. *Spring, 81,* 165–176.
Ulanov, A. B. (1971). *The feminine in Jungian psychology and in Christian theology.* Northwestern University Press.
Woodman, M., & Dickson, E. J. (1997). *Dancing in the flames: The dark goddess in the transformation of consciousness.* A. A. Knopf.

Index

122–124, 129–130, 132, 134–136, 156, 163, 165–166, 168, 170, 171, 179, 192, 195, 199–200, 201, 203, 208–210, 216, 218; collective/cultural unconscious 8, 27, 31–32, 33, 38–39, 44, 60, 62, 63, 83, 152–153, 162, 213

violence 13, 16, 57, 59, 64, 75n1, 79–82, 86–87, 89, 90–91, 92, 137, 145, 155, 158n1, 164, 169, 171, 172–173, 175, 179, 182, 182n4, 190, 194, 208, 212, 218; female 41, 50, 51, 137, 165, 170, 175; male 66, 71, 82–83, 85, 89, 103, 155, 174, 182n4, 192–193; and pregnancy 82–83; *see also* domestic violence

voice 6, 46, 50, 63, 68, 71–72, 74, 87, 111, 124–125, 138, 156, 176, 180, 182, 190, 208, 217; *see also* silenced/silencing

Woodman, M. 31–32, 129–133, 147, 166, 177, 209, 215–216